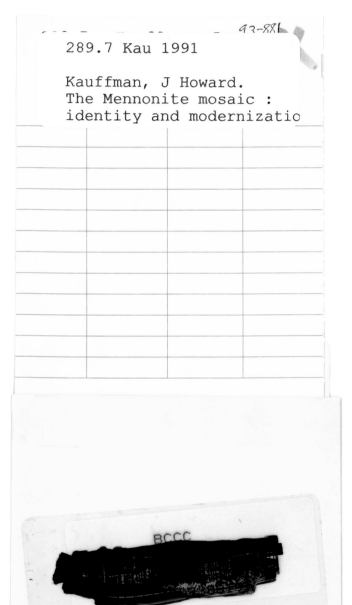

W9-ADJ-437

The

MENNONITE MOSAIC

Identity and Modernization

J. Howard Kauffman and Leo Driedger

Foreword by Donald B. Kraybill

HERALD PRESS
Scottdale, Pennsylvania
Waterloo, Ontario

Library of Congress Cataloging-in-Publication Data
Kauffman, J. Howard, 1919-
    The Mennonite mosaic : identity and modernization / J. Howard Kauffman
and Leo Driedger.
      p. cm.
    Includes bibliographical references and index.
    ISBN 0-8361-3567-9 (alk. paper)
    1. Mennonites—North America. 2. Brethren in Christ Church—North
America. 3. Anabaptists—North America. I. Driedger, Leo, 1928- . II. Title.
BX8116.K38 1991
289.7′73—dc20
                                      91-24568
                                         CIP

Cover photos from the files of Jan Gleysteen.
First photo on left, second row, by Rohn Engh.

THE MENNONITE MOSAIC
Copyright © 1991 by Herald Press, Scottdale, Pa. 15683
    Published simultaneously in Canada by Herald Press,
    Waterloo, Ont. N2L 6H7. All rights reserved.
Library of Congress Catalog Number: 91-24568
International Standard Book Number: 0-8361-3567-9
Printed in the United States of America
Cover and book design by Gwen Star

1 2 3 4 5 6 7 8 9 10 97 96 95 94 93 92 91

*To the
3,500 persons who
made this study possible*

Contents

Part II. Finding Sources of Identity

Part III. Consequences for Mennonite Life

List of Tables

List of Figures

Foreword

IN THE WORDS of Peter Berger,

> The forces of modernization have descended like a gigantic steel hammer upon all the old communal institutions—clan, village, tribe, and region—distorting or greatly weakening them, if not destroying them altogether.

What happens when the hammer of modernity strikes a traditional, religious group? How have North American Mennonites, and related groups who trace their roots to 16th-century Anabaptism, fared in their encounter with the forces of modernity? This book grapples with these and a multitude of other questions.

Based on responses from some 3,000 members of five Mennonite and Brethren-in-Christ denominations, Kauffman and Driedger take us on a grand tour of the more progressive North American Anabaptist groups. Complicated to outsider and insider alike, the progressive side of the Mennonite mosaic shines with clarity with the authors' careful description. Using the efficient methods of modern sampling techniques, 3,000 respondents speak for some 232,000 members of their denominations. We learn where Mennonites and their cousins live and what they do for a living. We learn what they believe and how they view abortion, homosexuality, and capital punishment.

The rich mine of data explored in this volume explodes many traditional stereotypes. Few Mennonites are farming. In fact, nearly three-fourths of one group are urbanites. Separatists who shun the modern world? Not these Mennonites, many of whom are penetrating the political realm in new ways. The members of all five groups are pursuing higher education in rising numbers. Has the pursuit of higher education secularized the Mennonite soul? The authors offer surprising results.

Kauffman and Driedger don't overwhelm us with trivial data. But they do present a wide array of facts on Mennonite beliefs and habits. The bits and pieces of data are, however, skillfully interpreted in the context of history, theory, and interrelationships.

A helpful historical overview of the five groups under study, of Anabaptist beginnings, and of key issues provides a context for interpreting responses to specific questions. A variety of theoretical perspectives illuminate the findings. Finally the authors trace the trail of relationships between the many variables included in the study. We discover, for instance, how beliefs about peace and nonresistance are linked to fundamentalism, Anabaptism, education, and urbanization.

Social comparisons lie at the heart of the sociological approach. Factual descriptions of a group take on new and richer meaning when contrasted with those from other groups. *The Mennonite Mosaic* provides comparisons at four levels.

First, it follows a similar profile of the same groups undertaken seventeen years earlier (Kauffman and Harder 1975). Thus we have a historical benchmark for longitudinal comparisons, allowing an assessment of trends and changes across the Mennonite landscape. Seventeen years may seem a short span to monitor change, but it does chart the changes of one generation. Remarkable is the rate of change in the Mennonite community in this brief span—including increasing urbanization, greater political involvement, changing gender roles, rising educational levels, and many other shifts.

Second, the analysis compares five Anabaptist denominations— each with different historical origins, theological slants, and ethnic strands. Inter-group comparisons allow the investigators to tease out the relative importance of denominational effects in contrast to demographic and socioeconomic forces.

Third, the profile offers U.S. and Canadian comparisons. To what extent have Mennonites been shaped by their respective political contexts?

Finally the authors present findings from national surveys of other religious groups in both Canada and the U.S. We discover the areas of continuity and discontinuity between Mennonites and other religious bodies. In all these ways *The Mennonite Mosaic* rests solidly in a framework of comparative analysis.

A variety of persons will benefit from the fruits of this major and commendable effort. Mennonite and Brethren in Christ church leaders will find it indispensable for tapping sentiments and trends across the church. Officers of church institutions will discover both the effects and perceptions of their work. It should serve them well as they map out future program plans.

Lay persons across the church will read the book with interest to learn about their cousins in the faith across North America and to find where they fit in the larger scheme of the Anabaptist world. *The Mennonite Mosaic* will also enjoy a welcome beyond the denominations it surveys. Leaders in other denominations will use it as a trustworthy guide to contemporary Anabaptist life and thought. Moreover, the scholars who monitor and research religious groups will digest it with enthusiasm.

The Mennonite Mosaic will be significant, possibly *the* landmark work, in the world of Mennonite and Brethren in Christ studies in the late twentieth century. Anchored in the best binational Mennonite data sets (1972 and 1989) it will have to be reckoned with by scholars both within and without Anabaptist groups.

Kauffman and Driedger distill thousands of responses to hundreds of questions, present them in a concise and interesting fashion, interpret them in a sophisticated theoretical context and draw striking conclusions. They manage to do so in a highly readable fashion. Their polished text flows with ease. It is of course a pleasure to commend such a work.

—*Donald B. Kraybill, Director*
The Young Center for the Study of Anabaptist
and Pietist Groups
Elizabethtown College
Elizabethtown, Pennsylvania 17022

Authors' Preface

THE PAST THREE DECADES have brought a great increase in the store of information about religious bodies in Canada and the United States. Some of this increase stems from surveys of the members of specific denominations. Some arises out of periodic surveys of national populations by major polling agencies. Key surveys include (for people in the United States) the Gallup polls conducted by the American Institute of Public Opinion, Princeton, New Jersey, and the General Social Surveys conducted by the National Opinion Research Center in Chicago.

Contrary to the U.S. census, the decennial census in Canada includes a question on religious affiliation. This makes it possible to compare religious bodies on a number of demographic variables. Private research in Canada supplements the census data and widens coverage of religious topics. The surveys reported on by Reginald Bibby (*Fragmented Gods*, 1987) are a notable example.

The Mennonite and Brethren in Christ denominations are too small for a significant number of members to be caught in the samples of national polls. Consequently, obtaining statistical information about Mennonite beliefs and practices is possible only through denominational surveys, two of which provide the basis for this volume. These surveys of churches in Canada and the United States make it possible to plot a North American Mennonite profile that can be compared with the characteristics of other Christian denominations.

The idea of a survey of the beliefs and practices of Mennonite church members first arose 20 years ago. It resulted in a "Church Member Profile," whose findings were analyzed and reported in Kauffman and Harder, *Anabaptists Four Centuries Later* (1975). A new survey, done 17 years later and called Church Member Profile II, has made it possible to identify trends in Mennonite life and thought.

Such a survey is a kind of thermometer, taking the religious temperature of church members at a particular time. Valid comparisons between two surveys are possible when the samples are taken from similar populations and the same questions are asked. The two Mennonite surveys compared 3,591 respondents in 1972 with 3,083 in 1989. In both cases respondents represented five related denominations: Brethren in Christ Church, Evangelical Mennonite Church, General Conference Mennonite Church, Mennonite Brethren Church, and Mennonite Church. Roughly two-thirds of the 1989 questionnaire repeated items from the 1972 instrument. The remainder introduced new dimensions for further study. (For details on the survey methods, see the appendix.)

A major purpose of the later survey was to gain clues about the impact of modernization on members of Mennonite and Brethren in Christ churches. What happens to their religious identity when church members become urbanized, achieve higher educational and income levels, and enter occupations that involve them much more extensively within the networks of industry, commerce, and the professions?

The surveys were designed to provide information of use to a wide range of church boards, agencies, and programs, many of which were consulted in the planning stages of the project. In addition, we hope this volume, by providing a view of several small religious bodies that differ in some significant ways from other Christian denominations, will make a serious contribution to the sociology of religion.

An Administrative Committee, representing the participating denominations, provided direction and general oversight for the 1989 survey. The members were Leo Driedger, chair, representing the General Conference Mennonite Church; Glen A. Pierce, Brethren in Christ Church; Donald W. Roth, Evangelical Mennonite Church; Abram G. Konrad, Mennonite Brethren Church; Edward B. Stoltzfus, Mennonite Church; and Elizabeth G. Yoder and Richard A. Kauffman, representing the Institute of Mennonite Studies, which provided some helpful administrative services. The Administrative Committee employed Howard Kauffman, director, and Leland Harder, associate director, to supervise the project.

We are deeply grateful for the encouragement of the chief administrative officers of the participating denominations and for the denominational financial contributions they arranged. We are also deeply grateful to several agencies that provided additional funds for the project: Mennonite Mutual Aid Association, Mennonite Central Committee, Schowalter Foundation, DeFehr Foundation, and Brotherhood Mutual Insurance Company.

Planning for the project received assistance from a "Consultation on Church Member Profile II." In this two-day workshop, some 40 scholars and church administrators explored the theoretical facets of Mennonite identity and modernization. The papers presented at the workshop were edited by Leo Driedger and Leland Harder and published by the Institute of Mennonite Studies in a volume entitled *Anabaptist-Mennonite Identities in Ferment* (1990).

Donald B. Kraybill, Abram G. Conrad, and Edward B. Stoltzfus gave valuable counsel on portions of the manuscript. We gratefully acknowledge the volunteer help of 40 "research visitors," each of whom administered questionnaires to the respondents in several of the 153 participating congregations. We thank Wilma Cender, Daniel A. Liechty, Tamara Loewen, Darlene Driedger, and Mary Ellen Martin for their assistance at various stages of the project.

—*J. Howard Kauffman*
Leo Driedger
February 1991

PART I

Sorting Forces
of Change

CHAPTER 1

The Challenge
of Modernization

THE ANABAPTIST ANCESTORS of the Mennonites and Brethren in Christ emerged from a caldron of religious, political, economic, and social change in the 16th century (Clasen, 1972). The discovery of America by Columbus in 1492 was only one manifestation of change. A revolution took Europe from landed feudalism to new opportunities via the sea, which offered new contacts and trade with other peoples of the world. The printing press revolutionized communication, from tedious handwriting to the printed page, with its potential for mass circulation.

Many Anabaptist craftsmen and women were at the cutting edge of this revolution, part of 16th-century modernization. They were only one radical religious manifestation of this social ferment of the 1500s, and their voices were diverse in those pluralist times (Clasen, 1972; Stayer, et al., 1975:83-121).

The electronic revolution represented by the computer is likewise transforming the latter part of the twentieth century. A global network of instant communication is at our fingertips. While only 35 percent of the Mennonites in North America lived in cities of 2,500 or more as late as 1972 (Kauffman and Harder, 1975:54), by 1989 one-half (48%) were urban. One-fourth of males were farmers in 1972; that figure declined to 15 percent in 1989. Today four times as many Mennonites (both males and females) are in the professions (27%) as are working the land (7%).

Change is clearly evident as Mennonites are exposed to the forces of modernization, secularization, and assimilation in settings where many religious denominations are clearly headed away from tradition, the sacred, the community, and traditional identity (Driedger and Harder,

1990). Can distinct identities still be found? Do Mennonites still aspire to be a leaven in society? What does the Mennonite mosaic look like today?

Chapter 1 offers a glimpse of the total Mennonite mosaic. Various chapters will elaborate on specific parts of the model we present here. Later sections of this chapter will introduce (1) the forces of modernization in North America that are reshaping Mennonites, and (2) the sources of Mennonite identity to be elaborated on in chapters 3-7.

Pages from the Past

The 16th-century Anabaptists were part of a larger set of religious movements in the political, economic, and social ferment of the time. These innovators had their origins in many countries of continental Europe, so that there were plural versions of their newly found insights and faith. They were seen as radicals persecuted by both Catholics and Protestants, who felt threatened by their radical faith and lifestyles. Too much change in volatile situations causes those who want order and stability to be nervous. Persecution drove many Anabaptists from the urban commercial fray into centuries of being the "quiet in the land," tucked away toward the periphery of society as tillers of the soil.

Sixteenth-Century Urban Anabaptists

Cornelius Krahn (1980:6) found that

> the Anabaptist Mennonite movement started primarily in larger cities such as Zurich, Bern, Strasbourg, Emden, Amsterdam, Leeuwarden, Groningen, Leyden, Rotterdam, Antwerp, Brussels, Munster, and Cologne. In the Swiss, South-German, and Austrian cities, the Anabaptist movement was crushed and survived only in remote areas. It was different in the Netherlands.

Of the 13 cities Krahn lists, only two were Swiss. The majority were North European, part of the commercial Hanseatic League, which flourished in the thirteenth and fourteenth centuries. While Anabaptists in Central Europe fled the cities, in the northern cities they survived first as an underground movement, later as a tolerated minority, and finally as a recognized religious group (Krahn, 1981:92).

Urbanism among Mennonites of the Low Countries is as old as Mennonitism itself. Today there are some 2,500 Mennonites in Amsterdam and some 2,300 in Haarlem. There are more than 1,000 in each of a number of other cities (Krahn, 1980:6). In the sixteenth century Amsterdam and Rotterdam were part of the Hanseatic League, whose ships plied the North and Baltic seas between the various ports of Bergen, Oslo, Stockholm, Copenhagen, Danzig, Amsterdam, Rotterdam, and London. While Menno Simons himself emerged out of rural Friesland, he nevertheless served Mennonites in many urban centers of the six-teenth century.

W. L. C. Coenen (1920:1-90) made a study of the Anabaptist martyrs in the Netherlands and found that not one of the 161 martyrs was a farm-er. Among the 58 occupations found were 27 weavers, 17 tailors, 13 shoemakers, six sailors, five carpenters, five goldsmiths, five hatmakers, four bricklayers, three bakers, three leather dealers, three teachers, three saddlers, and three potters (Krahn, 1980:8). Most of them, as crafts-people, industrial workers, and businessmen, were part of a more urban commercial society. There were also Mennonites in rural areas in North Holland, Friesland, and Groningen. Persecution drove some eastward into Prussia, mostly into the countryside but also to the suburbs of cities such as Altona, Hamburg, Danzig, Marienburg, Elbing, and Konigsberg (Penner, 1978). Many became middle-class citizens.

Paul Peachey's (1954:102-27) study of the social origins of the Swiss Anabaptists lists 762 Swiss individuals who were connected with the Anabaptist movement in Central Europe; 150 of these were urban (20%). There were 612 villagers and peasants (80%), whom he classified as rural. The peasants made up about three-fifths of the total number of persons listed, or about 460. Of the 150 who were urban, 20 had been clergy (14 priests and 6 monks), 20 were urban lay intellectuals (includ-ing Grebel, Manz, Enck, and Hugwald), 10 came from the nobility, and 100 were citizens and/or urban craftspeople. Among those who were in the crafts, tailors and bakers were most common.

Most of the urban leaders of clerical, intellectual, and noble back-ground disappeared within two years (1525-27), through martyrdom, early natural death, recantation, exile, or some unknown destiny. Thus the Swiss Anabaptist movement was only one-fifth urban to begin with, and almost completely rural two years later and thereafter. Severe perse-cution made an urban foothold impossible. The early Anabaptists were more urban in northern than in southern Europe, and these differences can also be found in North America, as we will see.

The Rural, Agricultural Retreat

The persecuted Anabaptists in Switzerland, Austria, and South Ger-many were indeed much safer as they fled up the mountainsides and into the valleys of the rugged Alpine regions. Mountains tended to serve as barriers to social interaction when transportation was undeveloped; even today the various segregated valleys have some distinctive cus-toms. In Switzerland four official languages (German, French, Italian, Romansch) still survive. The terrain supports residential segregation, tranquil rural life, and parochial ethnocentrism.

These conditions prompted the Swiss Anabaptists to develop a stronger separatist doctrine than did the Dutch. The Swiss experience contributed to the development of a "two-kingdom" ethic, emphasizing the separation of church and state. The Swiss Anabaptists believed that the followers of Christ are "called out" from "the world" to lives of holiness as members of the kingdom of God. While acknowledging the legitimacy of government over the "affairs of the world," the Anabaptists asserted the primacy of the claims of God over the claims of government. This separation was later expressed in the United States in the form of a general avoidance of participation in the political process; and the separatists viewed the rural environment as securing less involvement with the secular and morally compromising world of commerce, industry, politics, and entertainment typical of the city (Driedger and Kauffman, 1982:270-75).

Central Europe was the heart of the noncommercial, nonindustrial feudal age. The commercial activities of the Roman Empire in the Mediterranean filtered only slowly from the seaports of Venice and Genoa northward across the Alps into Central Europe. Likewise, as the new commercial center shifted to the Baltic Sea and North Europe in the 15th and 16th centuries, urbanization penetrated the European heartland much more slowly.

The South German Anabaptists in the cities were crushed and fled up the mountainsides and into the rural valleys. The mountainous terrain promoted segregation and slowed communication and social interaction. The urban industrial complexes of first the Roman age in the Mediterranean, and later of the 16th century commerce and industry of northern Europe, never did influence this central part of continental Europe as deeply as they did other areas. It was out of this setting that the Swiss Mennonites, with a separatist, two-kingdom ethic, came largely to America, a few to Canada.

The Hanseatic League was established in the thirteenth century to do commerce in northern Europe, in the area around the North and Baltic seas. By the 14th and 15th centuries there were 70 member Hanseatic city-states. They stretched from London in the west to Novograd (in western Russia) in the east, from the northern city of Bergen, Norway, south to Leipzig, Germany, and Cracow, Poland (Breasted and Huth, 1961:38). The silk- and linen-making crafts spread into France and the Netherlands as an important part of this North European trade. The Anabaptists emerged, during the preindustrial age (1500-1785), as craftspeople in this commercial region of northern Europe.

With the invention of the steam engine in 1790, the revolution of modern technology began. Machine power increasingly replaced animal and human muscle power. Industry moved from small "gemeinschaft-like" (face to face) settings into larger factories. Because its coalfields, the source of energy, gave England an enormous advantage, it began to dominate industrial technology. By this time the Anabaptists had moved eastward into the Danzig (Gdansk) area, in what is now Poland (Klassen, 1989). Nationalism also rose with industrialization. The pressures of the Prussian state, of which Danzig was then a part, forced large numbers of Mennonites to move farther eastward into the Ukraine, now part of the Soviet Union. Mennonites first moved to Russia in 1789, just before the steam engine was invented. Many Mennonites, however, stayed in the Netherlands and the Danzig area.

Northern Europe, especially the Vistula Delta, was the area from which most Russian Mennonites came. They began to leave Prussia in 1789 and 1803 to form the Chortitza and Molotschna settlements in the Russian Ukraine. Here they became largely farmers on the interior steppes, but their commercial and industrial skills led them also to develop business and commerce related to agriculture (Toews, 1981:289-371). Some left Russia less than 100 years later, immigrating to Canada and the United States in 1874. Others followed in the 1920s. Still others immigrated to Canada in the late 1940s and early 1950s. Their early Dutch urban proclivities lasted through the Russian agrarian period, making them more prone to urbanization in Canada (Urry, 1989).

Of the two major Mennonite branches that emerged in Europe—the Swiss and South German farmers, and the North European entrepreneurs—we would expect the North European Mennonites to have had a greater tendency than the South European Mennonites to move into cities in North America (Driedger and Kauffman, 1982:269-90). This early basic dualism is only one variation of the pluralist Anabaptist movement in the past, and we expect it to have continued into the present.

Denominational Heritage and Sampling

In 1989 there were 856,000 baptized Mennonite adults in the world, of whom 300,500 were located in North America—266,100 in the United States and 114,400 in Canada (Lichdi, 1990:327). In 1972 Kauffman and Harder (1975) reported findings from a sample of 3,591 church members in five North American denominations: Mennonite Church, General Conference Mennonite Church, Mennonite Brethren Church, Brethren in Christ Church, and Evangelical Mennonite Church.[1]

In 1989, seventeen years later, a second survey was made of the same five denominations, with responses from a sample of 3,083 members aged 13 and over. The two samples of the same five denominations permit us to identify changes after a period of seventeen years. A more detailed comparison of the historical origins of these five denominations appeared in Kauffman and Harder's (1975:31-50) original study. Here we can only briefly summarize the origins of each denomination. In 1990 these five denominations, with 232,275 adult members in Canada and the United States, represented 61 percent of the 380,500 North American Mennonites and Brethren in Christ (Lichdi, 1990:404-15).

The Mennonite Church (MC), with 102,276 members in 1989 (Lichdi, 1990:413), is the largest Mennonite denomination in North America, described (arguably, perhaps) by Robert Friedmann (1949:251) as "the guardian proper of the tradition of the fathers." Most of the members are of Swiss-South German origin. They first arrived in the United States about 300 years ago and are now located mostly east of the Mississippi River. Only 10 percent are located in Canada, mostly in Ontario. Many are of Amish background, greatly concerned with non-conformity and still the most rural, but presently changing rapidly.

The name "Mennonite Church" gradually evolved over the past century as denominational organizations emerged. Often called by some the "Old Mennonites" or the traditional church, they strongly identify with the Mennonite heritage and traditions (Kauffman and Harder, 1975:32-35; Schlabach, 1988:14).

The General Conference Mennonite Church (GC) is the second largest Mennonite denomination in North America, with 62,806 members (Lichdi, 1990:404, 415), 53 percent located in the United States and 47 percent in Canada, the majority west of the Mississippi. In 1860 General Conference Mennonite Church was formed by Mennonites from South Germany who had settled in Illinois and Iowa between 1830 and 1850 along with some Mennonites who broke away in 1847 from the "Old" Mennonites, what is now Franconia Conference in eastern Pennsylvania. Its leaders wanted to form a general conference, promote education and missions, and follow the principle of "unity in essentials, liberty in nonessentials, and love in all things" (Kauffman and Harder, 1975:36). The GCs are regarded as the most liberal. The majority are of Dutch-Russian background, with a sizable Swiss minority. The two largest bodies, MC and GC, are presently cooperating extensively in many areas and programs. They are seriously discussing the possibility of greater integration and potential for union.

The people in the Mennonite Brethren Church (MB), with a membership of 43,452 in North America (Lichdi, 1990:412), are almost all of Dutch-Russian heritage. They are located more in Canada than in the United States, mostly west of the Mississippi River. The MBs originated in Russia in 1860, when they separated from the older Kirchliche (ecclesiastical Mennonite) body, which they claimed had strayed far from the

New Testament church. Wanting more emphasis on conversion and evangelism, they lamented the "open godless living" of the old church (Kauffman and Harder, 1975:39-42). The MBs have been slower to cooperate with other Mennonites and have been somewhat more open to link with other Christian evangelicals.

The Brethren in Christ Church (BIC), with a membership of 19,853 in 1989 (Lichdi, 1990:410) is an attempt at synthesis of Anabaptism and Pietism that began in the 1770s in Pennsylvania. The BICs, who emphasized pietism, conversion, and sanctification, grew out of congregations of the "River Brethren," who were gathered from MC, German Baptist, United Brethren, and Wesleyan churches (Kauffman and Harder, 1975:42-45). They are active in the National Association of Evangelicals as well as the Mennonite Central Committee and the Mennonite World Conference. They are located mostly east of the Mississippi, largely in the United States, with some in Ontario.

The Evangelical Mennonite Church, the smallest of the five denominations studied here, had a membership of 3,888 in 1989 (Lichdi, 1990:415). Of Swiss background, its members are located mostly in the American Midwest, with none in Canada. Its roots were in the Old Order Amish church. Originally called Defenseless Mennonites, the Evangelical Mennonites presently represent a variety of backgrounds as a result of evangelism (Kauffman and Harder, 1975:45-48). The EMCs struggle much with their Anabaptist-Mennonite identity and are drawn to more conservative, non-Mennonite evangelicalism.

These brief sketches provide only a glimpse of how these five denominations originated. Their backgrounds vary, and we expect to discover considerable differences between them in attitudes, beliefs, and general activity. The extent of similarities and contrasts awaits our analysis.

The Forces of Modernization

With the invention of steam power in 1790, the revolution of modern technology began, replacing muscle power with machine power, and became a "silent technological transition" (Gendron, 1977:40-61). This industrial transition has gone through a series of stages to what Miller and Form (1980:40-41) called the emergent postindustrial age beginning after World War II, in the 1950s.

This new age requires atomic energy—supplemented by solar, geothermal, and fusion energy—automation in factories, highly trained engineers, and skilled technicians (Smucker, 1980). High-speed computers, video cassettes, cable television, and fax communication via electronic and magnetic media are now in common use. Mennonites as a whole have also increasingly entered this modern age. Let us look at the characteristics of these trends and at the extent of the modernization of Mennonites in North America.

Indicators of Modernization

The notion of modernization has its roots in the thinking of 19th-century philosophers and social scientists who noted a fundamental shift in social life after the beginnings of industrialization in 1790. Early social theorists such as Comte, Marx, Durkheim, Weber, Toennies, and Simmel were all concerned with trying to understand what the profound technological changes were doing to primary social relations, often referred to as *gemeinschaft*, or social solidarity (Kraybill, 1990).

The term *modern* derives from a Latin word meaning "in this time." Marion Levy (1972) argues that modernization is simply the ratio of inanimate to animate sources of power. Peter Berger and others (1973:9) define modernization as "the institutional concomitants of technologically induced economic growth." Technology is the key in both definitions. As social organization is revamped it alters ways of thinking and consciousness. Modern life is not likely to become solitary, poor, nasty, brutish, and short—but crowded, affluent, rational, stratified, mobile, and bureaucratic (Levy, 1972).

There are also degrees of modernity, depending on many factors, which we need to explore. Donald Kraybill (1988; 1990) lists a dozen characteristics which he thinks help delineate this broad concept: differentiation, pluralism, rationalization, functional ties, secularization, futuristics, individuation, abstraction, rapid change, choice, tolerance, and uncertainty. Ted Koontz (1989:404-05) proposes 17 indicators of modernization. Among these are education, socioeconomic status (SES), and mobility, which we will use in creating a model.

In Figure 1-1 we have plotted five dimensions of modernization—urbanization, rationalization, specialization, stratification, and mobility—which we think will have effected a considerable change among the five denominations of our 1989 sample. Each dimension will be discussed in some detail. The following appear to be good structural indicators of the five dimensions selected to measure degree of modernization: percentage of Mennonites who are urban, years of education, types of occupation, amount of income, and extent of residential change. We expect that as the indicators of modernization increase, they will add to Mennonite pluralism. Pluralism seems to be a consequence of increased modernization among Mennonites.

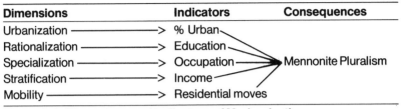

Dimensions	Indicators	Consequences
Urbanization ———————>	% Urban	
Rationalization ———————>	Education	
Specialization ———————>	Occupation ——————>	Mennonite Pluralism
Stratification ———————>	Income	
Mobility ———————>	Residential moves	

Figure 1-1. Dimensions and Indicators of Modernization

The five dimensions of modernization are also positively related to each other, as illustrated in Figure 1-2. The correlations between education and the other four indicators are all positive.[2] Let us examine each of the five dimensions, the indicators, and the expected consequences of pluralism in more detail.

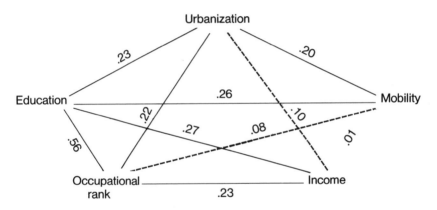

Figure 1-2. Correlations Between the Five Major Modernization Indicators

Extent of Urbanization

The early Anabaptists were extensively involved in European cities where they emerged. Swiss and South German Anabaptists were severely persecuted, and soon they had to retreat to rural areas, but Dutch and North European Anabaptists remain urban to this day (Driedger and Kauffman, 1982). However, many of the latter fled eastward and retreated to agricultural life. Thus the Mennonites who came to the United States and Canada were largely rural agriculturalists, and most remained on the farm until World War II.

These North American Mennonite and Brethren in Christ agriculturalists have begun to move to the cities (Driedger, 1988; Peachey, 1963). The 1972 survey of the Brethren in Christ and four Mennonite denominations in Canada and the United States showed that one-third

(35%) of the members lived in urban centers of 2,500 or more (Kauffman and Harder, 1975:54-55).[3] The extent of urbanization varied considerably by denomination, with more than one-half (56%) of the Mennonite Brethren and only one-fourth (26%) of the members of the Mennonite Church living in centers of over 2,500 (see Table 1-1). It was clear that by 1972 considerable urbanization had occurred.

Table 1-1. Percent Urban, Five Denominations, 1972 and 1989

Denominations	1972 N=3,591	1989 N=3,083
Mennonite Brethren	56	73
General Conference Mennonite	40	53
Evangelical Mennonite	39	47
Mennonite Church	26	37
Brethren in Christ	30	32
Five denominations	35	48

Seventeen years later, urbanization had increased substantially.[4] In 1989 about one-half (48%) lived in centers of 2,500 or more. Three-fourths (73%) of the Mennonite Brethren and over one-half (53%) of the General Conference Mennonites lived in urban centers. During this 17-year period urbanization among the Mennonite Brethren increased by 17 percent, and among the General Conference Mennonites by 13 percent. The largest denomination (MC), which was the most rural in 1972 (26%), has also begun to urbanize, with over one-third (37%) of its members urban in 1989. Evangelical Mennonites showed moderate change (39 to 47% urban). The Brethren in Christ remained stable over the 17 years (30 and 32%).

We expect these major changes over one generation to have had a profound influence on Mennonite life and thought. Such changes occurring recently make the Mennonites one of the best groups for studying the effects of change and modernization. Controlling for variations of change in urbanization by denomination will provide us with interesting comparisons, which we will discuss in greater detail in chapter 10. In chapter 2 we will further analyze these changes nationally, regionally, and denominationally. We expect such increased modernization to have brought about more openness and pluralism (Driedger, et al., 1978:294-311).

Education and Rationalization

Many of the early Anabaptist leaders had studied theology and attended universities. As the Mennonites retreated to rural areas they continued to value basic education, for reading and writing, but became suspicious of higher education. The Low German saying *"je geleheda, je vekeheda"* (the more learned, the more confused) conveyed an attitude toward higher learning that has endured in many Mennonite communities until recently. Agricultural Mennonites usually had six to eight years of schooling. However, with urbanization came a greater interest in education.

Table 1-2 shows the educational attainment of church members in 1972 and 1989. In 1972 one-third (32%) of all Mennonites had obtained higher education (college and beyond); this did not vary greatly by denomination.

Table 1-2. Educational Attainment by Denomination, 1972 and 1989

Level attained	1972					
	MB	GC	EMC	MC	BIC	Total
Elementary (grades 1-8)	24	19	15	28	20	24
Secondary (grades 9-12)	41	42	49	46	49	44
College (grades 13-16)	20	22	24	17	19	19
Graduate school (1+ years)	16	17	12	9	12	13
Total percentages	101	100	100	100	100	100
	1989					
Elementary (grades 1-8)	8	10	4	15	8	11
Secondary (grades 9-12)	32	37	39	41	48	39
College (grades 13-16)	33	32	37	24	28	29
Graduate school (1+ years)	27	21	20	20	16	21
Total percentages	100	100	100	100	100	100

By 1989 one-half of the respondents reported at least one year of college attendance. Sixty percent of the Mennonite Brethren went to college, as did many Evangelical Mennonites (57%). Somewhat fewer than half of the respondents in the Mennonite Church (44%) and Brethren in Christ (44%) reported at least some undergraduate education. In one generation the percentage of those attending college for at least one year had risen from 32 to 50 percent. One-third (36%) of rural-farm Mennonites had attained at least some undergraduate study, compared with two-thirds (64%) of the Mennonites in large metropolitan centers.

Occupation and Specialization

The early Anabaptists were at the cutting edge of occupational specialization; many of them were craftspeople, no longer working on the land. However, with persecution this situation soon changed, especially in southern and eastern Europe, where most of the Anabaptists became farmers. Most Mennonite immigrants to Canada and the United States pioneered as farmers and played an important role in opening up virgin lands to cultivation. After World War II the occupational diversity greatly increased. In 1989 there were four times as many in the professions (28%) as in farming (7%), counting both males and females.

Table 1-3 shows that in 1989 more than one-fourth (28%) of the Mennonites and BICs in North America were in professional occupations, more than in any other occupational category. Professionals have almost doubled, from 16 percent in 1972 to 28 percent in 1989. In 1989 more than one-third (36%) of the males and one-fifth (21%) of the females were in the professions, largely in teaching, medicine, and social services. One in 10, mostly male, were in business; and about as many, mostly female, were in sales and clerical work. For both males and females farming has declined, from 11 percent in 1972 to 7 percent in 1989, although 15 percent of the males are still in farming, down from 23 percent in 1972.[5]

Table 1-3. Occupation by Sex, 1972 and 1989

Occupational class	1972			1989		
	Male N=1589	Female N=1858	Total N=3447	Male N=1401	Female N=1613	Total N=3014
Professional	23	10	16	36	21	28
Business proprietor or manager	8	1	5	16	4	9
Sales/clerical workers	5	8	7	6	15	11
Craftspeople	11	0	5	10	1	5
Machine operators	8	2	5	6	1	4
Service workers	2	4	3	3	5	4
Farmers	23	0	11	15	1	7
Laborers	5	1	2	2	1	1
Housewives/husbands	0	60	32	1	45	25
Students	14	14	14	5	7	6
Total percentages	100	100	100	100	101	100

Forty-five percent of the women in the 1989 sample listed themselves as housewives, and 7 percent (mostly teenagers) as students.[6] Almost one-half (48%) of the women were in the work force, slightly lower than the national figures for Canada (53%) and the United States (57%). Mennonite women in the work force almost doubled (26% to 48%) between 1972 and 1989; more than half were in the urban work force. The percentage of Mennonite women who reported being (primarily) housewives declined from 60 to 45 percent. Increased urbanization and education have opened up new opportunities in a variety of specialized occupations. We expect that this occupational diversification has altered Mennonite attitudes and behavior and contributed to greater pluralism.

Income and Stratification

Karl Marx argued that industrialization stratified individuals into rich and poor classes. To what extent has increased education and specialization of occupation resulted in greater differences in Mennonite income? In the 1972 study Evangelical Mennonites had the highest median household income, and the General Conference Mennonites the lowest.[7] That is no longer the case. In 1989 the Mennonite Brethren, who were also the most urban and the most educated, had the highest median income, and the General Conference Mennonites still had the lowest. One-fourth (26%) of the Mennonite Brethren households earned more than $50,000 (4% earned more than $100,000), and only 5 percent had an income of under $10,000. Only 16 percent of the General Conference Mennonite households earned over $50,000 (2% over $100,000), and 7 percent had an income of less than $10,000.

Table 1-4 shows that the median Mennonite household income was between $30,000 and $40,000 dollars. Nineteen percent earned above $50,000 and 3 percent above $100,000; 5 percent earned below $10,000. Farmers represented the largest range of income, with 10 percent earning under $10,000 and 7 percent, $100,000 or more. One-fourth (25%) of the Mennonite households in which the respondent's occupation was business proprietor or manager reported earnings above $50,000, while one-third (34%) of the farmers were earning less than $20,000.[8] The range of incomes was very large, with those in business and the professions representing one-third of all Mennonites and earning the highest incomes.

Mobility and Residential Stability

Mennonites have made many migrations during their 465-year history. The early Anabaptists often fled from persecution, and in many lands they were barely tolerated because of their religious beliefs. Their nonviolent position and refusal to serve in the military required many moves.

Table 1-4. Mennonite Household Income by Occupational Status, 1989

	Percent by income level								
	Under $10,000 N=153	$10-19,999 N=447	$20-29,999 N=719	$30-39,999 N=526	$40-49,999 N=397	$50-74,999 N=365	$75-99,999 N=99	$100,000 plus N=79	Total N=2784
Profes-sionals	3	10	23	22	18	18	4	2	29
Business owners/ workers	3	8	18	23	16	18	8	7	10
Sales/ clerical workers	3	13	26	22	17	15	4	1	11
Crafts-people	7	23	23	20	15	10	2	0	5
Machine operators	4	25	30	20	14	7	1	0	4
Service workers	8	21	32	17	15	6	1	0	4
Farmers	10	25	33	10	8	4	2	8	8
Laborers	6	32	17	24	10	5	0	7	1
Housewives/ husbands	10	22	30	15	9	9	3	2	24
Students	4	16	21	15	18	20	3	3	4
Percent of total	5	16	27	19	14	13	3	3	100

As Mennonites and BICs have begun to modernize, we would expect that those living in the city would also be more mobile. As shown in Figure 1-2 the relationship between urbanization and mobility is significant ($r=.20$). Three times as many Mennonites in large cities (21%)—compared to the farm residents (7%)—had lived in the same community for less than a year.

The reverse was also the case, with 29 percent of the farm residents having lived in their present communities for more than 20 years, and only 11 percent of Mennonites in large cities having done so. Mennonites with more education and in the professions also moved much more often than the less educated and the farmers. There is, however, no correlation between level of income and mobility. Mennonites in business earned the most and also stayed in one community longer, unlike professionals, who earned somewhat less but moved more.

Age is an important factor in mobility, and the two correlate highly and negatively ($r= -.36$). This means that older people are less mobile. Mennonites in their twenties are very mobile. By contrast, four times as many over the age of 50 lived in one community for 20 years or more. Also, the clergy moved more often than laypeople. Mobility is highly correlated with youth, the pastoral ministry, higher education, urbanization, and the professions.

Linking Modernization and Identity

So far we have explored the dimensions of modernization which we expect will have affected Mennonite identity. We will devote chapters 3-7 (part two of this volume) to developing the concept and dimensions to be analyzed in part three. However, let us at least introduce the concept of identity and illustrate how it links with modernization.

We expect that Mennonites will have become more pluralistic—as the title, *Mennonite Mosaic*, implies—with the changes that have occurred. Several books that address the issue of Mennonite identity appeared in recent years, such as *Why I Am a Mennonite*, edited by Harry Loewen (1988), *Mennonite Identity*, edited by Calvin Redekop and Samuel Steiner (1988), *Mennonite Identity in Conflict*, by Leo Driedger (1988), and *Anabaptist-Mennonite Identities in Ferment*, edited by Leo Driedger and Leland Harder (1990). They all clearly show that North American Mennonites are in the process of redefining who they are and what their distinctive contribution in modern societies might be.

Dimensions of Identity

Figure 1-3 presents the dimensions of Mennonite identity and some of the indicators which will be used to analyze the variations. The Anabaptists originated in 16th-century Europe as part of the Protestant Reformation (Stayer, 1975; Klaassen, 1990). We will examine measures of some of the original Anabaptist religious beliefs among today's Mennonites, as well as subsequent religious developments in North America (Kraus, 1990). The first central dimension of Mennonite identity to be discussed will be *religion*; religious beliefs and practice will be important indicators in our analysis of this dimension in chapter 3.

The reconstruction of a believers' *community* was a second part of the early radical Anabaptist movement. According to Hans Denck, "*Christ sein heisst Christum im Leben nachfolgen*," meaning that to be Christian involves following Jesus in everyday life. Discipleship was translated into primary communities of gemeinschaft, fellowship, and mutual aid. In chapter 4 we will examine the current Mennonite community to see to what extent these early practices are still followed, and to what extent Mennonite communities have changed. Is it still possible to create believers' communities today? To what extent is peacemaking a central part of such communities, in both the country and the city?

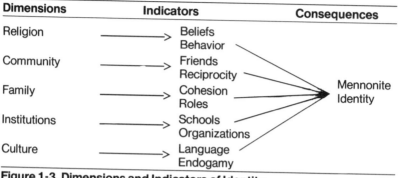

Figure 1-3. Dimensions and Indicators of Identity

In the 16th century many Anabaptist *families* fled from place to place to escape horrific persecution and martyrdom. The treks into East European countries and Russia and finally to North America forced the Mennonites into renewed pioneering efforts. The retreat to an agrarian lifestyle brought with it large extended families, strongly patriarchal, in which women's and children's roles were often subservient.

As Mennonites become increasingly urban, as formal education and income increase, as occupational roles change, with more and more women joining the work force, the functions and structure of the modern family also change. In chapter 6 we will explore the changing roles and the extent of family cohesion and solidarity as separation and divorce increase.

In many places Mennonites have organized and supported in-group *institutions*—including their own Bible schools, high schools, colleges, and seminaries—to teach their heritage and theology. Various mutual aid and service agencies have also emerged to reinforce the influences of the church, family, schools, and other organizations. On the steppes of Russia, Mennonites were "institutionally complete," to use Breton's (1964) term; as a minority group they created all of their own, separate institutions. To what extent do such Mennonite organizations still exist, and how effective are they? To what extent are such in-group institutions still a source of Mennonite identity and solidarity?

Moving from country to country, Mennonites frequently changed their identity and language, and often they brought with them distinctive cuisine and dress, which resulted in unique Mennonite *cultural* patterns. Their children were encouraged to marry within their own religious and cultural groups; endogamy (marriage within the group) was preferred and sometimes enforced. Most Mennonites in North America have adopted English as their language, as well as the prevailing English cultural patterns of North America. In the rural setting distinctive culture was an important part of Mennonite identity. In chapter 7 we will see to what extent a distinctive cultural pattern is still a part of Mennonite peoplehood and identity in North America, and we will look at the different cultural versions in the various regions as well.

Processes of Dialectical Change

Having presented the dimensions of modernization and the dimensions of Mennonite identity, we wish to predict in what ways they might be related, which we will call processes of dialectical change, as shown in Figure 1-4. We expect that urbanization and education will have influenced Mennonite religiosity and community in the direction of *secularization*, which Mennonite religious beliefs and community will have sought to combat. Thus, secularization and *sacralization* are in conflict, in a dialectical process (back and forth influence), resulting in modification and/or renewal (Driedger and Harder, 1990:1-10; Hamm, 1987).

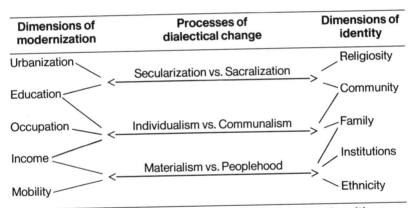

Figure 1-4. Linking Dimensions of Modernization and Identity with Processes of Change

We expect the dimensions of education, occupation, and income (indicators of social status) will have led to greater *individualism*, which Mennonite communities and family will, again, have sought to counteract in the struggle to maintain distinctive identity. As individualism and *communalism* come into conflict, adjustments and changes will again occur. In rural Mennonite communities family and communal identities may be stronger, while in urban communities individualism may be more influential.

We also expect that the income and mobility dimensions of modernization will have affected Mennonite institutions and ethnicity. This seems to be a battle between *materialism* and a distinctive Mennonite *peoplehood* and communal emphasis. Mennonite schools, businesses, and arts—together with cultural elements of language, cuisine, in-group friends and organizations—presumably are designed to create in-group networks which enhance Mennonite identity. Mennonites' mobility and economic well-being increase with attractions elsewhere. The three processes of dialectical change basically represent the encounter between Mennonite values and those of the larger society.

The Influence of Modernity on Identity

We will have more opportunity to show the effects of the five modernization variables on Mennonite attitudes and behavior throughout this volume. However, let us briefly present several items to illustrate the effects of education, occupational status, and higher income on Mennonite identity.

The diversification of attitudes is evident when we combine education, occupation, and income in what sociologists call a socioeconomic status or social-class scale. We expect that respondents who score high on education, income, and occupation will demonstrate very different attitudes and behavior than those who score low on all three. Using a few select issues—introduced more fully in later chapters—Table 1-5 illustrates these differences.

Table 1-5. The Relation of Socioeconomic Status to Political Behavior and Social Attitudes

	Socioeconomic status				
Scale	Low N=477	Lower middle N=537	Upper middle N=483	High N=510	Pearson's r
	(Percent)				
Strong on fundamentalism	33	26	17	8	-.31
Favor political participation	13	21	28	38	.28
Favor racial equality	16	24	33	54	.34
Favor expanded roles for women	19	28	38	56	.29
Favor greater women's roles in church leadership	19	33	43	63	.36
Memberships in four or more community organizations	6	14	20	39	.35
Own many mass media devices	5	11	19	21	.28
Total SES scores	24	27	24	25	

Mennonites of low socioeconomic status (SES) scored higher on fundamentalist theology, hence the significant negative correlation between these scales. While one-third (33%) of the low-SES Mennonites scored high on fundamentalism, only 8 percent of the high-SES Mennonites did so. Fundamentalism does not appeal to many higher-status Mennonites. We will analyze the different types of theology more carefully in chapter 3.

Mennonites of high socioeconomic status are much more liberal in their attitudes and involvement in social issues. Three times as many (38%) high-status Mennonites as low-status Mennonites (13%) favored political participation. Attitudes favorable toward racial equality were held by even more higher-status Mennonites (54% compared to 16% for lower SES). Three times as many higher-status respondents also favored expanded roles for women (56 to 19%), and even more favored greater women's roles in church leadership (63 to 19%). Higher-status Mennonites were also six times (6 to 39%) as involved in organizational memberships and had a high rate of ownership of mass media devices (TV, radio, VCR, video camera, computers) four times (5 to 21%) that of lower-status respondents. These few items clearly illustrate that there are substantial differences between Mennonites of high and low status.

Throughout this volume we wish to show the extent to which the five indicators of modernization affect Mennonite beliefs, values, attitudes, and behavior. We expect that in many areas modernization will have led to greater secularization, individualism, and materialism. However, we also expect that the negative influences of modernization will have been resisted through strong religious commitment, community solidarity, family networks, Mennonite institutions, and a consciousness of peoplehood. In the following chapters we will observe where changes are occurring, the degree to which Mennonites are becoming more pluralistic, and the extent to which they have the will to survive.

Summary

The early Anabaptists were at the cutting edge of the religious, political, economic, and social ferment of the 16th-century Reformation. Many were craftspeople in urban areas, but many others were driven by persecution into agricultural areas on the periphery of the various societies in which they survived. Since then, Mennonites in North America have again become half urban, with one-third of their members in the professions and business ownership and management. Only 23 percent live on farms, and only 15 percent of the males are farmers by primary occupation.

Modernization and industrialization are profoundly affecting Mennonites. Using data from the 1989 church member survey, we explored the impact of five dimensions of modernization: urbanization, rationalization, specialization, stratification, and mobility. Indicators of these five dimensions of modernization—degree of urbanization, amount of education, occupational status, level of income, and permanence of residence—are all highly correlated, indicating that they are indeed related aspects of modernization.

Of the five denominations studied in 1972 and 1989, the Mennonite Brethren have changed the most over the 17 years and have become the most modernized of the five Mennonite groups. In 1989 they were the most highly urbanized, the most highly educated, the most strongly represented in the professions and business, and had the highest average income. The Brethren in Christ, on the other hand, were the least urbanized and educated, and their incomes and occupational levels were the lowest; they had experienced the least change since 1972.

We expected that modernization would lead to greater differentiation of Mennonites and Brethren in Christ, resulting in more heterogeneity and pluralism. That is indeed the case. Mennonites of higher socioeconomic status are less attracted to fundamentalist theology, favor more political participation, are more supportive of racial equality, and are more heavily involved in social organizations and ownership and use of mass media devices.

If modernization has these liberalizing tendencies, where are the sources of retention of a distinctive Mennonite identity in the future? In this chapter we could only outline five factors—religion, community, family, Mennonite institutions, and ethnic culture (peoplehood)—which could be essential in retaining Mennonite solidarity and identity. These five factors will be dealt with in greater depth in chapters 3-7. Having introduced the challenge of modernization in chapter 1, we will next look at the regional settings in North America in order to provide an additional context for the discussion of Mennonite identity and the consequences of modernization in succeeding chapters.

CHAPTER 2

Sketching the Regional Settings

IN CHAPTER 1 we suggested that modernization is increasingly making Mennonites in North America more pluralistic and heterogeneous. In this chapter we wish to explore whether such pluralism is also evident in the various regions of North America. We need to map the Mennonite settings historically, demographically, and regionally to provide a general context for subsequent discussion of various issues regarding pluralism.

North American Mennonite Beginnings

In chapter 1 we began with the early Anabaptist ancestors in Europe. Here we trace early North American beginnings and the move westward, comparing the Swiss and the Dutch immigrations as well as American and Canadian variations (Redekop, 1989).

Moving East to West

With a few exceptions the South European Mennonites came to North America from 1700 to 1830, most of them to the United States, and settled east of the Mississippi River; and to this day they are located mainly in the eastern half of the United States (MacMaster, 1985).[1] The first South European Mennonites arrived in southeastern Pennsylvania in 1683.[2] (This area still has the largest concentration of Mennonites in North America [Ruth, 1984].) One hundred years later, during the American Revolution, a group of South European Mennonites migrated to southern Ontario; they were the first Mennonites to arrive in Canada. Between 1800 and 1850 a second migration headed west and crossed the

Allegheny Mountains into Ohio, Indiana, and Illinois (MacMaster, 1985; Dyck, 1967). Later a relatively small group moved to Kansas, and a few to Alberta. By the 1880s the rural South European Mennonites who came directly from Switzerland and South Germany in the 18th century were fanning out westward and establishing scattered settlements in Missouri, Iowa, Kansas, Nebraska, and Oregon (Driedger and Kauffman, 1982:273). Only about 10 percent entered Canada.

While the largest megalopolis (Boston-New York-Philadelphia-Baltimore-Washington) in the world was in the making, Mennonites were living nearby, a few miles from Philadelphia. In Canada the Mennonites of South European origin were located in midwestern and southern Ontario, the country's greatest industrial area. Toronto and the nearby U.S. cities of Chicago, Detroit, and Cleveland were expanding into metropolises (Fretz, 1974; 1989). These urban centers transmitted their communications and values into the rural areas where South European Mennonites farmed. One could only expect that Mennonites would also increasingly migrate to the cities as many of the general rural population moved to urban centers, unless the factor of rural South European origin acted as a deterrent.

In contrast to the South European Mennonites, the North European Mennonites came to the New World much later. They settled basically west of the Mississippi; they migrated to Canada in greater numbers than did the South Europeans; and to this day they are heavily concentrated in the North American prairies region. The first Russian Mennonites arrived in 1874 and settled primarily in Manitoba and Kansas; a few settled in Minnesota (Epp, 1974). Manitoba and Kansas are still the two largest North European Mennonite centers. Later, the descendants of these Mennonites, as well as new immigrants of the 1920s, moved westward, until large numbers reached British Columbia, California, and—to a lesser extent—Washington and Oregon. In short, the North European Mennonites who came from Russia fanned westward again, and very few moved eastward (a few Russian Mennonites of the immigrations of the 1920s remained in Ontario). The overlap of eastern South European Mennonites and western North European Mennonites is minimal (Driedger and Kauffman, 1982:273).

Metropolitan centers in the West developed fairly late, industrialization did not expand as fast as in the East, and generally the prairies are more sparsely populated. Although the urban centers near rural Mennonite concentrations—Minneapolis, Winnipeg, Wichita, Saskatoon, Calgary, Vancouver, and Fresno—are growing, they are newer and less industrialized. Here, too, we expect Mennonites to migrate to the cities, but not as extensively, unless the factor of urban North European origin still acts as a stimulus.

Differential National Settlement Patterns

The differential residential patterns of Mennonites in the United States and Canada were demonstrated in the previous section. Prior to the twentieth century both countries welcomed immigrants to fill their vast open spaces. In the 1920s, however, American immigration policy changed, and acceptance of new immigrants was severely restricted. Canadian immigration policy has remained fairly open to this day, with selective restrictions from time to time. Thus, after 1920 most Mennonite immigrants settled in Canada, and a vast majority of these were of North European background. Since then, Canada has become the home of a large number of North European Mennonites, 80 to 90 percent being of Dutch origin and coming to Canada via Prussia and Russia (Francis, 1951; 1955).

In the 1920s (50 years after the Russian immigration beginning in 1874), some 20,000 Russian Mennonites arrived in Canada and settled mostly on the prairies (Epp, 1974:282). After World War II, between 1947 and 1961, 12,000 more Russian Mennonites arrived and settled in the western provinces (Epp, 1982:67-90). These two major migrations of Mennonites to Canada were possible because of greater openness in Canadian immigration policy, although even the Canadian doors closed after each of these major migrations. While the immigrants of the 1920s originally settled mostly on farms, the immigrants of the 1950s settled mostly in cities. While the first Russian immigrants were reluctant to move to the cities, immigrants of the 1920s, who had engaged in technological farming in Russia, were more open to urban life, and immigrants of the 1950s, having been scattered around Europe by the Russian Revolution and the two world wars, were ready to move directly to Canadian cities (Toews, 1981:289-371; Urry, 1989). Thus the two waves of Mennonite emigrants from Russia came to Canada, bypassing the United States. These urban-prone Mennonites accelerated Canadian Mennonite urbanization (Driedger and Kauffman, 1982:269-90).

While recent Mennonite immigration is peculiar to Canada because of its more liberal immigration policy, a second factor has differentiated the two nations. Americans have historically prided themselves in their ethnic melting-pot ideal of immigrants from all over the world gathering to mold a new nation. Since assimilation was the aim, ethnic origins were played down (Newman, 1973). Canada has always been more oriented toward cultural pluralism. The native Indians still occupy much of the landmass in the northlands; the French, who represent one-fourth of the population, perceive of themselves as a distinct society; the empire loyalists, who settled in Ontario and the Maritime provinces, exhibit strong British loyalties; and the many others who came to Canada more recently also maintain their own vibrant identities (Driedger, 1989). While two official languages are legally perpetuated in Canada, the government promotes a multicultural policy. It is more popular to be ethnically distinct in Canada than it is in the United States (Driedger, 1987).

We do not know to what extent Mennonites in Canada acquired a more open attitude toward pluralism, and to what extent they were therefore more willing to risk exposing themselves to city life. Were Canadian Mennonites less stigmatized and therefore more open to enter nonagricultural occupations? Were educational, economic, political, and social institutions in Canada more open to having a variety of people compete and contribute? It may also be that, since the West was in stages of new growth, and since status and prestige were less established than in the East, Mennonites gained easier access into life in the national arena.

Our review of the development of historical Mennonite roots leads us to expect that (1) Mennonites of North European origin will have been more likely to urbanize than South European Mennonites; (2) western Mennonites (of North European origin) will have been more open to urbanize than eastern Mennonites (South European); and (3) Canadian Mennonites (mostly of North European origin, and more recent immigrants) will have been more urban than American Mennonites. Will our 1989 data support these predictions?

The Regional Settings

In Figure 2-1 we have plotted four regions in the United States and three in Canada where Mennonites and Brethren in Christ are heavily concentrated. Mennonites in the American East are located east of the Allegheny Mountains, heavily concentrated in Pennsylvania and Virginia, and not far from Philadelphia (MacMaster, 1985). Mennonites in the American Midwest, between the Alleghenies and the Mississippi River, are concentrated in Illinois, Indiana, and Ohio—with Chicago as the metropolitan center. For Mennonites living on the American prairies, between the Mississippi River and the Rocky Mountains, Wichita is the urban center. West of the Rockies, American Mennonites live along the Pacific Coast, with Fresno as their most prominent center (Toews, 1975). The three Canadian Mennonite regions are clearly centered around Kitchener-Waterloo in Ontario, Winnipeg and Saskatoon on the prairies, and the Fraser Valley and Vancouver on the West Coast (Fretz, 1989; Driedger, 1988).

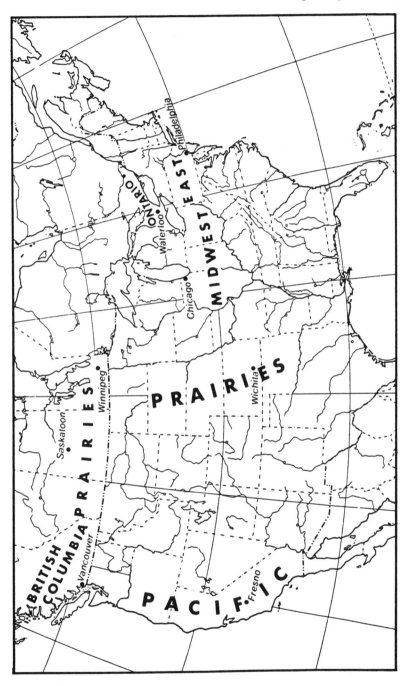

Figure 2-1. American and Canadian Mennonite Regions and Metropolitan Centers

Denominational Concentrations by Region

The Swiss and South German Mennonites who settled in the eastern United States in the 18th century still predominate in the American East and Midwest, most of them affiliated with the Mennonite Church. The Brethren in Christ are also a significant group in the East, but the others are hardly represented. General Conference Mennonites are the second largest group in the Midwest, although a relatively small group. The Evangelical Mennonites, a small group, are concentrated in the Midwest. (See Table 2-1.)

Table 2-1. Distribution of Participating Denominations by Nation and Region

Denominations	United States				Canada			Total
	East	Midwest	Prairies	Pacific	East	Prairies	Pacific	N=3040
Menn. Church	70	75	33	30	46	7		45
General Conf.	5	14	50	7	24	59	31	27
Menn. Breth.			17	56	18	34	69	18
Breth. in Christ	25	3		7	12			8
Evang. Menn.		8						2
Total percentage	100	100	100	100	100	100	100	100

Half of the Mennonites on the American prairies are General Conference Mennonites, and one-third are part of the Mennonite Church, with a significant number of Mennonite Brethren. The other two groups, with only a few scattered, small congregations on the prairies, were not represented in the sample. On the American Pacific Coast the Mennonite Brethren are a clear majority, while almost one-third belong to the Mennonite Church. The Mennonite Church predominates in the East and the Midwest, and the General Conference Mennonites and the Mennonite Brethren are clear majorities on the prairies and the Pacific Coast, respectively, in the United States.

In Canada none of the five groups holds a majority in the East (primarily Ontario), but the Mennonite Church (46%) is the largest group, with substantial clusters of General Conference Mennonites (24%, Mennonite Brethren (18%), and Brethren in Christ (12%) (Fretz, 1989). As in the pattern on the American prairies, the General Conference Mennonites are a majority on the Canadian prairies, with one-third strongly represented by the Mennonite Brethren. On the Canadian Pacific Coast this configuration is reversed, with the Mennonite Brethren constituting two-thirds and the General Conference Mennonites one-third.

To summarize, we have defined basically four different geographical regions—with the Mennonite Church predominating in the American East and Midwest, east of the Mississippi; the General Conference Mennonites a majority on the American and Canadian prairies; the Mennonite Brethren predominant on the Canadian and American Pacific Coast; and a multi-Mennonite grouping in eastern Canada, mostly in Ontario. It is interesting that the Mennonite Church is so predominant in the eastern United States, while in eastern Canada we have the most heterogeneous mix of Mennonites, which J. Winfield Fretz (1989:89-129) describes under the categories of progressive, moderate, and conservative. Not surprisingly, in Ontario and other eastern provinces some of these groups have formed a new alignment—the Mennonite Conference of Eastern Canada.

Rural-Urban Variations by Region

In chapter 1 we suggested that urbanization acted as an influence toward greater modernization. Is this influence felt equally in the seven different regions of North America? From our earlier discussion of the greater urbanization of North European Anabaptists, we would expect Dutch-Prussian-Russian Mennonites to move to the cities more readily than Swiss and South German Mennonites.

Table 2-2 shows that Mennonites in our sample are fairly evenly distributed among six categories, ranging from the farm to the metropolis, but there are striking regional variations. In 1989 two-thirds of the American Mennonites in the East (67%) were rural, and one-third lived in cities (one-fourth in small cities). In 1972 four out of five (79%) were rural, so they have urbanized somewhat, but are still the most rural (Kauffman and Harder, 1975). They are mostly of Swiss and South German origin and belong largely to the Mennonite Church. Eastern American Mennonites are unique in that one-third (34%) lived in rural, nonfarm settings. Even though most do not farm, they prefer country living to city life. Few (9%) were living in larger cities.

American Mennonites in the Midwest are similar to eastern Mennonites except that more live on the farm (27%), and not as many (23%) are rural nonfarm residents. Two-thirds (65%) are rural, and more prefer the small city to the metropolis. These American Mennonites east of the Mississippi are definitely the most rural, confirming our expectations that Mennonites of Swiss and South German origin do not move to the city as readily (Driedger and Kauffman, 1982; Juhnke, 1989).

One-third (32%) of American Mennonites on the prairies live on the farm, and another third (35%) live in the city. These prairie Mennonites are the most rural-farm of any in the seven regions, and they are about as urban as eastern and midwestern Mennonites.

Table 2-2. Rural-Urban Residence by Nation and Region, 1989

Residence	United States				Canada			Total
	East	Midwest	Prairies	Pacific	East	Prairies	Pacific	N=3006
Rural farm	21	27	32	9	29	16	8	23
Rural nonfarm	34	23	9	6	8	3	9	17
Village (under 2,500)	12	15	24	2	16	6	6	13
Small city (2,500-25,000)	24	22	21	18	9	22	18	21
Med. city (25,000-250,00)	6	10	6	25	32	20	43	15
Metropolis (250,000-plus)	3	3	8	40	7	33	16	12
Total percentage	100	100	100	100	100	100	100	100

The American Mennonites on the Pacific Coast clearly represent a very different residential pattern than do those in the other three American regions. More than four out of five (83%) are urban, and 40 percent live in a large metropolis; they are heavily concentrated in Fresno, California. Only 9 percent live on farms. The trend toward high urbanization was already clearly evident in 1972, and it has escalated since. These American Mennonites on the West Coast are largely Mennonite Brethren who originated in Holland, coming via Russia to settle west of the Mississippi 100 years ago. Why have so many Mennonite Brethren moved to the city, and why have they moved to the Pacific Coast in greater numbers than any of the other denominations?

Do the three Canadian regions follow the American Mennonite residential patterns? Similar to Mennonites in the American Midwest, 29 percent of the Mennonites in Ontario live on farms, but only eight percent live off farms outside villages. Unlike the eastern American Mennonites, almost half (48%) of the Ontario Mennonites are urban, a majority of them living in the medium-sized city of Waterloo-Kitchener (11 congregations) (Driedger, 1990). Earlier we said that they are the most heterogenous denominationally. They have only gradually become more urban since 1972; their Swiss origin appears to restrain their urbanization.

Mennonites on the Canadian prairies are quite different from those on the American prairies. Only half as many (16%) live on the farm, and half as many (25%) are rural. Three-fourths are urban—with the strongest preference for the metropolis of over 250,000 (33%)—and are heavily concentrated in Winnipeg (47 churches) and Saskatoon (14 churches) (Driedger, 1990). As late as 1972, 42 percent of the Mennonites on the Canadian prairies still lived on the farm, and over half (56%) were rural. With the trend to larger, mechanized farms, more and more have moved to metropolitan centers, such as Winnipeg, Saskatoon, Calgary, and Edmonton.

Since only North European Mennonites are located on Canada's West Coast in British Columbia, and since a majority are Mennonite Brethren as on the American Pacific Coast, have they also urbanized as fast? Mennonites on the Canadian Pacific Coast are almost as urban (77%) as their American counterparts (83%). Only 8 percent live on the farm, and 43 percent live largely in the various suburbs of greater Vancouver, which had a population of 1.2 million in 1981. The medium city (any of the Vancouver suburbs) and metropolis categories could really be collapsed, so that one could say that 59 percent live in the greater Vancouver metropolis of over one million. Moving to large cities has greatly escalated since 1972, when 42 percent of the Mennonites in British Columbia were urban (Driedger and Kauffman, 1982).

Political Involvement by Region

Since one's politics are often influenced by regional issues and the circumstances at municipal, state/provincial, and national levels, it seems appropriate to examine politics by region. We have collapsed the American East and Midwest into a new category, the American East, and the prairie and Pacific regions in both countries into the categories of American West and Canadian West. In our discussion so far we have implied that Mennonites of North European ancestry may be more open to involvement and participation in political affairs. Are there such differentiations, and if so, does openness to greater involvement manifest itself in liberal or conservative terms?

Table 2-3 shows great variation in Mennonite attitudes toward political issues. Most Mennonites believe that they should study political issues (79%) and vote in municipal, state/provincial, and national elections (84%). The figures in 1972 were 68 and 76 percent, respectively, so there has been a considerable increase. Many are still reluctant to favor political action, although over half (56%) favor *some* action, while in 1972 only 32 percent felt this way. However, only a minority (39% in 1989; 25% in 1972) favor having their congregations endorse specific candidates for office and discuss politics from the church pulpit (28% in 1989; 16% in 1972). Mennonites today are generally more willing than they were in 1972 to participate in politics, but they wish to do so selectively.

Two-thirds (65%) of the 1989 respondents voted in most elections, while fewer than half (46%) of the 1972 respondents did so; these figures indicate a considerable increase in political participation. Almost half (48%) favored conservative political parties, and only 10 percent favored liberal parties (23% took no position at all, and others favored liberal Republicans or conservative Democrats in the United States or other minority parties in Canada).

Table 2-3. Political Attitudes and Participation by Region, 1989

Political issues	American		Canadian		Total
	East	West	East	West	N=3083
	(Percent)				
Political attitudes					
Should vote in elections	77	82	87	93	84
Should study political issues	72	82	78	83	79
May hold government office	68	77	82	89	78
Should witness to the state	71	79	75	72	75
Encourage political action	49	58	59	56	56
Should endorse candidates	33	42	41	39	39
May discuss politics from pulpit	25	29	36	26	28
Political participation					
Voted in most elections	47	65	67	85	65
Favor conservative Republicans (U.S.) or Conservatives (Canada)	49	46	31	62	48
Favor liberal Democrats (U.S.) or NDPs in Canada	6	10	18	10	10
Have held government office	3	6	2	3	4
Total	23	46	9	22	100

While Mennonites are willing to participate more today than formerly, they are doing so from a very conservative political base. Theron Schlabach (1988:149-50) claims that eastern Mennonites in the Lancaster and Franconia Conferences voted Whig and Republican as early as the 1840s, and some helped prominent Republicans to get elected. According to James Juhnke (1975:50-54), Russian Mennonites in Kansas also voted mostly Republican. Among the 1989 respondents, 4 percent (125 individuals) had at one time held an elective or appointive local, state/provincial, or national government office. In the 1972 sample 98 individuals (3%) had held such an office.

There are important, interesting regional variations which tend to confirm our hypothesis that Mennonites of Dutch origin are more willing to enter the political fray than are Mennonites of Swiss origin. American Mennonites east of the Mississippi scored below average on every one of the 11 indicators of political involvement in Table 2-3. There are also differences between the American East and the Canadian West in many cases.

Of significance is that two-thirds of the Mennonites in the Canadian West voted for conservative candidates, considerably above the general regional average. Among those who voted in 1989, 72 percent of American Mennonites voted for George Bush as president, and 60 percent of the Canadian Mennonites voted for Brian Mulroney as prime minister. Participation in politics has increased since 1972, but political conservatism overall has remained about their same. Interestingly, western Canadians vote most conservatively, and eastern Canadians vote most liberally, while Americans from both East and West fall between the two extremes.

Influence of Swiss and Dutch Origins

Driedger and Kauffman (1982) have suggested that the original Swiss-South German branch of the Anabaptists—compared to the Dutch branch—remained more rural and that these different origins continue to influence the attitudes and behavior of Mennonites in North America today. In his recent book, *Vision, Doctrine, War*, on the history of American Mennonites between 1890 and 1930, James Juhnke agrees that these two different origins still influence attitudes and behavior. In the opening chapters of this volume as well, we have implied the existence of these differences. Until now no one has been able to measure directly the effects of these Swiss and Dutch origins. In this 1989 study we can do so since we asked the respondents about their European origins.[3]

Distribution of Mennonite Origins

In the past we assumed that American Mennonites east of the Mississippi were largely of Swiss origin and west of the Mississippi of Dutch origin. Table 2-4 shows that in the regions east of the Mississippi the majority (59 and 71%) are of Swiss origin and that Mennonites of Dutch origin (27 and 19%) are relatively less represented.[4] Well over one-half (56 and 58%) in the regions west of the Mississippi are of Dutch origin, with a substantial minority of Swiss origin (31 and 21%) as well. Since data on European origins were not collected in 1972, no trends could be plotted.

In Canada the patterns of settlement are rather different. Mennonites of Dutch origin comprise 46 percent of Mennonites in Ontario; those of Swiss origin, 38 percent. As expected, Dutch Mennonites predominate on the prairies (88%) and the Pacific Coast in British Columbia (80%).

Forty-eight percent of the respondents in the total 1989 sample indicated that they were of Dutch origin; 40 percent checked Swiss. We think the Dutch proportion is inflated; some respondents of Swiss origin, thinking of themselves as "Pennsylvania Dutch," apparently checked "Dutch" instead of "Swiss" (see note 4 above). A further analysis of our data led us to believe that the Mennonites of Swiss origin are a bit more numerous than those of Dutch origin.

Table 2-4. European Origins of Mennonites by Region, 1989

Origin	United States				Canada			Total
	East	Mid-west	Prai-ries	Pacific	East	Prai-ries	Pacific	N=2848
Swiss	59	71	31	21	38	7	5	40
Dutch	27	19	56	58	46	88	80	48
Other	14	10	13	21	16	5	15	12
Total	100	100	100	100	100	100	100	100

The 419 Mennonites whose origin was other than Swiss or Dutch represented a substantial 12 percent of the 1989 sample. These Mennonites are a heterogeneous group. Four percent reported their background as British, ranging—by regions—from 2 percent in the Canadian prairies to 9 percent in Ontario. Unfortunately, the 1989 sample included only 14 blacks, nine Hispanics, and three Asians—too few for a reliable analysis of the attitudes and beliefs of these new Mennonites.[5] In his census of the Mennonite Church, Michael Yoder (1982) was able to include other Mennonites, with very interesting results. As new Mennonites from other backgrounds join Mennonites of Swiss and Dutch origins, heterogeneity and pluralism will no doubt increase. Blacks and Hispanics are more prominent in the United States, and native Indians and Chinese are more prominent in Canada. In chapter 7 we will have more opportunity to discuss these differences.

General Differentiations by Origin
    The five denominations in the 1989 sample, who represent roughly two-thirds of all Mennonites and Brethren in Christ in North America, vary greatly as to background. Initially almost all of the Evangelical Mennonites were of Swiss background, but in 1989 they had one of the strongest representations from other backgrounds, with very few of Dutch ancestry (see Table 2-5). The Mennonite Brethren are the reverse, with 84 percent of Dutch background and very few of Swiss origin. In their origins, General Conference Mennonites are more like the Mennonite Brethren; and the members of the Mennonite Church and the Brethren in Christ are more like the Evangelical Mennonites.
    Nearly two-thirds (63%) of the American Mennonites are of Swiss origin, one-fourth are of Dutch origin, and the remainder represent other backgrounds. Among Canadian Mennonites the opposite is true, with three-fourths (79%) of Dutch origin (almost all having come via Prussia

and Russia), with only 16 percent of Swiss origin, and even fewer of other backgrounds.

Table 2-5. Mennonite Origins by Denomination and Nationality, 1989

Denominations	Swiss	Other	Dutch	Total
		(Percent)		
Evangelical Mennonite	79	21	0	100
Mennonite	82	9	9	100
Brethren in Christ	65	24	10	100
General Conference	19	7	74	100
Mennonite Brethren	7	9	84	100
Nationality				
American Mennonites	63	12	25	100
Canadian Mennonites	16	5	79	100

Almost two-thirds of the Dutch Mennonites and more than one-third of the Swiss Mennonites are urban; "other" Mennonites are about half urban. More than one-third (38%) of the Swiss respondents were baptized at a very young age—before the age of 13—while only 12 percent of the Dutch Mennonites were baptized this young. The early Anabaptist insistence on adult baptism seems to be more observed by the Dutch than the Swiss (although the age at which adulthood begins may be debated).

Origins and Political Issues

Table 2-3 shows that Mennonites vary considerably by region in their attitudes toward and involvement in political issues. Generally those in the American East are the most reluctant to get involved in politics; this reluctance increasingly fades as we move westward. We reported above that those east of the Mississippi are largely of Swiss origin, and suggested that ethnic/national background influences one's stance on issues. Table 2-6 shows that that is indeed the case and that the particular European background of Mennonites is a factor.

Dutch Mennonites are usually more willing than Swiss Mennonites to vote in elections, study political issues, hold office, witness to the state, encourage political action, endorse candidates, and discuss politics from the pulpit. The differences between the Swiss and Dutch are statistically significant on most of these issues. The attitudes of newer Mennonites (the "other" category) are most similar to the attitudes of the Dutch Mennonites.

With respect to actual political participation the results are much different. More Dutch Mennonites (84%) voted in elections than did Swiss Mennonites (51%), but they voted more heavily in favor of conservative Republicans (56 to 43%) in the United States, and Conservative and Social Credit candidates in Canada, than did the Swiss Mennonites. Slightly more Swiss Mennonites (12%) favor liberal Democrats in the United States, and the New Democratic Party in Canada, than do the Dutch Mennonites (9%). The actual participation of other Mennonites resembles that of the Dutch, being more liberal in that respect than the Swiss. While the Dutch Mennonites score much higher on the political participation scale, they vote more conservatively. Greater participation does not translate into more liberal attitudes.

Table 2-6. Political Attitudes and Participation by Mennonite Origin, 1989

Political issues	Swiss	Other	Dutch	Total
		(Percent)		
Political attitudes				
Should vote in elections	76	88	93	84
Should study political issues	75	82	86	80
May hold government office	67	87	89	78
Should witness to the state	77	78	76	77
Encourage political action	50	62	61	56
Should endorse candidates	34	43	44	39
May discuss politics from pulpit	27	31	29	28
Scored "high" on the political action scale	35	46	45	40
Political participation				
Voted in most elections	51	69	84	67
Favor conservative Republicans (U.S.) or Conservatives (Canada)	43	43	56	49
Favor liberal Democrats (U.S.) or NDPs (Canada)	12	15	9	10
Have held government office	5	2	5	5
Scored "high" on the political participation scale	14	30	30	22

We expect that a variety of American and Canadian differences—in urbanization, European origin, political involvement, education, etc.— have influenced their respective attitudes and behavior. These general national variations can be pursued in detail as we go on to discuss the issues of theology, family, community, institutions, and ethnicity.

The Mennonite Brethren, over half living in Canada, are naturally influenced more by Canadian historical and social patterns, while the Mennonite Church, with 90 percent of its members living in the United States, is largely influenced by the American scene. We expect the differences between Mennonite Brethren and the Mennonite Church to be significant.

Summary

While in chapter 1 we presented the challenges of modernization represented in urbanization and stratification, in this chapter we have sketched the regional settings of Mennonites from east to west in both the United States and Canada. We began by tracing the North American beginnings in eastern Pennsylvania and the migrations northward into Ontario and westward into the Midwest, the prairies, and the Pacific Coast. We found that these settlement patterns varied by denomination in the four American and three Canadian regions.

The five denominations represented in the 1972 and 1989 samples follow very different regional patterns. The members of the Mennonite Church are heavily concentrated in the United States, east of the Mississippi. The Evangelical Mennonites reside mostly in the American Midwest; the Brethren in Christ in the American and Canadian East. The General Conference Mennonites and Mennonite Brethren are mostly located on the American and Canadian prairies and the Pacific Coast, west of the Mississippi. Mennonites in the American East are the most rural; Mennonites become increasingly urban as we move westward. Two-thirds of all Canadian Mennonites are urban, and they also become increasingly more urban as we move from east to west.

These historical immigration and regional patterns are reflected in political attitudes and participation. Since 1972 Mennonites have become more willing to get politically involved, but this varies by region. Eastern American Mennonites are more reluctant to get involved in politics than are western Mennonites, and Canadians are more willing to participate than are Americans. Generally Mennonites tend to vote conservatively, although urban and younger Mennonites are beginning to move further left of center.

Mennonites of Swiss origin differ in some significant ways from Mennonites of Dutch/Prussian/Russian origin. Swiss Mennonites—located mostly in the East—are less urban, more heavily concentrated in the United States, and more reluctant to become involved in the political process. Dutch Mennonites, who are more urban and more heavily concentrated in the western regions of the United States and Canada, are more willing to engage in political action. More political involvement, however, does not necessarily mean less conservatism. Dutch Mennonites vote somewhat more conservatively than Swiss Mennonites. North American Mennonites vary considerably by region in historical beginnings, denominational concentrations, urbanization, and political involvement.

PART II
Finding Sources of Identity

CHAPTER 3

The Sacred and Secularization

IN PART ONE we asked the basic question of how modernization has affected Mennonite identity, and what are the possible consequences for the Mennonites and Brethren in Christ in North America.

In chapter 1 we said we expected the influence of modernization would be countered by Mennonite identity in the struggle between the sacred and secularization, the community and individualism, and peoplehood and materialism. In chapter 2 we began to explore how Swiss/Dutch origins and national and regional North American settings might vary with respect to Mennonite identity and diversity.

In part two (chapters 3-7) we will concentrate on the five dimensions of Mennonite identity: the sacred, the community, the family, institutions, and ethnicity. This chapter will focus on the sacred and secularization. Figure 1-4 outlined the five dimensions of modernization and the five dimensions of Mennonite identity, and showed the expected struggle or dialectic between the two forces of secularization and sacralization. We expect that urbanization and education, especially, will affect religious commitment, to which subject we now turn.

Recently Werner Packull (1990:1-22) suggested that we are between paradigms and that Anabaptist studies are at a crossroad. Historians and theologians are reexamining what happened in the 16th century when the various Anabaptists emerged, and are suggesting that there may not have been only one "Anabaptist Vision" as Harold S. Bender indicated in the 1940s, but a polygenesis, or multiple beginnings which were much more diverse and differentiated theologically than was first thought (Stayer, et al., 1975). The 1972 survey of North American Mennonites by

Kauffman and Harder (1975) used Bender's Anabaptist Vision as a model, working from a normative Anabaptist set of beliefs and principles. Since we wanted to identify changes since 1972, we asked the same questions in 1989, which we will present in this chapter. However, we also tried to broaden the study to take into account more recent findings regarding pluralism and change. We agree with Packull (1979:313-29; 1990:5-6) that the Reformation was not only a theological event, that we must move beyond Weberian and Troeltschian ideal types, and that we must give social history and sociology a more important place. A new, more plural paradigm seems to be emerging.

In 1988 alone, four books were published on Mennonite identity, asking such questions as "Who am I?" "What am I?" and "Why am I a Mennonite?" (Driedger, 1988; Loewen, 1988; Redekop and Bender, 1988; Redekop and Steiner, 1988). Two other books concerned with Mennonite identity were published in the past two years (Juhnke, 1989; Driedger and Harder, 1990). What is the meaning of this search for identity? The process of modernization seems to be changing religion, families, communities, institutions, and culture—calling for a reexamination of relevance and loyalties (Kraybill, 1988:153-72). New evidence on religious pluralism, urbanism, and religious participation may be helpful (Stark, et al., 1980; Wuthnow, 1981; Finke and Stark, 1988; Quin, et al., 1982; Breault, 1989).

Elements of the Sacred Canopy

In *The Sacred Canopy* Peter Berger (1967) introduced a general conceptual frame that is most useful for discussing the five dimensions of Mennonite identity to be covered in this and the following chapters. Berger (1967:19, 21) suggests that everyone, as an individual, needs to construct a world of identity—as well as to establish identification with a larger community—that involves "an ordering of experience" into "a meaningful order, or nomos, [which] is imposed upon the discrete experiences and meanings of individuals." "To participate in the society is to share its 'knowledge,' that is, to co-inhabit its nomos."

Berger says that humans must socially construct a core of values and impose a meaningful order upon reality. The individual must belong to and identify with others; this requires constructing a meaningful social world as well as becoming part of a larger, meaningful social order (Berger and Luckmann, 1966). To be separated from society exposes the individual to a multiplicity of dangers that cannot be dealt with by the individual alone.

To bridge the gap between the conceptual and the practical, Berger (1967) introduces the idea of a "sacred canopy" (a tentlike roof used by the Jews) as a symbol of protection against terror. The canopy used by the Jews is like a large blanket, with a long pole or stake attached to each corner to make a covering for protection. It symbolizes the tents that the Hebrews used during their desert wanderings to protect themselves from the wind, sand, cold, and storms, as bedouins still do today.

While the canopy protects the people and valuables inside, the poles that hold up the covering are also important. One or two stakes are hardly adequate; usually four or more are needed. The stakes can be replaced by new ones, and the various components of the canopy are adjustable (Driedger, 1980:343). The canopy is also mobile. It can be folded, transported, and pitched again in new places. Nomos-building can be seen as pitching a sacred canopy, which shields the individual or group from terror and meaninglessness (Driedger, 1980; 1988). The canopy houses a "reality," or a meaningful order, or nomos.

In his 1980 study Driedger (1980:341-56) compared the native Indians, Hutterites, and Jews and found that over time they have approached reconstruction of their canopies in three different ways. When the Europeans came to North America, the native Indians, still in the food-gathering stage, were soon shunted onto segregated reserves. Encroaching agriculture destroyed their buffalo and hunting grounds, and the Indians were forced to reconstruct entirely their sacred canopy of religion, economics, and way of life. Many Indians have found it very difficult to develop a renewed, changed nomos—to reconstruct their sacred canopy.

The Hutterites, on the other hand, largely transferred their canopy— their communal religion and agricultural way of life—onto the North American prairies, without great adjustments. The Jews arrived from shtetls in eastern Europe and transformed their religion and way of life into modern urban canopies (Driedger, 1980; 1988).

When Mennonites came to North America, largely as agriculturalists, they, like the Hutterites, transferred their religion and way of life largely intact (often into villages). However, now that half of the Mennonites are urban they are in the process of reconstructing their sacred canopies—adjusting and sometimes changing their stakes to make the canopies more secure—as needed in the new, urban settings.

In part two of this volume we will treat religious commitment, family, community, institutions, and culture as five different poles holding up the canopy that protects Mennonite identity. Each of these dimensions is very important to the maintenance of Mennonite identity. In this chapter the focus will be on religion.

The Mennonites began as a radical religious movement in 16th-century Europe, and they have always considered religion a central feature of their origin, identity, and way of life. Religion is certainly one of the most important stakes in the Mennonite sacred canopy; many people see it as the center pole, and all other poles as secondary or even of little importance.

We will examine here the various dimensions of religion—the lesser pegs, holding ropes that further balance and steady the religion pole (Kauffman, 1979:27-42). The religious pegs that we will examine—beliefs, devotionalism, experience, practice, and knowledge—have also been developed by other scholars (Lenski, 1963; Stark and Glock, 1968; Bibby, 1987; Hamm, 1987).

In 1961 Gerhard Lenski published *The Religious Factor*, a study of contemporary religious commitment and practice in Detroit that spawned considerable interest in the study of religion. He introduced four major dimensions—orthodoxy of religious beliefs, devotionalism, associationalism, and communalism—which Charles Glock, Rodney Stark, and associates (1965; 1967; 1968) used and expanded in a series of volumes based on general surveys of religion in the United States. More recently Reginald Bibby (1987) used similar categories to measure religious commitment in three national surveys in Canada (1975, 1980, and 1985).

Kauffman and Harder (1975) used Lenski's four dimensions in their 1972 survey of Mennonites in North America, and we used these same dimensions in our 1989 survey, so that we now have comparable data over a generation. In subsequent parts of this section we present our findings on Mennonite religious beliefs, devotionalism, religious experiences, associationalism, and Bible knowledge. In section two we examine the role of Anabaptism in Mennonite mobility and religious commitment, and in section three we review the influences of urbanization, socioeconomic status, and mobility on religious commitment.

Religious Beliefs

In their 1972 survey Kauffman and Harder (1975) used a scale measuring general orthodoxy of beliefs that included many of Stark and Glock's (1968) basic Christian doctrinal items—belief in God, Jesus, miracles, Satan, and life after death. Table 3-1 lists (in abbreviated form) the seven questionnaire items that comprise the scale on general orthodoxy of beliefs. The table shows that in 1989 88 percent or more of the Mennonites and Brethren in Christ in North America held to these basic tenets of the faith, having checked the most orthodox response offered for each item. The data show that these beliefs remained very stable over the period between 1972 and 1989. On the basis of scale totals, the five Mennonite groups varied only slightly, with General Conference Mennonites scoring lowest; their response percentages ranged from 84 to 91. The

Evangelical Mennonites scored highest, with response percentages ranging from 95 to 99.
Compared to the respondents in Stark and Glock's (1968) original
survey, Mennonites in 1972 were more orthodox than all Catholic and
mainline Protestant groups except Southern Baptists (Kauffman and
Harder, 1975:107). According to a recent Gallup poll (Gallup and Jones,
1989), 71 percent of Americans believe there is life after death, and 34
percent believe that the devil is a personal being. Bibby's report
(1987:93) indicates that 79 percent of Canadians believe in the divinity of
Jesus and 65 percent believe in life after death.

Table 3-1. Responses to Items on General Orthodoxy

Orthodoxy items	1989					Totals	
	GC	MC	BIC	MB	EMC	1972	1989
	(Percent most orthodox response)						
No doubt that God exists	85	86	92	94	95	89	88
No doubt that Jesus is human and divine	84	86	93	95	96	90	88
Jesus will return to earth some day	84	89	95	97	99	90	90
Miracles are super-natural acts of God	87	90	97	96	99	90	91
The physical resur-rection of Jesus was a fact	90	90	94	96	97	91	92
Satan is an active personal devil	85	89	96	97	99	93	90
Definitely life beyond death	91	91	94	98	97	92	93

During the twentieth century various theological emphases have influenced Mennonites, fundamentalist theology being one of them (Hunter, 1983:35). Fundamentalism focuses on specific theological interpretations and emphases—on the virgin birth of Jesus, the Bible as the inerrant
and infallible Word of God, Christ as the only Savior from eternal punishment, and creation of the world in six 24-hour days. In addition, fundamentalists tend to exclude from church membership persons who do
not accept these fundamentals.
Table 3-2 shows the distribution of responses to the items in the fundamentalism scale.[1] In 1989 the majority of the respondents chose the
most orthodox responses regarding these beliefs; fewer held to the aforementioned fundamentalist beliefs than to the orthodox tenets. Fewer
than half believed that God created the earth in six 24-hour days, and

about two-thirds (63%) believed that eternal punishment will result if a person does not accept Christ as Savior. The percentages for several items have declined since 1972, especially for eternal punishment, the creation, and the inerrancy of Scriptures. Again the General Conference Mennonites were least fundamentalist and the Evangelical Mennonites were most fundamentalist in their beliefs.

Table 3-2. Responses to Items on Fundamentalism

Fundamentalism items	1989					Totals	
	GC	MC	BIC	MB	EMC	1972	1989
	(Percent most orthodox response)						
Jesus was born of a virgin	84	88	97	96	99	88	89
Should exclude from membership those who don't accept the fundamentals	74	78	88	93	96	*	81
Bible is inerrant Word of God	71	75	90	89	97	82	78
Accept Christ as Savior or suffer eternal punishment	52	60	75	78	84	74	63
God created the earth in six 24-hour days	43	47	56	44	63	50	46

*Not included in the 1972 survey.

In 1972 eight questionnaire items were used to test adherence to 16th-century Anabaptist beliefs. For the sake of comparability, these same items were used again in 1989 to form an Anabaptism scale.[2] Table 3-3 presents the items (in abbreviated form) in the Anabaptism scale, with the percentages of respondents who agreed with the statements.

Most respondents affirmed four basic beliefs, the first four in the table: adult baptism, the lordship of Christ, church discipline, and opposition to war. While the percentages believing in adult baptism and church discipline were relatively unchanged from 1972 to 1989, the numbers holding to the lordship of Christ and nonparticipation in war have declined. Differences between the five denominations were slight with respect to adult baptism. Although a majority of the GC, MC, and MB respondents were opposed to taking part in war, only a minority were opposed among the BIC (39%) and EMC (11%).

The second half of Table 3-3 shows the strength of four other Anabaptist beliefs, emphasized less by Mennonites of North European background than by those of South European background. Most early Anabaptists believed that Christians could not hold some governmental offices because it would compromise some of their beliefs; a majority (59%) of the Mennonite respondents in 1989 agreed, but that is a decline from 74 percent in 1972. A large majority of the members of the Mennonite Church (71%) and a minority (31%) of the Evangelical Mennonites wished to limit participation in government. One-half were against the swearing of oaths, with the General Conference Mennonites and the Mennonite Church strongest in their opposition. Fewer than half (45%) wanted to emphasize following Jesus in evangelism and works of mercy. Only one-third were against taking others to court, with the Mennonite Church (41%) strongest on that point.

Table 3-3. Responses to Items on Anabaptism

Anabaptism items	1989					Totals	
	GC	MC	BIC	MB	EMC	1972	1989
	(Percent agreeing)						
Baptism is unnecessary for infants and children	81	85	79	89	85	82	84
Should follow the lordship of Christ even if persecuted	62	63	67	75	75	72	66
Church discipline is necessary for the unfaithful	55	55	66	78	60	60	60
Christians should take no part in war	65	78	39	56	11	73	66
Christians cannot perform in some government offices	52	71	48	49	31	74	59
It is against God's will to swear civil oaths	64	59	32	54	31	66	57
Must follow Jesus in evangelism and deeds of mercy	47	46	39	47	37	52	45
Should not take a person to court even if justified	31	41	30	32	28	36	35

While most Mennonites are similar in their strong adherence to the tenets of general orthodoxy, there is a much greater spread of views regarding fundamentalism and Anabaptism. We have included a look at these contrasting beliefs since they tend to polarize Mennonites under modern influences. The scales for general orthodoxy, fundamentalism, and Anabaptism, reviewed above, will figure prominently in our discussion of Mennonite religious identity later on.

Devotionalism

A second measure of religious commitment (used by Lenski, 1961; Stark and Glock, 1968; Bibby, 1987; and Kauffman and Harder, 1975) is the practice of religious devotions. Table 3-4 presents seven indicators of devotionalism. Three-fourths of the sample in 1989 engaged in daily private prayer, two-thirds read the Bible weekly, and as many often asked God for guidance in major decisions of life. Over one-half (56%) held private or family devotions once a week or more often. Generally the practice of devotions was as high in 1989 as in 1972. However, the frequency of grace at meals and group worship (other than grace at meals) declined somewhat. As was the case regarding orthodoxy of beliefs, GC and MC members ranked below average and MB and EMC members above average.

Gallup and Jones (1989:38) reported that among their national sample of Americans in 1986 76 percent agreed that "prayer is an important part of my daily life," and 88 percent responded positively to the question "do you ever pray to God?" More women (93%) reported praying than did men (83%). One-third of American adults read the Bible weekly or more often in 1986, slightly up from an earlier survey in 1978 (Gallup and Jones, 1989:40).

Table 3-4. Responses to Items on Devotionalism

	Percent in 1989					Totals	
Devotionalism items	GC	MC	BIC	MB	EMC	1972	1989
Pray privately daily or more	75	77	78	83	86	77	78
Say grace at all meals	75	65	66	80	69	83	70
Read Bible weekly or more	58	62	63	75	72	67	63
Often ask God for guidance in making decisions	59	62	65	70	74	61	63
Private or family devotions weekly or more often	49	56	57	69	59	60	56
Feel close to God	51	53	54	55	67	53	53
Household has group worship	35	29	34	44	31	45	34

Bibby's (1987:68) national survey of Canadians in 1980 showed that 77 percent prayed at least occasionally and 39 percent did so once a week or more. Only 10 percent said grace at *all* meals; 22 percent at least once a week. Fifty-one percent "never or hardly ever" said grace, and 55 percent "never or rarely" read the Bible privately (9% at least weekly). Mennonites engage in prayer and Bible reading much more often than their national populations.

Religious Experience

Table 3-5 presents six indicators of religious experience, the third dimension of Mennonite commitment. We again compare the five denominations over the span of a generation, from 1972 to 1989. The first four items have to do with positive experiences, and the last two with negative experiences. Most respondents (89%) in 1989 felt that they had a purpose and goal in life, and almost as many (82%) had had at least one conversion experience, up slightly from 1972. Over half (53%) felt close to God, and almost half (47%) claimed they had received "the baptism of the Holy Spirit."

In 1989 one-fourth of the respondents sometimes had doubts about their salvation, and 16 percent were often discouraged in their Christian life; the percentages in 1989 were considerably lower than in 1972, when 42 percent had doubts and 24 percent felt discouraged. As Mennonites and Brethren in Christ have become more urban and educated, do they feel less restricted than when they were in rural enclaves? Have their religious consciences become less sensitive? Have they acquired greater assurance of salvation?

Table 3-5. Responses to Items on Religious Experience

Religious experience items	Percent in 1989					Totals	
	GC	MC	BIC	MB	EMC	1972	1989
Am conscious of a goal and purpose in life	87	87	87	94	91	85	89
Had a conversion experience	71	82	91	95	91	79	82
Feel close to God	51	53	54	55	67	53	53
Received the "baptism of the Holy Spirit"	51	48	56	33	44	*	47
Sometimes have doubts about salvation	31	28	24	17	16	42	26
Often feel discouraged in living a Christian life	19	12	13	18	15	24	16

*Not included in the 1972 survey.

The five denominations vary. The Evangelical Mennonites had the fewest doubts about salvation, and the Brethren in Christ and members of the Mennonite Church were least often discouraged in the Christian life. The Mennonite Brethren scored highest on conversion experiences (95%) and purpose in life (94%). The Brethren in Christ scored highest on "baptism of the Holy Spirit" (57%).

Church Participation

While devotionalism is ritual practice related to building up the vertical relationship between the individual and God, church participation (or associationalism) denotes social relationships within religious organizations. Early researchers often limited the operational definition of associationalism to frequency of church attendance. We prefer a broader definition that includes attendance at church, Sunday school, and weekday meetings, and holding leadership positions in the congregation. Moreover, we added items probing the members' interest in serving their congregations—in line with abilities—and their sense of the importance of church participation.

A scale measuring church participation (associationalism) was derived by combining the responses to the six items listed in Table 3-6. Church participation in 1989 was very similar to that in 1972 except for somewhat lower attendance at Sunday school (71% regular attendance in 1989 compared to 80% in 1972). Regular attendance at Sunday worship services was common to almost all (92%) of the Mennonites and Brethren in Christ in 1989, while a strong third regularly attended weekday meetings. As with the beliefs items, General Conference Mennonite members scored below average and the Evangelical Mennonites above average. There were no denominational differences in the responses to the item probing the importance of church participation. Regarding interest in serving the congregation, differences were slight in the GC-EMC pattern noted above.

Table 3-6. Responses to Items on Church Participation

Church participation items	Percent in 1989					Totals	
	GC	MC	BIC	MB	EMC	1972	1989
Attend church "almost weekly" or more often	88	92	92	96	96	93	92
Church participation is "very important" or "fairly important"	90	90	91	92	92	87	90
Attend Sunday school at least "most Sundays"	54	81	79	67	85	80	71
Interested in serving the congregation	63	66	67	74	73	68	68
Have held leadership position in congregation within the past three years	59	60	65	65	68	57	61
Regularly attend weekday meetings	30	37	36	42	53	36	36

Bible Knowledge

Church leaders have expressed the concern that knowledge of the Bible may be declining among Mennonites. In 1989 we used the same eight-item test of Bible knowledge that Kauffman and Harder had adopted in 1972. The short multiple-choice questions required the respondents to correctly identify the eight items (listed in Table 3-7) by choosing one of four responses in each case.

In 1989 at least four out of five respondents correctly identified Zacchaeus, the Macedonian call, Pentecost, and the Samaritans. Smaller proportions were able to identify King Herod, Gethsemane, Bartholomew, and the exile, the last being confused by some respondents with the exodus of the Israelites from Egypt.

Scores on the test ranged from zero to eight in both 1972 and 1989, with mean scores of 5.7 in 1972 and 5.6 in 1989, a difference too small to be statistically significant and leading to the conclusion that Bible knowledge has not diminished in recent years.

Anabaptist Commitment

How do the several dimensions of religious commitment (religiosity) relate to each other? To examine the relationships between these dimensions (variables or scales), we relied heavily on correlation coefficients (Pearson r), which show the strength of the relationship between two variables.[3]

Table 3-7. Responses to Items on Bible Knowledge

Bible knowledge items	Percent correct in 1989					Totals	
	GC	MC	BIC	MB	EMC	1972	1989
Zacchaeus	89	92	89	95	91	92	91
Macedonian call	81	82	79	89	85	82	83
Pentecost	84	76	76	84	73	74	80
Samaritans	79	80	78	83	76	79	80
King Herod	80	75	71	81	80	79	77
Gethsemane	68	65	68	68	71	67	67
Bartholomew	49	60	62	56	58	61	57
The exile	43	45	41	51	40	47	45

Does it make a difference whether Mennonites adhere more strongly to one or another among the Anabaptist, general orthodoxy, and fundamentalist beliefs systems? Should we expect scores on these three dimensions to be positively or negatively related? Are these dimensions antithetical or complementary in their interrelations? And if Mennonites adhere to one of these more strongly than to the others, does that make a difference in their beliefs and attitudes on many other dimensions?

Positive correlations were obtained between these three scales, indicating that they are not antithetical. The correlation coefficient between Anabaptism and general orthodoxy was .23; between Anabaptism and fundamentalism, .21. (In 1972 these values were .23 and .26, respectively.) Thus, Anabaptist beliefs are somewhat related, but not strongly, to orthodoxy and fundamentalism. However, orthodoxy and fundamentalism are strongly related to each other (r=.71; .72 in 1972).

Beliefs and Commitment

Figure 3-1 compares the Anabaptist, orthodox, and fundamentalist beliefs by indicating how they intercorrelated with other dimensions of religious commitment. All three belief systems were positively related to

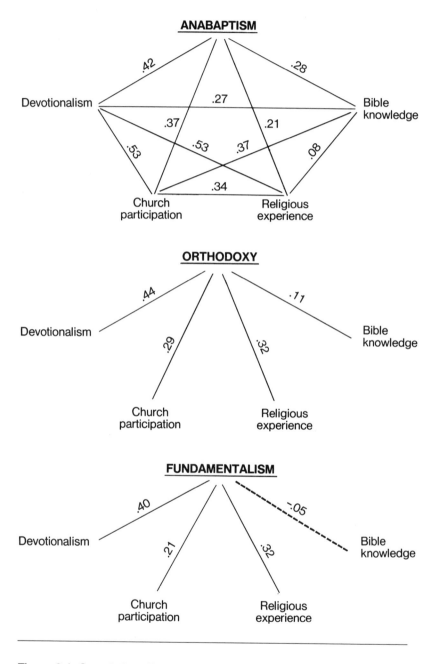

Figure 3-1. Correlations Between Measures of Religiosity

devotionalism (r=.42, .44, and .40). Thus, in devotional practices there were no significant differences between the adherents to these three beliefs systems.

Mennonites with a strong commitment to 16th-century Anabaptism tended to score higher on church participation (r=.37) than did those who were strong on orthodoxy (.29) and fundamentalism (.21). Mennonites strongly committed to Anabaptism attended church and Sunday school more regularly, were more involved in church leadership, and showed stronger interest in serving their congregations.

The relationship between religious belief and experience was moderately positive for all three types of beliefs (.21, .32, .32), but Mennonites of orthodox and fundamentalist leanings scored higher on this scale than did those of Anabaptist orientation. Anabaptism and Bible knowledge were significantly related (.28), but orthodoxy and fundamentalism were weakly related (.11 and -.05) to Bible knowledge.

The intercorrelations between the four indicators of religious commitment (devotionalism, church participation, religious experience, and Bible knowledge) were all positive, ranging from .08 to .53, suggesting that they are all valid measures of religiosity. The Bible knowledge variable is the least valid, however, since the correlations with other variables were weakest—a finding noted by Kauffman (1979:29) in his review of research by other investigators.

We conclude that Anabaptist beliefs are more strongly related than general orthodoxy and fundamentalism to three of the four indicators of religious commitment, suggesting that adherence to Anabaptism is the best orientation for tying together the elements of religiosity.

Anabaptism and Outreach

The early Anabaptists were deeply committed to extending their newly found faith to others in the form of evangelism, but they were equally concerned with the application of their faith to the issues of the day. Our research has included the development of measures of several forms of outreach: evangelism, peacemaking, service to others, and support of the work of the Mennonite Central Committee. How do twentieth-century Mennonites link their Anabaptist beliefs to these elements of outreach?

An evangelism scale was constructed from three items, asking how frequently the respondents had witnessed orally to their faith, invited persons to attend church services, and attempted to lead someone to Christ. The peacemaking (pacifism) scale probed opposition to war and militarism, and readiness to promote peacemaking principles. The scale measuring service to others included items that asked the respondents to indicate the degree of importance they attached to being at peace with others, treating others properly, using resources for the good of others, and doing volunteer work; also the frequency with which they did volunteer work and visited the sick. Finally, the "MCC support scale" probed favorableness toward the work of the Mennonite Central Committee, an agency of the Mennonite churches that has 1,000 volunteers in 50 countries carrying out a variety of relief and service projects.

Figure 3-2 shows that all three beliefs systems related positively and similarly to evangelism (.26, .25, and .24). Only Anabaptism correlated positively with peacemaking (.48), while orthodoxy and fundamentalism related negatively (-.17 and -.30). Note that evangelism and peacemaking were not associated at all (r=.00), suggesting that these two arms of outreach are independent of each other. Since Anabaptism was significantly related to both, we conclude that Anabaptist Mennonites are unique in their attempt to bridge these elements of outreach, which some Christian groups see as unrelated or even in opposition to each other. Some of the most conservative, fundamentalist religious bodies are also the most militaristic and the least interested in finding peaceful solutions to conflict. Mennonites seek to take seriously both the spiritual and social worlds (Klaassen, 1973; 1990).

In Figure 3-2 "Others" denotes the scale for service to others and "MCC" refers to the MCC support scale. Mennonites of all three belief patterns related positively to "others," but the Anabaptist group scored more strongly (.29) than the orthodox (.15) and fundamentalist (.07) groups. A similar pattern emerged regarding support of MCC, with Mennonites of a more Anabaptist orientation associating positively (.16) and Mennonites of more orthodox and fundamentalist leanings relating negatively (-.03 and -.15 respectively).

What do we make of all this? We conclude that Mennonites of a stronger Anabaptist orientation support a dual service thrust including evangelism (relating people to God) and peacemaking and MCC service (relating to the needs of others). Mennonites of more orthodox and fundamentalist orientation emphasize evangelism only. The fundamentalist respondents, in fact, were negatively related to both peacemaking and MCC work. It *does* make a difference what church members believe. Our findings indicate that differences in belief orientation have important effects on the attitudes and behavior of church members, as will be further revealed in subsequent chapters. Theological pluralism is clearly evident among the Mennonites and Brethren in Christ.

Theology and Secularism

In chapter 1 we introduced secularization as a factor related to ur-

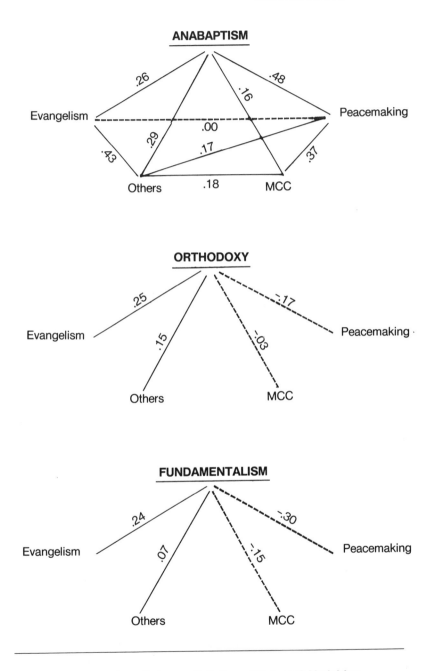

Figure 3-2. Correlations Between Beliefs and Outreach Variables

banization and other dimensions of modernization—secularization as opposed to sacralization, in a process of dialectical change that tends to reduce the strength of religiosity in the lives of people. Other forces often identified with modernization are individualism and materialism, which will be discussed in the next chapter. It is not clear whether secularism, individualism, and materialism can be regarded as partially defining modernization or whether they tend to flow from it.

Our model of modernization relies on demographic changes as the primary factors, since we can easily identify the demographic variations and trends among church members. We do not have adequate measures to classify church members in terms of other aspects of modernization, such as industrialization, increased technology, and increased bureaucratization of society. However, in chapter 6 we will note the extent to which the respondents in 1989 participated in community organizations and institutions—which bears some relationship to involvement in bureaucratic complexities.

Our preference is to regard secularism, individualism, and materialism as derived from modernization rather than a definition of it. We will refer to these dimensions as *concomitants* of modernization, relying on demographic changes as our primary factors in defining the process.

In the preparation of our questionnaire we made an attempt to construct a scale that would measure secularism. If church members could be ordered along a scale of lesser and greater secularism, it would then be possible to correlate levels of secularism with other variables in our study, particularly those variables in our model of modernization.

For Berger, secularization is the process by which sectors of society and culture are removed from the domination of religious institutions and symbols (Hunter and Ainlay, 1986:146). Since World War II there has been much debate as to whether the traits and symbols of contemporary culture are losing religious meaning, that is, whether secularization is increasing. Herberg (1955) and Yinger (1970:491) have noted a paradox—pervasive secularism amid mounting religiosity. The emergence of new religious movements in the 1970s and 1980s has occurred in spite of increasing secularization. Roof and McKinney (1987:8) "do not write off the modern world as an age of rampant secularization and religious decline as do many scholars and intellectuals." Wuthnow (1988:4) says that religion simply has not beat a humiliating retreat in the face of secularization.

In developing a set of questionnaire items that might logically indicate secularist attitudes, we relied heavily on ideas presented in *Habits of the Heart* (Robert N. Bellah, et al., 1985). Several dozen statements were formulated, with which respondents could agree or disagree. Some 28 of these were pretested, and the list was reduced to the nine that best withstood factor analysis. Table 3-8 presents the nine items together with the distribution of responses by denomination. No trends can be observed since this scale was not used in the 1972 survey.

Table 3-8. Responses to Items on Secularism

Secularism items	Percent agreeing					
	GC	MC	BIC	MB	EMC	Total
I believe that the pursuit of pleasure is a valid way to keep some balance and enjoyment in my life	36	33	31	31	27	33
When engaged in scientific endeavor, a scientist who is also a Christian must nevertheless suspend personal beliefs in the supernatural	16	12	12	10	11	13
Religious belief and moral conviction are plausible and justifiable only if they stand up to the rigors of logic and reason	16	10	8	7	7	10
Evangelism has so many negative connotations that we shouldn't even use the term	11	9	4	6	2	9
I tend to discount or rationalize the nature miracles described in the New Testament, such as walking on water and turning water into wine	8	6	3	3	1	6
[Disagree that] we should become more critical of the myriad of secular messages intruding upon our consciousness every day	4	5	7	5	3	5
The fact that the world has not come to an end as predicted in the New Testament probably means that it never really will	3	3	1	1	1	2
My doubts about traditional Christianity are so serious that I am unable to pray to God	2	1	1	2	1	2
I am moving toward a worldview that this life, the life experienced through our senses, is all there is	2	3	2	1	1	2

The table gives the percentages of respondents who chose the two most secular responses among the five possible responses: strongly agree, agree, uncertain, disagree, strongly disagree.[4]

In the case of several items, only a small proportion of the respondents chose the secular responses. Nevertheless, the range of scale scores was sufficient to afford an adequate basis for deriving correlation coefficients with other scales.

Correlations between secularism and residence, socioeconomic status, and mobility provide a sense of the relationship between secularism and modernization. The relevant coefficients are as follows: residence, .02; SES, -.16; and mobility, -.07. Since these coefficients are very low, and in two cases negative, we infer that secularism is quite independent of demographic factors. We conclude that secularism depends on factors other than demographic changes associated with modernization—for example, degree of commitment to religious beliefs.

Correlations of secularism with the three beliefs scales yielded the following results: Anabaptism, -.35; orthodoxy, -.42; and fundamentalism, -.34. The negative correlations obtained from the measure that we had constructed demonstrate that secularism is antithetical to all three beliefs systems. As expected, secularization is a force in society that tends to reduce adherence to Mennonite beliefs, whether these be of the Anabaptist, general orthodox, or fundamentalist variety.

In line with our expectations, secularism also correlated negatively with religious practice: church participation, -.44; devotionalism, -.45; religious experience, -.27; and Bible knowledge, -.38. Thus, secularization is clearly at odds with the principal measures of religiosity. Respondents scoring higher on secularism rated much lower on religious beliefs and practices.

Sacred Commitment and Modernization

In chapter one we suggested that modernization (increased urbanization, socioeconomic status, and mobility) would seduce Mennonites away from the sacred into greater secularization, that is, decreasing religiosity. We can now test this assumption by noting the correlations between the indicators of modernization and the various measures of religiosity introduced earlier in this chapter.

Religion and Urbanization

Table 3-9 presents the correlations between the indicators of modernization and the three systems of beliefs and the four measures of religious practice. From the very low correlation (-.05) between urbanization and Anabaptism, we conclude that rural and urban Mennonites are very similar in their acceptance of 16th-century Anabaptist principles. On the other hand, increased urbanization was associated with declining orthodoxy (-.11) and fundamentalism (-.18), although these were rather low correlations.

Table 3-9. Correlations Between Modernization and Religiosity

Religious variables	Urbani-zation	SES	Mobility
Religious beliefs			
Anabaptism	-.05	-.01*	.02*
General orthodoxy	-.11	-.15	-.07
Fundamentalism	-.18	-.31	-.13
Religious practice			
Devotionalism	-.04*	.01*	-.01*
Church participation	-.10	.16	.08
Religious experience	-.06	-.04*	.00*
Bible knowledge	.05	.30	.12

*Not statistically significant at the .01 level.

The associations between residence and devotional practices (-.04) and between residence and religious experience (-.06), although negative, were so low as to be negligible. There was a weak negative relationship (-.10) between urbanization and associationalism, indicating that church participation diminishes slightly with increased urbanization. Bible knowledge was slightly higher (.05) among urban respondents, but this was due more to the higher education among urban members than to residence per se.

In summary, rural and urban differences with respect to religious beliefs and practices were so small as to be almost neglible. The differences that were statistically significant suggest that urbanization has a slightly downward influence on religious beliefs and practices.

Religion and Socioeconomic Status

Socioeconomic status—our second indicator of modernization, which combines education, income, and occupational rank—was not significantly related to Anabaptism, devotionalism, and religious experience. It had a negative impact on orthodoxy (-.15) and especially fundamentalism (-.31). However, it yielded a considerable positive influence on church participation (.16) and Bible knowledge (.30).

Further analysis in chapter 11 indicates that these negative and positive values are due more to the influence of education than to either income or occupation. Advanced education is particularly negative toward fundamentalism, and individuals with higher educational achievement tend to become involved in teaching and other leadership roles in the congregation. Consequently, higher socioeconomic status indicates more leadership, which may demand regular attendance, and greater knowledge of the Bible.

Religion and Mobility

How does mobility, as a third indicator of modernization, affect religious beliefs and practices? Movers tend to be younger and more highly educated than the less mobile, but they are not likely to have achieved higher socioeconomic status, thus making it difficult to predict how mobility will affect the religiosity of church members.

The correlations with mobility (reported in Table 3-9 above) were rather similar to the values for SES, except that the negative associations with orthodoxy and fundamentalism, and the positive correlations with associationalism and Bible knowledge were less strong than for SES. Thus, mobility's effect on religious beliefs and practices is weak, somewhat less than the effect of higher socioeconomic status and, except for associationalism, rather similar to the impact of urbanization. The more mobile respondents were no different on Anabaptism, devotionalism, and religious experience than the less mobile.

In conclusion, the forces of modernization as measured by demographic changes have no negative or positive effects on Anabaptist beliefs, devotional practices, or religious experience. They do result in diminished adherence to general religious orthodoxy and, especially, fundamentalist beliefs. Modernization tends toward greater Bible knowledge, but has mixed effects on church participation.

Summary

In part two we examine five dimensions of Mennonite identity: religion, community, family, institutions, and ethnicity. In this chapter we focused on religion, using Berger's analogy of a sacred canopy, or tentlike cover, which may serve to protect a people's identity. Religion is one of the poles or stakes that hold up the canopy or covering; many Mennonites think it is the most important pole.

In examining Mennonite commitment to religion we used Lenski's four dimensions of religiosity, supplemented by concepts borrowed from the work of Stark and Glock. The five dimensions are religious beliefs, devotionalism, religious experience, church participation, and Bible knowledge. Each can be thought of as a peg holding the ropes or braces of the central pole—religious commitment—of the sacred canopy.

We identified three types of religious beliefs—doctrinal orthodoxy, fundamentalism, and Anabaptism—each of which was operationalized in the form of a scale composed of a number of questionnaire items. Of these three, Anabaptism emerged as the least affected by modernization. On these three beliefs scales, the respondents in 1989 were virtually unchanged from those in 1972.

Scores on devotionalism were relatively unchanged from 1972 to

1989. The responses on several other aspects of religious practice were unchanged, but two questions revealed that in 1989 there were slightly fewer doubts about personal salvation and there was less discouragement in living the Christian life. Although attendance at church services declined slightly, participation in leadership roles in the church increased slightly, and there was an increase in the sense of importance attached to church involvement. Scores on the Bible knowledge test in the two surveys were quite similar. In summary, religious commitment in 1989 was about the same as in 1972.

The respondents who scored high on Anabaptism scored higher on Bible knowledge and most items regarding church participation than did those who scored high on orthodoxy and fundamentalism. The three beliefs groups scored similarly on devotionalism and evangelistic outreach. Respondents strong on Anabaptism scored higher than the other two groups on peacemaking, service to others, and support for the work of the Mennonite Central Committee. Mennonites who scored high on general orthodoxy and fundamentalism tended to score lower than others on measures of peacemaking and support for MCC.

All three beliefs systems had strong negative correlations with secularism, indicating that secular views are inimical to these different theological orientations. With respect to measures of the transcendental relationship to God (devotionalism, religious experience, evangelism) the three beliefs systems were similar. With respect to social outreach in the form of peacemaking and service to others, those strong on Anabaptism clearly showed a higher concern and interest. We conclude that an Anabaptist orientation succeeds best in synthesizing the two dimensions— the transcendental relationship to God and immanent relationships with fellow human beings.

The effects of modernization on religious commitment vary. While Anabaptism is unaffected by urbanization, higher socioeconomic status, and mobility, orthodoxy and fundamentalism are negatively affected by all of these. Insofar as Anabaptism is concerned, modernization has not weakened the religion pole supporting the Mennonites' sacred canopy. If there are any detrimental effects stemming from the factors of modernization, they apparently are offset by other poles that support the sacred canopy.

CHAPTER 4

Community and Individualism

IN THE PREVIOUS CHAPTER we introduced Berger's concept of a "sacred canopy" under which a people establishes a core of values and constructs a meaningful order out of their collective experience. We posited several "stakes" which hold up the corners of the canopy: religion, community, family, culture, and social institutions. In this chapter we focus on the second of these—community. How do Mennonites and Brethren in Christ relate to the church communities of which they are a part? What tensions exist between individual expressions and commitment to community? Is community a vital factor in holding up the Mennonite canopy?

Community in a Mennonite Context

The Meaning of Community

The concept of "community" has been used in many ways. It can be applied to anything from a Hutterite colony to the European Economic Community. Thomas Bender (1982:5) noted that one investigator found no less than 94 meanings given to the term. "The most common sociological definitions used today," wrote Bender, "tend to focus on a community as an aggregate of people who share a common interest in a particular locality." But, he noted further, community is more than a place. It has an experiential dimension, implying a special quality of human relationships. It is "a network held together by shared understandings and a sense of obligation."

Thus community may be defined geographically or ideologically. A Mennonite community is often identified by its locality—for example, the Steinbach community, or the Hillsboro community, where many Mennonites reside and one or more churches can be found. The most elemental type of church community is the Hutterite colony, where locality and church are one and the same. With a Mennonite population of over 20,000 and nearly 50 congregations, is Winnipeg also a Mennonite community? (Driedger,1990).

In the *ideological* sense, a community is composed of people who know each other, share understandings, and have a sense of obligation to each other. This is the meaning of *gemeinschaft* as developed by Toennies (1965), who lived and wrote in Germany in the 1880s. The German rural village is a "gemeinde," a church or parish. As Harold Bender (1945) argued, the Mennonite understanding treats community and church as almost synonymous. "And what more is a Christian community," wrote Bender, "than a fellowship of disciples of Christ sharing a common faith. . . ." It is primarily in this sense, as a church-oriented group of people sharing a common religious faith, that we use the word community in this chapter. In chapter 1 community as *locality* entered the discussion as the rural-urban variable.

As analyzed by Berger and Luckmann (1966), society (and we would add community) is a human product, the result of "externalization," a process whereby individuals working collectively ("outside" their subjective selves) over long periods of time construct the norms, values, and organizations that constitute society. In turn each individual is a product of society. Through the process of "internalization" society's norms and values become the individual's own.

In the earliest years of life the individual experiences society primarily through the family, the subject of the next chapter. Growing older, children come increasingly into contact with a wider range of values and social organizations in the community. Although the values, ideas, and beliefs of a community are generally understood, and individuals are expected to conform to them, Kraybill (1988:155) pointed out that "a modicum of freedom prevails allowing 'real' choices among a variety of culturally constrained options." Freedom of choice for individuals is always freedom within cultural limits set by the family and community.

It is at the nexus of individual and community that tensions arise over the amount of freedom allowed the individual. Communities, particularly churches, vary greatly in the degree to which they permit or encourage individual freedoms. Hutterites believe that "the collective will is more important than the separate individuals who compose it" (Hostetler, 1974:235). From infancy the young Hutterite is taught to fit into the group pattern. Little room is left for a creativity that would involve innovations.

Most communities, of course, do not limit the individual so strictly. Nevertheless, no individual is so free from controls that he or she can violate the social norms with impunity. The price of peace is a certain degree of conformity to social norms. Otherwise conflict results, as documented in Driedger's analysis of a situation in Saskatchewan in which a conservative congregation resisted the innovations of one of its families (Driedger, 1988:61). Conversely, a community lacking innovations soon becomes ossified and stultifying, and ultimately deteriorates. The price of conformity has often been a lack of vitality and progress.

Redekop (1989:130) noted that the community has always been an influential factor in the thought and life of Mennonites. The community performs many functions for its members and "is the foundation for the existence of Mennonite society." Mennonite communities have tended to be rural, isolated, and somewhat segregated, with significant ideological boundaries; Driedger (1988) referred to them as "ethnic enclaves."

During the 1940s a "Mennonite Community Movement" emerged which questioned the ability of Mennonites to maintain their religious identity if they became urbanized. The emphasis was on strengthening the agricultural base of the rural community and the socioreligious health of the congregation.[1] Professionals (teachers, doctors, nurses) were encouraged to practice their professions in small communities rather than in large cities. Small industries were encouraged so that church members would not need to move to the city for employment. This emphasis on maintaining the small community, with a rather ingrown focus, can be called "communalism," loyalty to a social group based on religious principles. The Mennonite community movement stressed communalism, while wondering whether it could survive the large city context (Fretz, 1956).

Several decades later, following de facto urbanization of Mennonites, the threat of Mennonites becoming "lost" in the city has receded. There are many examples of thriving churches in urban areas. Driedger (1988:190) argues that instead of becoming lost in the city, Mennonites have been able to enter a greater diversity of occupations and "have become in a way liberated from homogeneous agricultural occupational confines." Also, an emphasis on missions and foreign service necessitates a "go forth" message in place of a "stay at home" theme (Kauffman, 1966).

A Measure of Communalism

A communalism scale, utilized in both 1972 and 1989, provides a test of communal thinking among church members. The scale measures "in-groupness," a strong sense of identity with one's background and church affiliation. A person who scores high on the scale has always been a member of the same denomination and wants to continue that membership, had parents of the same background, has his or her closest friends in the same denomination, has a feeling of satisfaction with the denomination, and "fits in well" with his or her congregation. Table 4-1 summarizes the scale items and the variation of responses for the participating denominations in the two surveys.

Table 4-1. Responses to Items on Communalism by Denomination

Item	Percent in 1989					Totals	
	MC	GC	MB	BIC	EMC	1972	1989
Both parents members of respondent's denomination	72	70	61	43	35	78	67
Respondent never a member of another denomination	80	78	69	52	46	85	74
At least four or five best friends belong to same denomination	50	44	48	31	35	47	46
Prefer own denomination and want to remain a member	81	77	72	73	72	77	78
"Very much" or "a good deal" of satisfaction with being known as a Mennonite or Brethren in Christ	55	60	52	59	50	52	56
Fit in "very well" or "fairly well" with my congregation	85	82	84	85	89	80	84

The proportion of respondents who had parents of the same denomination varied from 72 percent for the Mennonite Church (MC) to 35 percent for the Evangelical Mennonite Church (EMC). A similar variation (from 80 to 46%) was found in the denominational background of the respondent, reflecting the greater commitment of the EMC and Brethren in Christ (BIC) to bringing in members from other denominational backgrounds. With respect to preference for in-group friendships, less variation was evident, with MC and BIC at the extremes. On the other scale items, variations were minor and patterned slightly differently in regard to denominational variations.

As to trends it is clear that somewhat smaller proportions of members were from Mennonite or BIC background in 1989 than in 1972. Otherwise little change occurred in the 17-year interim, except for a very slight increase in the proportion of members feeling satisfied with their denomination and congregation.

A Measure of Separatism

We probed a second aspect of in-groupness called "separatism." This concept is rooted in a "two kingdom ethic," a belief in a strong church-world dichotomy found in some sectors of the Mennonite and Brethren in Christ populations, as noted in chapter 1. Whereas communalism is based on certain religious *experiences* of the respondents, separatism is a part of the belief system. Nevertheless we expected the two measures to be interrelated since both communalism and separatism tend to be sectarian and emphasize strong boundary maintenance.

"Separation from the world" has been a strongly held biblical principle throughout Anabaptist-Mennonite history. It has been incorporated into a number of confessions of faith. The first of these was the Schleitheim Confession (more properly the "Brotherly Union") of 1527, whose article IV, on "Separation from the World," reflects a sharp differentiation from "the world" that was persecuting the early Anabaptists. In reviewing the confession Hostetler (1987:87) noted that the article "implies two worlds or two kingdoms. . . . Separation from the religious establishment was a rigorous judgment that invited the animosity of both Catholic and Protestant authorities."

The Dutch-oriented Dordrecht Confession of 1632 stressed repentance and reformation of life as the fruit of repentance, but spoke less directly about separation from the world than about the separation of erring members—via the ban—from fellowship with the church. Throughout their history, the Mennonites of Dutch origin have tended to emphasize the church-world dichotomy somewhat less than have their kin of Swiss origin (Driedger and Kauffman, 1982; Juhnke, 1988). In North America they have become more urbanized and more politically active than the Swiss Mennonites, who immigrated earlier and settled in the eastern United States, as noted in chapter 2.

Further indication of these differences appears in two recent confessions of faith representing the BIC and MC groups. Article 16 of the 1963 *Mennonite Confession of Faith* states: "We believe that there are two opposing kingdoms to which men give their spiritual allegiance, that of Christ and that of Satan." The BIC "Doctrine" (1973) states: "Separation from the world is normal for the Christian because God's children enjoy a transferred citizenship, belonging to a kingdom different from this present evil world."

Separatism among Mennonites has historically been more spiritual and ideological than sociological or geographical. Except for Hutterites, Old Order Amish, and the Mennonites in their tightly knit, ethnically distinct village communities of Prussia, Russia, and Canada, Mennonites, both in Europe and in North America, have lived among people of other faiths, particularly in cities. They have intermingled with others in agriculture, commerce, industry, schools, recreation, community voluntary associations, and ecumenical organizations. Nevertheless, the idea of two kingdoms persists in the minds of many members, as shown in Table 4-2.

Table 4-2. Responses to Items on Separatism

Items	MC	GC	MB	BIC	EMC	Total
	(Percent agreeing)					
There is a clear difference between the "kingdom of God" and the "kingdom of this world"	93	88	95	93	95	92
Christians should avoid involvements in the "kingdom of this world" as much as possible	59	55	60	62	68	58
There is an inner contradiction between following Christ and the exercise of leadership in government	38	28	21	22	13	30
There is no great tension between church and world, between the commandments of Christ and the laws of my society	(Percent disagreeing)					
	82	79	86	85	87	82
How much if any conflict do you experience between your Mennonite or BIC beliefs and practices and the attitudes and practices of the larger society?	(Percent "much" or "some")					
	57	55	71	57	62	59

Members of all five denominations (92%) appear to believe that the "kingdom of God" and the "kingdom of this world" are clearly different. The dilemma of being "in the world but not of it" is not easily resolved, as indicated by a smaller proportion (58%) who believe they should avoid involvements in the world. Their responses do not, of course, reveal which particular involvements they would avoid and which they would not.

Only 30 percent of the respondents viewed participation in government as contradictory to following Christ—suggesting that most members did not regard the "world" and the government as the same thing. Eighty-two percent expected tension between church and world, but fewer (59%) actually experienced noticeable conflict with the larger society in regard to religious beliefs and practices.

Once again denominational differences were small, but on the basis of these items it appears that separatism is strongest among the MB and EMC groups, except in the case of government. Trends cannot be observed, since none of these items were included in the 1972 survey.

When the items were combined to form a separatism scale, individual scores ranged from 7 to 24, within possible limits of 5 and 24. For all denominations 80 percent of the scores ranged from 15 to 20. Mennonites of Dutch origin scored a bit lower on the scale than did those of Swiss origin, as expected, but the differences were relatively small. Variations by age-groups and other demographic variables will be noted in chapter 11.

Memberships in Community Organizations

A different but somewhat related concept of in-groupness called "in-group identity" will be introduced in chapter 7, where the concept of "peoplehood" is developed. At this point we introduce evidence that Mennonites are increasingly participating in community organizations that extend their social contacts beyond the denominational in-group.

The respondents were asked to record the number of memberships they held in each of 15 types of community organizations. Table 4-3 reports the percentage of respondents who belonged to one or more clubs in each type of organization.

Table 4-3. Memberships in Community Organizations, 1972 and 1989

Type of organization	Percent in 1989					Totals	
	MC	GC	MB	BIC	EMC	1972	1989
School service clubs	18	16	15	19	18	24	17
Youth groups	17	14	18	21	23	23	17
Farm organizations	10	11	6	8	15	12	9
Sports clubs	16	14	15	18	20	12	15
Professional or academic societies	17	18	20	15	16	11	18
Major political groups	8	10	10	19	10	7	10
Hobby or garden clubs	7	7	6	7	6	6	7
Literary, art, etc., groups	6	6	5	4	4	6	5
Business corporations (officers)	9	6	7	7	8	5	8
Labor unions	5	6	10	7	5	5	6
Service clubs (Rotary, etc.)	5	8	4	4	4	3	5
Fraternal groups (lodges)	2	3	0	3	1	2	2
College fraternities or sororities	2	2	1	3	3	1	2
Veterans groups	1	2	1	2	2	1	1
Physical fitness clubs	14	11	13	11	13	*	13

*Not included in the 1972 survey.

A comparison of the 1972 and 1989 total columns shows a drop in memberships in school and youth groups (from 24 and 23% to 17%);

this drop reflects the substantially smaller proportion of teenagers in the 1989 sample. Teenagers in 1989 were members of groups in larger proportions than were people in other age categories. Ninety percent of the teenagers in 1989 were members of at least one organization; the figure was 89 percent in 1972.

The decline in memberships in farm organizations reflects the decline in the proportion of church members who are farming. Otherwise, nearly all categories exhibit a gradually increasing involvement of Mennonites in out-group relationships. Later in this chapter we will note how involvement in community organizations is associated with other variables developed in this and earlier chapters.

The denominational differences were very small and, with only three exceptions, not statistically significant.

A memberships scale was constructed by giving each respondent a score equal to the number of memberships reported. Thirty-five percent reported no memberships at all (31% in 1972), another 24 percent reported one membership, and 41 percent reported two or more memberships.

Individualism in a Mennonite Context

Defining Individualism

Increasing attention has been given in recent years to the nature and growth of individualism in North American societies. A major contribution to our thinking on this subject was published in 1985 by Robert Bellah and his associates under the title *Habits of the Heart*. These authors viewed individualism as a major component of the American value system.[2] Modern societies have increasingly emphasized the rights and dignity of the individual, as a response to the often autocratic and arbitrary use of power and authority by heads of government and other organizations in past centuries. The authors "do not argue that Americans should abandon individualism," but they are concerned that individualism may be carried to excess and may undermine the foundations of community and social organizations.

Bellah elaborates on four types of individualism: biblical, civic, utilitarian, and expressive (1985:142-51). Biblical individualism, inspired by Reformation Christianity, emphasizes individual responsibility and voluntary participation but within a context of moral and religious obligation to God and community. Civic individualism has its roots in classical republicanism, which emphasizes the protection of individual rights and liberties but with citizen responsibility to work for the public good.

Utilitarian individualism is rooted in the philosophy of John Locke, who argued that "the individual is prior to society, which comes into existence only through the voluntary contract of individuals." It holds that individuals should be free to get ahead on their own initiative, unhampered by constraints imposed by others. Expressive individualism grows out of the personal desires and sentiments of individuals who seek whatever serves their self-interest and personal wishes at the moment.

Bellah feels that traditional civic and biblical individualism were held in check by sentiments of citizen responsibility to a larger whole—community and tradition. Modern individualism, particularly the expressive type, "has pursued individual rights and individual autonomy in ever new realms" (Bellah, et al., 1985:143). Bellah is fearful that unchecked modern individualism (both utilitarian and expressive) may undermine social consensus, removing the very basis for the rewards and approval that are so essential to individual well-being. The clash between autonomy and conformity "seems to be the fate of American individualism" (Bellah, 1985:149).

Gans (1988:98) is less pessimistic about modern individualism, but nevertheless observes, "Virtually all the critics agree that people should sacrifice some of their individual strivings for more communal concerns."

Religious writers are prone to view expressive individualism as a threat to the spiritual and moral fabric of the churches. Regarding mainline Protestantism, Roof and McKinney (1987:32) noted that Americans "enjoy a great deal of freedom to believe as they wish and to pursue spiritual quests as they please." Speaking for Canadians, Bibby (1987) referred to "religion a la carte," meaning that people tend to pick and choose what they want from a religious menu of beliefs and practices. Roof and McKinney (1987:32-33) say:

> Utilitarian aspects of individualism encourage the pursuit of self-interest and personal achievement and hold up these values as taking primacy over group loyalties. . . . Commitment to self has grown at the expense of community, disrupting especially loyalties to traditional religious institutions.

How much individualism would one expect to find within the Mennonite ethos? As Ainlay (1990a) reasoned, 16th-century Anabaptism demonstrated a biblical individualism, holding that individuals were personally responsible for faith and morals on the basis of Scripture alone, not on the basis of church tradition or priestly ministrations. Pietism, with its emphasis on inner spiritual renewal, also influenced Anabaptists and further reinforced their religious individualism.

However, Ainlay (1990a) noted that Friedmann (1944) saw Anabaptist individualism as limited by a sense of concern for the member, and submission of issues to the council of the congregation. Thus responsibility to the congregation, as the body of Christ, has the effect of limiting individual expression for those who would be accepted into the community of the committed.

Contemporary Mennonite pluralism shows varied approaches to the "individual versus community" dilemma. The more conservative groups afford their members less room for individual expression. The individual is superceded by the inherited tradition, which is reinforced by the congregation's leadership. In the more progressive groups, congregationalism prevails, but with a great amount of freedom for individual members to determine the content of their own faith, their religious practices, and their lifestyle, which are influenced, of course, by the teaching and preaching in church and Sunday school.

Ainlay (1990a:142) argues that individualism is not contradictory to Mennonite life and culture so long as it is moderated by biblical and civic traditions that are a part of the Anabaptist legacy. But "radical individualism—in either its utilitarian or expressive forms—which is excessively subjective, resulting in the fragmentation of the group, giving the self unquestioned priority over the collective interest of the group, is both contradictory and inimical to Mennonite life."

Although hard to measure, individualism may be increasing among Mennonites, according to Ainlay. He bases his assumption on the increasing bureaucracy of church structures, the shift from farming to professional and technical work, the increasing emphasis on self-reliance and independence in child rearing, the increasing emphasis on egalitarianism in social relationships, and the tendency of individuals to seek freedom from all forms of external control and constraint. Ainlay's question poses this dilemma, "How does one continue to advance the rights and opportunities of all people and yet avoid the traps of subjectivity?" (Ainlay, 1990a:146).

In view of the difficulties involved in operationalizing the concept in a form that could be incorporated into a survey questionnaire, we may be somewhat presumptuous in attempting to construct several measures of individualism. No attempt was made to do this in the 1972 survey. In 1989, however, we accepted the risk and challenge of plowing some new ground. Not finding an individualism index that could satisfactorily meet our needs, we gathered suggestions from several sources and developed three measures:[3]

1. An individualism scale, whose items tested the respondents' religious autonomy and desire to be free of churchly doctrines or controls in respect to personal faith and life. We believe it measures "religious individualism." The items appear in Table 4-4.

2. A personal independence scale, which is an attempt to measure

the extent to which the respondents valued independence, self-reliance, and freedom in matters of personal choice. We believe it is a test of "expressive individualism." The items, given in Table 4-5, reflect what Dueck (1988) had in mind when he wrote:

> Psychology tends to reflect and reinforce the individualism of North American societies. Human development theory follows the pattern from symbiotic relationship with mother to individuation, from dependence to independence, heteronomy to autonomy, from conformity to self-actualization.

3. A materialism scale, to probe the importance which the respondents attached to working hard, earning and saving money, and possessing things that money will buy—measuring something akin to "utilitarian individualism." Table 4-6 contains the items. As with the personal independence items, the respondents were asked to indicate how important each item was in their "own life and thought."[4]

We have chosen the term "concomitants of modernization" to refer to these three scales plus the secularism scale introduced in chapter 3. The literature is replete with arguments that these ideas are related to modernization. Since we prefer to think of modernization as characterized primarily by urbanization and the advances of education, science and technology, we regard secularism, individualism, and materialism as dependent rather than independent variables in relation to modernization.[5]

Since these measures were not included in the 1972 survey, no observations could be made as to trends. Neither could comparability with other religious populations be established, since no comparable scales were found in other surveys. Aside from providing a glimpse into contemporary Mennonite thinking, the value of these measures inheres mainly in facilitating intercorrelations with other scales that are central to the data analysis.

Measuring Individualism

Only one-fourth of the respondents took the position that the church should not be involved in one's personal affairs (Table 4-4). Fifty-nine percent disagreed, and 17 percent were "uncertain." Differences among the denominations were small. The last item in the table is something of an antithesis of the first, and only 9 percent of the respondents took the individualistic view opposing mutual admonition.

Over one-half (55%) of the respondents agreed that faith is a private matter—suggesting that church members take seriously the idea of individual responsibility for their beliefs. A somewhat smaller proportion (34%) saw religion primarily as a matter of personal choice. Presumably, most of the others saw their faith as under the canopy of communal commitment, and were willing to submit their views to the collective wisdom of a body of Christian believers.

Table 4-4. Responses to Items on Individualism

Items	MC	GC	MB	BIC	EMC	Total
	(Percent agreeing)					
In the last analysis faith is a private matter for each to decide and practice oneself	52	63	49	57	61	55
One's own religion should be more a matter of personal choice than directed by churchly doctrines and standards of behavior	37	37	27	31	29	34
It's not really the business of the church to be directly involved in my personal affairs	24	27	20	25	28	24
The phrase, "If it feels good, do it" is a good principle of life for the Christian today	4	5	1	1	0	3
For me to be a church member means to give and receive mutual admonition about how we live our lives	(Percent disagreeing)					
	8	12	9	9	11	9
Scale totals: Percent scoring "high"	18	21	11	12	12	17

Although the differences between the denominations were minor, the respondents within each denomination varied widely in their scale scores, from a low of 5 to a high of 20 and over, within possible limits of 5 and 25. Each denomination had within its membership persons representing the whole range of attitudes or values in respect to religious individualism—indicating a great deal of similarity among the denominations.

Measuring Personal Independence
Table 4-5 shows the extent to which the values of personal independence appear to be a part of Mennonite thinking. If we combine the responses of those who answered "very important" and "important" regarding each of the stated values, a large majority of the respondents can be said to have affirmed the value of being independent, self-reliant, and able to make their own decisions. However, only a third were ready to give unqualified assent to "being free to do what I want to do." Possibly this suggests too much latitude for unrestrained questionable behaviors.

Once again denominational differences were slight, but individual scores on the total scale ranged from 5 to 20, within limits of 4 and 20.

Eighty percent scored from 12 to 18, with the other 20 percent representing those members who value personal independence most and least highly.

Table 4-5. Responses to Items on Personal Independence

Items	Percent responding "very important" or "important"					
	MC	GC	MB	BIC	EMC	Total
Being able to make my own decisions	78	86	84	85	84	82
Being self-reliant	75	81	78	80	77	78
Taking care of my own needs— being independent	63	71	64	64	64	65
Being free to do what I want to do	32	40	33	33	31	34
Scale totals: Percent scoring "high"	20	30	24	22	24	24

Measuring Materialism

Finally, the evidence of materialism (or utilitarian individualism), as we have attempted to measure it, appears in Table 4-6. Financial security in old age seemed to be the most emphasized value, with 60 percent of the respondents viewing it as important or very important. The "latest clothing styles and fashions" (7%) and "the nicest home and furnishings" (8%) were the least valued of these items. Getting ahead financially, and earning and saving money were highly valued by from one-fifth to one-third of the church members.

Once again scale scores were derived by adding item scores. Total scores ranged from the minimum of 6 to the maximum of 30. The range of scores for the members *within* each denomination was at least 8 to 28, indicating a similar spread within all participating denominations.

Intercorrelation of Measures

Having constructed scales measuring four concomitants of modernization (secularization, individualism, personal independence, and materialism), we now turn to the question of how scores on these scales intercorrelate with scores on demographic and religiosity variables reported in earlier chapters. Table 4-7 reports the Pearsonian correlation coefficients which measure the degree of association between the relevant variables and scales, providing further evidence of the impact of modernization on Mennonites and Brethren in Christ.

Urbanization appears to bear no significant relation to these concomitants of modernization, since the correlation coefficients are close to zero. Contrary to what some have predicted, the move to cities has not made Mennonites more secular, individualistic, and materialistic.

Table 4-6. Responses to Items on Materialism

Items	MC	GC	MB	BIC	EMC	Total
	Percent responding "very important" or "important"					
Earning enough money to be secure in my old age	57	64	60	64	60	60
Working hard so as to get ahead financially	31	38	33	34	31	34
Saving as much money as possible	28	25	23	34	29	27
Earning as much money as possible	17	21	18	26	16	19
Getting the nicest home and furnishings I can afford	8	6	8	13	12	8
Being dressed in the latest styles and fashions	7	7	10	7	5	7
Scale totals: Percent scoring "high"	16	18	17	24	20	17

Likewise, these findings do not support predictions about adverse effects from increased education and higher socioeconomic status. Indeed, these demographic characteristics of modernization appear to have caused a reduction rather than an increase in the concomitants of modernization. Why do these findings not conform to past expectations? Are secularization, individualism, and materialism not really concomitants of demographic modernization, or are Mennonites different, experiencing diminished secularism, individualism, and materialism as they become more educated and upwardly mobile?[6]

One possible explanatory factor that the data do not control is loss of membership. Have the more secularized individuals dropped their Mennonite affiliation, leaving only the more highly educated members whose Mennonite identities are stronger? Even if this were true, there is no evidence that loss of low-identity Mennonites is greater among the more highly educated, or among those living in the city, than among others. Research on persons who are no longer members of Mennonite and BIC congregations is needed to probe this issue.

We are left with the conclusion that increased secularism, individualism, and materialism are not concomitants of the demographic modernization of contemporary Mennonites. The first generation of higher status, urban Mennonites may have sufficient religious commitment and community supports to combat countervailing forces. Will this also be the case several generations later?

Table 4-7. Intercorrelation of Concomitants of Modernization with Other Variables

Variable	Secu-larism	Indivi-dualism	Personal indepen-dence	Materi-alism
Modernization				
Residence (urbanization)	.02	-.06	.03	-.03
Educational achievement	-.20	-.21	-.06	-.12
Socioeconomic status	-.16	-.17	-.02	-.04
Mobility	-.07	-.09	-.09	-.11
Beliefs				
Anabaptism	-.35	-.42	-.19	-.23
Orthodoxy	-.42	-.23	-.10	-.04
Fundamentalism	-.34	-.14	-.04	.06
Bible knowledge	-.38	-.35	-.18	-.26
Religious practice				
Associationalism	-.44	-.47	-.24	-.21
Devotionalism	-.45	-.38	-.16	-.18
Religious experience	-.27	-.21	-.05	-.06
Mennonite identity				
Communalism	-.03	-.13	-.02	.00
Separatism	-.39	-.31	-.14	-.16
Memberships	.08	.06	.06	.08

Note: To be statistically significant at the .01 level, coefficients must be less than -.045 or greater than .045.

Driedger has suggested elsewhere (1989:229) that a modernized ethnic group may find a way to save itself from loss of identity even though deeply involved in the urbanized industrial and bureaucratic social systems. Networks of social relationships can be built with the conveniences of modern transportation and communication. As middle-class urbanites and suburbanites, Mennonites have avoided the more socially disorganized segments of the urban centers, and they appear to be able to transfer their unique beliefs and practices from rural areas to those parts of the city offering the amenities (housing, schools, shops, etc.) that support a middle-class way of life.

Secularism, individualism, and materialism are clearly detrimental to religious beliefs, as indicated by the substantial negative correlations with the variables of Anabaptism and other religious beliefs. Likewise, they are negatively related to the scales measuring religious practice. Among the measures of Mennonite identity, only the separatism scale has substantial negative correlations. The fact that we expected these negative correlations with the concomitants of modernization tends to argue for the validity of our measures.

Summary

In the mid-20th century the movement of Mennonites from rural to urban areas spawned, particularly in the United States, a Mennonite community emphasis designed to promote communalism. The intent was to foster loyalty to the small religious community as a bulwark against the threats of modernization associated with urbanization.

Nevertheless, the urban movement continued. Casting their lot increasingly with the cities, Mennonites have become more pluralistic and have found ways to cope with the urban environment (at least those portions which are not socially disorganized) by building churches and networks of communication, fellowship, and mutual aid.

A major threat to communalism is the gradual development of individualistic emphases that put self-interest ahead of commitment to community values and sentiments. In this chapter we presented several measures of individualism and communal commitment that test the impact of modernization on community loyalties. It was assumed that several concomitants of modernization (secularism, individualism, and materialism) would be positively associated with demographic components of modernization (urban residence, increased education, higher socioeconomic status, and residential mobility).

Urban Mennonites scored no higher than rural Mennonites on scales measuring secularism, individualism, personal independence, and materialism. Furthermore, these concomitants of modernization were *negatively* correlated with more education, higher socioeconomic status, and mobility. We cannot speak for other populations, but these findings do not support the assumption that demographic modernization yields greater secularism, individualism, and materialism among Mennonite and Brethren in Christ church members.

As expected, these concomitants of modernization were negatively related to religious beliefs and practices, but this counteraction occurred within all categories of age, residence, education, socioeconomic status, and mobility. Insofar as secularism, individualism, and materialism are threats, their roots must be found in other explanatory variables, such as lack of religious commitment and failure to practice the spiritual disciplines of worship and faithful church attendance.

CHAPTER 5

Changing Family Patterns

PERHAPS NO SOCIAL INSTITUTION has been more profoundly affected by the forces of modernization than has the family. The family is both a foundation stone of society and a frontline defense against the negative impacts that the larger society might have upon its members. From the standpoint of the individual, the family is both a launching pad and a refuge from the impersonal forces that threaten a person's security. The family is one of the most important stakes supporting the Mennonite sacred canopy, perhaps more important even than community.

How Are North American Families Changing?

Differing Views

The impact of modernization on the structure and quality of family life has been widely debated. More than 50 years ago Goodsell (1934:482) concluded:

> The family of the twentieth century is markedly unstable; it would seem that in some instances it has paid for the independence of its members the costly price of its very existence or its existence in a changed and incomplete form.

Others (Ogburn, 1933; Sorokin, 1941:776; Zimmerman, 1947; Goode, 1964:108) also were pessimistic about prospects for the modern family, citing a decline of the kinship system, increased marital breakdown, earlier separation of children from parents, weakening of the social mores undergirding the family, and the transfer of family functions to other groups and agencies.

Some students of the family, however, found reasons for hope in the emerging features of family life. Burgess and Locke (1953:22) believed that marriage was becoming less patriarchal and more equalitarian, resulting in a greater sense of companionship in marriage. Folsom (1943) saw increased democracy in family functioning as a gain. Duvall (1971) found a trend from "traditional" to "developmental" patterns in child-rearing that would improve the emotional well-being of children as they moved through their developmental stages.

More recently, family sociologists and psychologists have continued to view the decline of patriarchy as a gain—patriarchy being replaced with increased gender equality in marriage and more freedom for self-expression among the children. According to Nye and Berardo (1973: 22), "the institution of the family is not dissolving, but changing rather rapidly in its functions, roles, and values."

From a conservative viewpoint these changes are simply evidence of the deterioration of family mores. Small but increasing proportions of adults are satisfying their needs for social and sexual intimacy in arrangements outside of marriage. Some of the manifestations of these changes are living together unmarried, having children outside of marriage, and homosexual "marriages." In the past 40 years the proportion of births to unwed mothers in the United States has gone from 4 to 25 percent (National Center for Health Statistics, 1990:32).

What for some persons is deterioration, for others is liberation. Schulz (1982:385-86) noted that we live in a pluralistic culture with regard to family lifestyles; "those who see 'crises' do not like this variety. Those who find pluralism desirable speak of the adaptive capabilities of families."

Current family theorists focus less on what has been happening historically to the family as an institution and more on understanding the dynamics of family interaction, individual development, and gender role identities. In reviewing the recent growth of family theories, Holman and Burr (1984:33) note the decline of institutional theory and the ascendancy of interactionist, exchange, and systems theories. Although these latter are important for analyzing families at a particular time, they tend to avoid value judgments regarding long-term gains and losses in family life.

Religion and Family Changes

Mennonites, ever inclined to make value judgments, want to know whether we are gaining or losing in reference to strongly held traditional family values such as kinship loyalties, premarital chastity, the permanence of marriage, and religious socialization of children.

The emphasis on maintenance of traditional values creates a tension with the modern emphasis on individualism, as presented in the previous chapter. D'Antonio and Aldous (1983) note that religion tends to bolster traditional family values. On the contrary, according to these authors, modernization emphasizes individual freedom, "the right of the individual to escape or transcend any group loyalties in order to create an individually designed life plan—a career" (1983:28).

Concern for traditional family values is not limited to conservative religious groups. In their 1988 survey, the Gallup organization found that 94 percent of the American public would welcome "more emphasis on traditional family values," up from 91 percent in 1978 (Gallup and Jones, 1989:102).

In view of the continuing debates over the future of the family, it may be well to reflect on where we have come from. Leslie (1979: 211) has caught the essence of family patterns of the rural past, a picture that Mennonites may well have fit into a couple generations ago:

> The arduous conditions of life, the detailed division of labor within the family, and the emphasis on productivity did not encourage concern with the quality of emotional relationships. The relevant considerations in evaluating a husband were whether he owned property, was hard-working, sober, God-fearing, and just. Women were supposed to be good housekeepers, morally upright, strong, and equipped to bear and rear children. Assuming these qualities, the differences between persons were minimized; one did not expect great and continued emotional satisfaction in marriage. Similarly, children were trained to be industrious, obedient, and well mannered. Whether they were well adjusted and happy was not considered.

Today less than 5 percent of North American families are fully farm families. The traditional, patriarchal family of frontier days still exists, as a typical family pattern, only in isolated pockets of rural society, as in the Appalachian highlands or among the Old Order Amish. Currently this pattern is favored by some very conservative fundamentalist religious groups. Patriarchy is not well suited to an urban environment, where families no longer form production units, and where family members tend to be dispersed because of their occupational, educational, and recreational roles and functions. Adaptation to the urban environment necessitates modified patterns of family life.

Were the prophets of doom a half century ago correct in their predictions? The family system is still very much with us. Marriage seems to be as popular as ever, if we can judge by the tendency of many divorced persons to move back into marriage at the first opportunity. Intimate companionship is still a basic human need, and the social mores still hold that legal marriage is the appropriate setting for satisfying this need.

Perhaps Everett Dyer's summary (1979:449-51) expresses it well. He sees strong evidence that the family will survive. Monogamous marriage and the nuclear unit will remain the predominant form. The long-range trend toward companionate marriage will continue, with more flexibility and interchangeability of roles. Many continuing problem situations will require frequent adjustments on the part of individual family members. "The family has survived a variety of experiments and efforts to reshape it in recent history, but always, so far, after the experimental fervor has declined, there has been a gradual return to more conventional family patterns" (Dyer, 1979:451).

Mennonite Views on Marriage and Divorce

In chapter 1 we introduced five indicators of modernization: urbanization, education, income, occupational status, and mobility. How have these factors affected family life and thought among Mennonites? In this chapter we will seek answers to this question, attempting to identify those trends which seem to be positive, and those which seem to be negative, for the achievement of Mennonite family values. Is the Mennonite family still a powerful stake in support of the sacred canopy?

The family is the primary agent in the transmission of values from one generation to the next, followed by church, school, and community. The family is also the context in which adaptations to changing social and cultural conditions must be made. As we examine Mennonite family patterns we will discover changes that reflect adaptations to the external environment, such as the decline of patriarchy and changing attitudes toward the permanence of marriage. We will also note the impact of shifts in family residence and occupational status. Is there a continuing Mennonite family identity in the face of social and cultural modernization?

Changing Family Norms

Two important factors help explain the background of contemporary Mennonite family patterns: (1) Mennonite understandings of the ethical norms set forth in the Bible and (2) the pervasive influence of the rural farm environment both in Europe and—under pioneer conditions—on the North American continent. These factors have persisted well into the middle of the twentieth century, with gradual modifications in recent decades.

With respect to biblical norms, Mennonites have emphasized the sacredness of the marriage vows, the permanence of marriage, the sinfulness of fornication and adultery, the family "headship" of the husband-father, the need for children to be taught to be dutiful and obedient, the priority of family needs over individual preferences, and the responsibility of family members to care for the special needs of kin. Additionally there has been a strong work ethic and a desire to be good stewards of the resources which God has given to all. Despite considerable rural strictness in group controls over individuals, the ethic of love was emphasized as the standard in all personal relationships, however imperfectly achieved.[1]

In regard to the rural farm environment, Mennonites were affected in much the same way as other North Americans were, as described above. The farm family was a production unit, and the husband-father was seen as the supervisor and, by extension, the head of all the family activities outside the household, if not within it as well. Varying degrees of patriarchy developed in the rural social setting. Much role differentiation developed also, as each family member was assigned specific duties in an effort to achieve maximum efficiency. With much work to be done, there was little time for recreation or for cultivating relaxed interpersonal relationships. Affection was more assumed than expressed. Companionship in marriage was a by-product of integrated work roles rather than a conscious objective.

As noted above, students of the family have considered the decline of patriarchy a gain. To test this thesis, Kauffman (1960) surveyed 149 midwestern Mennonite families in order to compare the more traditional, patriarchal families with the more "emergent" (democratic, equalitarian) types. With regard to sharing authority between spouses, Mennonite families ranged from those in which a strongly patriarchal pattern was evident to a few in which the wife was recognized as dominant. About one-third of the respondents claimed that they and their spouses shared authority equally. As measures of "family success," the study focused on three interpersonal dimensions: (1) husband-wife, (2) parent-child, and (3) child-peer.

The comparison of traditional, patriarchal families with emergent-type families led to results generally favoring the emergent families. On all three scales measuring interpersonal relations, the emergent families scored somewhat higher. In a measure of the children's acceptance of Mennonite values, however, there was no significant difference between traditional and emergent families. The patriarchal families did not score highest on any of the measures of success used in the study.

Viewpoints on Marriage

How have Mennonites responded to the social forces affecting marriage and family life in 1972 and 1989? Mennonite attitudes toward the permanence of marriage are revealed in the responses to the question "Which statement best expresses your view of marriage?"

Table 5-1 indicates that almost three-fourths (72%) of the respondents viewed marriage as a lifelong commitment, not to be broken except by death. Almost all of the remainder (27%) accepted divorce if all attempts at reconciliation had failed.

Table 5-1. Attitudes Toward the Permanence of Marriage by Denomination and Year

	1989					Totals	
Response	MC	GC	MB	BIC	EMC	1972	1989
	(Percent agreeing)						
A lifelong commitment never to be broken except by death	71	64	81	77	78	77	72
A lifetime commitment, but may be broken only if every attempt to reconcile disharmony has failed	28	35	18	22	21	22	27
A commitment to remain married as long as the partner is compatible	1	*	*	*	1	1	1
A commitment to remain married until one partner wishes to break the marriage	*	*	*	0	0	*	*
Totals	100	100	100	100	100	100	100

*Less than 0.5 percent.

Clearly the prevailing view has not changed much in 17 years. About 5 percent have shifted to accepting divorce if efforts at reconciliation have failed. Those selecting the first response ranged from 63 percent for the 30-49 age-group to 84 percent for the 70 and over group. In both surveys the older groups held the most traditional views opposing divorce; however, among the older groups the proportions opposing divorce were lower in 1989 than in 1972. As in 1972, gender differences were statistically insignificant.

Denominational differences were rather small. GCs (35%) were most willing to accept a broken marriage, and MBs (18%) were least willing. Only one percent of the respondents took more liberal views toward marriage breakup.

Divorce and Remarriage

The conditions of modern life seem to militate against the permanence of marriage. Over the past two decades Mennonites and Brethren in Christ have had to grapple with issues related to divorce and remarriage more frequently than in former times. They have not escaped the national trends toward higher divorce rates, although their sacred canopy has kept their rates far below those of the national populations.

In 1989 4.2 percent of our respondents had experienced divorce or separation, a majority of whom had remarried. This rate was about four times the one percent reported in 1972. Among the 1989 respondents, the percentage ever divorced or separated ranged from 3.5 for the GC to 6.6 for the BIC and EMC. If we omit those 1989 respondents who never married and include only those aged 30 and over, the percentage ever divorced or separated was 5.1.

The national rates stand in sharp contrast. According to the General Social Survey, nearly one-third (32.5%) of adults (aged 18 and over) in the United States have experienced divorce (National Opinion Research Center, 1989:529). Cherlin (1981:25) estimated that 48 percent of Americans who married in the late 1970s will experience divorce—assuming that the annual divorce rates remain constant, as was the case during the 1980s. Divorce rates are somewhat lower in Canada, currently about half the U.S. rate (Driedger, et al., 1985:370). Using data from the 1981 Canadian census, Driedger (1985:374) compared the divorce rate for Mennonites with the rates for 18 other religious bodies. Only two groups—"Reformed Bodies" and Hutterites—had lower rates than Canadian Mennonites.

Are modernization factors causing an increase in the dissolution of Mennonite marriages? A look at the residence categories shows that the ever-divorced or -separated percentage was 3.0 for church members who were living on farms, compared to 6.6 for those who were living in large cities. Thus, urbanization appears to be a factor. Education was also related to divorce rates, with only 1.8 percent of the respondents experiencing marital breakup among those who did not go beyond the eighth grade, while 5.9 percent of those who went to college (but not beyond) broke up. However, the age factor explains part of this difference, since the older groups averaged less education.

Because of traditional attitudes opposing divorce, divorced Mennonites have often found it difficult to retain fellowship within their congregations. However, since the 1970s this situation has been changing and divorce is being regarded as forgivable, like other sins. Congregations, and individuals within congregations, may vary considerably in how much readiness there is to accept the divorced on an equal basis with all other members. Variant attitudes are revealed in the percentage of members who regard divorce as "always wrong."

Table 5-2 reports on the attitudes toward divorce and the remarriage of divorced persons, with variations by level of education. For each item, the respondent was asked to choose from among four responses: always wrong, sometimes wrong, never wrong, and uncertain. The table gives only the percentages for the "always wrong" responses.

Table 5-2. Attitudes Toward Divorce and Remarriage by Education and Year

| | Percent responding "always wrong" | | | | | |
| | Educational level | | | | Totals | |
Item	Elem.	H.S.	College	Grad	1972	1989
Divorce (because of adultery)	43	24	12	10	33	20
Divorce (for other causes)	52	36	31	27	49	35
Remarriage while first spouse is still living	59	38	23	17	60	31

Clearly church members think somewhat differently about divorce for cause of adultery than for other causes. The attitude that divorce for the cause of adultery is always wrong declined from 33 percent in 1972 to 20 percent in 1989. In the case of divorce for other causes, the decline was from 49 to 35 percent. In both cases many respondents regarded it as "sometimes wrong," that is, under some conditions. In both cases 11 percent were "uncertain."

As a modernizing factor, education has a major effect on attitudes toward divorce and remarriage. For the three items presented, the proportion of respondents who did not go beyond elementary school answering "always wrong" was two to four times as high as for those who attended graduate school. Since age and educational achievement are inversely related, some of the educational variation can be attributed to the age factor. That is, since the elementary and high school categories contain larger proportions of older persons, the higher percentages in those categories can be partly attributed to age.

Urbanization was also associated with greater acceptance of divorce and remarriage. Smaller proportions of city residents responded "always wrong" than did those in rural areas, but the differences between residence categories were not so great as between the educational categories.

Currently the greater problem is how to regard the remarriage of divorced persons. Some conferences and congregations have developed procedures for working with couples who wish to marry when divorce has been involved. Such procedures involve counseling the person or persons to determine whether there has been satisfactory closure to the previous marriage(s) and whether careful consideration is being given to the probability of success in a new marriage. Thus Mennonites have not abandoned their serious view of the marriage vow.

The respondents were asked, "Under what conditions would you approve admitting to membership in your church a person who is divorced and remarried (with first spouse still living)?" The response categories were (in condensed form): (1) under no conditions, (2) if divorce was due to adultery, (3) if confession and restitution were made, (4) no confession, but promise of future faithfulness to church doctrines, and (5) belief in Christ, without reference to divorce.

The findings (summarized to save space) were as follows: (1) Ninety-five percent would accept such remarriages if certain conditions were met, with 23 percent making no conditions other than faith in Christ. (2) From 1972 to 1989 there was a slight shift toward more acceptance of remarried persons. (3) Higher education was strongly associated with greater acceptance. (4) Residents of cities were slightly more accepting than those living in rural areas. (5) Within each denomination, respondents varied greatly in their attitudes toward the remarriage of divorced persons.

Exogamous Marriage

Although Mennonites have generally discouraged exogamous marriage (marriage of persons from differing religious or ethnic background), the proportion of such marriages has increased over the years. Urbanization and increased higher education among Mennonites have brought them into increasing contact and communication with potential mates from other backgrounds.

Driedger (1988:136) reported Canadian census data indicating that exogamous marriages among Mennonites in Canada increased from 7 percent in 1921 to 39 percent in 1981. He noted that, of 12 major religious bodies, only Jews, with 30 percent, had a lower proportion of exogamous marriages. Three fourths of Lutheran and Presbyterian marriages were exogamous. Of the 12 bodies, Mennonites were the most rural, a factor which minimizes exogamous marriage.

As observed in 1989, 38 percent of (U.S. and Canadian) Mennonite and BIC spouses did not belong to the same denomination at the time of their wedding, up from 27 percent in 1972. However, at the time of the survey only 9 percent of the married respondents were members of different denominations. This percentage was the same in both years, indicating the continued tendency for spouses to bring their memberships into the same church sometime after marriage. Doubtless in some cases the couple joined the church of the non-Mennonite spouse.

Only 14 percent of the 1989 respondents agreed with the statement that "unless a Mennonite has good reasons, he/she should not, under any circumstances, marry outside the Mennonite (or BIC) church." Perhaps some of the 71 percent who disagreed would discourage interfaith marriage but would not want to be this rigid in their position.

Marriage of church members from different denominations varies considerably by denomination. The proportion of persons whose spouses did not belong to the same denomination at the time of their wedding varied from 33 percent for the MC to 58 percent for the EMC. The latter have been much more successful in bringing into their denomination persons from other backgrounds.

Increasing intermarriage is evident in the age distribution of the respondents. By age categories, the following proportions married spouses of another denomination: 20-29, 43 percent; 30-49, 47 percent; 50-69, 30 percent; and 70+, 28 percent.

Surprisingly, residence was not a factor in explaining differences in intermarriage rates. There was no significant difference between rural and urban respondents in the proportion of persons who married spouses of a different denomination. Intermarriage was lower (25%) for those respondents who did not go beyond the eighth grade, compared to 40 percent for those who went to high school and beyond.

National differences were significant. Only 34 percent of Canadians, but 41 percent of Americans intermarried. The proportion of intermarriages for the 1989 Canadian respondents under the age of 30 was 44 percent; under the age of 50, 42 percent. These results compare roughly to the intermarriage rate of 39 percent noted above for Mennonites in the 1981 Canadian census.[2]

The significant relationship between exogamy and marital breakup rates is interesting. Nine percent of the exogamous marriages ended in divorce or separation, but only 2 percent of the endogamous marriages did so. Thus, exogamous marriages had a breakup rate four times that of endogamous marriages.

Family and Household Characteristics

The impact of modernization on Mennonite and Brethren in Christ families is also revealed by a look at the demographic characteristics of families in 1972 and 1989. We will examine trends in marital status, age at marriage, number of persons in household, household income, and employment patterns. Most striking among these trends is the increased employment of women, particularly of married women.

Marital Status

Table 5-3 gives the marital status of church members in 1972 and 1989, with a breakdown by gender. Nine percent more males than females were married (to their original spouses) and 6 percent more females than males were widowed. These were the only significant gender differences, and they reflect the longer life span of females. Also, males showed a greater tendency than females to marry again after divorce or the death of the spouse.

Table 5-3. Percentage Distribution of Respondents by Marital Status and Gender

Marital status	1989		Totals	
	Male	Female	1972	1989
Single	13.4	14.1	23.2	13.8
Married to original spouse	80.4	71.7	71.5	75.8
Widowed	1.4	7.3	3.2	4.5
Widowed and remarried	1.7	1.6	1.2	1.6
Divorced	.7	2.0	.3	1.4
Divorced and remarried	2.2	2.8	.5	2.5
Separated	.3	.4	.2	.3
Totals	100.1	99.9	100.1	99.9

The drop in the proportion of singles (from 23 to 14%) reflects the much lower proportion of teenagers in the 1989 sample. The 1972 teenagers were a part of the "baby boomers," born in the high birthrate years of the 1950s. The 1989 teenagers were born in the 1970s, years of low birthrates. There was no evidence that the difference in the proportions of singles and married persons is due to any change in the proportion of people who ever marry.

The small increase in the proportions of the widowed and those widowed and remarried reflects the increased proportion of older persons in the church member population. In 1972 the proportions having experienced divorce and/or separation totaled one percent; in 1989 it was 4.2 percent—a significant increase, as noted in the previous section.[3] These figures reflect not only an increase in the occurrence of divorce among Mennonites, but also the increasing acceptance of divorced persons within the congregation; earlier some of these persons would have transferred their membership elsewhere.

Age at Marriage

The median age at marriage was 22.3 years, slightly lower than the median of 22.5 for 1972. In 1989 males had married at a median age of 23.2 years; females at 21.3 years. In 1972 the comparable ages were 23.4 and 21.7 years. Thus the trend appears to be toward a slightly younger age at marriage.

However, a look at age categories tells a more accurate story. The median age at marriage by age categories was as follows: 20-29, 22.2 years; 30-49, 22.0 years; 50-69, 22.3 years; and 70+, 23.6 years. Thus the decline in age at marriage ended with the baby boomers, who are aged 30 to 49. Those who are younger are marrying at a slightly older age.

Family Size

Statistics on family size are usually given either as the number of persons living in a household or as the number of children born to a family. We shall note both characteristics.

The average number of persons living together in one household has been declining, perhaps largely because of the decline in birthrates. In 1989 the number of persons per Mennonite household ranged from one to nine, with a mean of 3.2, down from a mean of 4.5 in 1972. Single person households increased from 4 to 7 percent of all households. The shift to smaller households may be due in part to increased affluence, making it possible for a dwelling unit to be maintained by fewer persons.

Fifty-two percent of all respondents were living in households occupied by a married couple with one or more children or other persons living with them. Another 30 percent were living as a married couple with no others present, three-fourths of these being couples over the age of 50 who had reached the "empty nest" stage of their lives. The 7 percent who lived alone included 85 singles, 101 widowed, 10 divorced, and 9 other persons.

National birthrates are usually given as the number of children born per year per 1,000 population. Since births in the United States are not reported for religious and ethnic subgroups, comparable data cannot be obtained for Mennonites. The next best measure of reproduction is the number of children born to families, normally reported as the number of children born to women.

The 1982 census of the Mennonite Church (Yoder, 1985:335) reported an average of 2.3 children born to all women aged 20 and over; a 2.8 average for all ever-married women. Ever-married women over the age of 50 in 1982 averaged from 3.5 to 3.9 children within ten-year age cohorts. The 30-39 age-group averaged only 2.3 children per woman, although their childbearing may not yet be complete. Yoder compared the Mennonite data with data for the U.S. population and concluded that the younger families (as of 1982) were having no more children than families in the national population. In earlier decades Mennonite birthrates had been 40 to 50 percent higher than those of the national population; thus Mennonite rates have clearly declined more rapidly than the rates for the general population.

Our 1972 survey data yielded an average of 2.8 children born to all women aged 20 and over. In 1989 the average was 2.6; for the 30-49 age-group it was 2.3, the same as in Yoder's 30-39 age-group in 1982.

Family Income

In 1988 the median household income of all families and single-person households in the survey was $31,123; in 1971 it was $9,608. Adjusting the 1988 median income by the increase in the U.S. Consumer Price Index since 1971 resulted in a 17 percent increase in real income over the 17 years, or an increase averaging one percent per year.[4] Several factors, not precisely measured, may have affected the trend. In 1988 a larger proportion of married women were employed, thus raising the average household income. A larger proportion of the 1989 respondents were in their retirement years, which would tend to lower the average income. Perhaps Mennonite family incomes have kept pace with the general increases in Canada and the United States.

Household incomes in Canada averaged $34,845. In the United States the average was $29,741. At the exchange rate of U.S. $.85 for one Canadian dollar, the Canadian household income was equal to U.S. $29,618, almost identical to the American average. Thus Mennonites in the two countries have essentially the same incomes.

Employment of Married Women

A very significant trend is the increased employment of Mennonite women. The employment of all women went from 45 percent in 1972 to 56 percent in 1989. In both years many of these were employed only part time. For the sake of comparison, the employment rate for all Mennonite males was 88 percent in 1972 and 86 percent in 1989, including part time employment. This slight decline is related to the increased proportion of unemployed, retired men in the 1989 sample, an increase even greater than the decrease in the proportion of unemployed male students.

In his chapter on "Love and Marriage," Bellah (1985:111) comments on the increasing employment of women in America:

> Women have entered the work force in increasing numbers, so that now the majority of married women and mothers work. This they do partly to express their feelings of self-worth and desire for public involvement, partly because today many families would not survive without two incomes, and partly because they are not at all sure their marriages will last. The day of the husband as permanent meal-ticket is over, a fact most women recognize, however they feel about "women's liberation."

Our survey instrument did not probe reasons for employment, but it is likely that Mennonite women do not differ much from other women in this regard, except that, given the low divorce rates for Mennonites, there may be less uncertainty about the survival of their marriages.

Table 5-4 gives trend data for the employment of Mennonite women. In 1989, 29 percent of the women were employed full time and 27 percent part time, for a total employment rate of 56 percent. In 1972, 20 percent were employed full time and 25 percent part time, for a total of 45 percent. Thus, there has been an 11 percent increase in employment, and the full-time rate now exceeds the part-time rate, a shift from 1972.

Table 5-4. Employment of Mennonite Women, 1972 and 1989

	Percent	
	1972	**1989**
Percent of all women employed	45	56
Full time	20	29
Part time	25	27
Percent of nonretired married women employed	40	62
Full time	16	33
Part time	24	29
Farm residence, full or part time	24	56
Nonfarm, full or part time	48	64
Percent employed among married women with one or more preschool children (under grade one)	*	47
Full time	*	19
Part time	*	28

*Not obtained in 1972.

Comparable data for the United States indicates that in 1988 56.6 percent of all females aged 16 years and over were in the labor force (Johnson, 1990:61). Thus, Mennonite women are employed at the same rate as women in general in the United States.

The employment rate for *married* women was 52 percent (not shown in table), slightly lower than for all women. When retired married women were removed from the calculation, the percentage employed rose to 62, compared to 40 percent in 1972. In 1972 the rate of employment (outside the home) for farm women was half that for nonfarm women. By 1989 the rate for farm women had almost caught up with the nonfarm rate (56 versus 64%), a striking commentary on the change in the work patterns of farm women.

Some readers may be particularly interested in the employment rate of mothers of preschool children. The 1989 survey shows that 47 percent were employed, more than half of them only part time. This rate was not obtained in 1972. In 1988, 56.1 percent of mothers with children under the age of six in the United States were in the labor force (Johnson, 1990:61). Mennonite mothers with preschool children, by comparison, are substantially less employed.

Changing Role and Authority Patterns

Two basic themes of Western "enlightenment" are liberty and social equality. These themes have become increasingly integrated into Western style democracy over the past 200 years. They gradually led to the demise of slavery, to the development of public schools in which all children would have equal access to education, to the franchise for women, and to the civil rights movement of the 1950s and 1960s. More recently the women's rights movement of the 1970s and 1980s has developed these themes, calling for freedom from male oppression and for equal opportunity with men in all segments of society (Kephart, 1981:201-22). These movements have influenced Mennonites too, within as well as beyond the family.

Gender Role Identities

Patriarchy is increasingly regarded as an outmoded reflection of male dominance, a theme for literary humor in the form of "Papa is all." In the 1940s and 1950s family "headship" was still acceptable, but on the basis of leadership rather than domination. Nowadays family leadership is frequently called into question if it implies some type of unequal sharing of responsibilities and duties.

Much discussion has been going on within Christian circles in an effort to determine the extent to which equality in marriage is biblical. Was the social equality of the Western enlightenment rooted in Christian doctrine or in secular humanism? Or possibly in both?

How a particular couple shares leadership depends on a number of factors. What kind of model did their respective parents provide, and how did they react to that model? How strongly do they believe in the principle of gender equality in marriage? And, most important, what kind of personality does each bring to the marriage? By the time they consider marriage, their personalities have become rather fixed, with some persons inclined to have aggressive, "take charge" traits and some tending to sit back and let others lead.

Regardless of parental models or belief in gender equality, an aggressive husband and a retiring wife are not likely to develop an equalitarian marriage. And if the wife evidences the "take charge" traits, while the husband is a hesitant, retiring person, the family will likely be matriarchal. Prevailing principles of gender equality notwithstanding, developmental processes continue to result in a wide range of personality types, and we are not likely to soon see the development of some type of uniformity in the way modern couples work out the issue of gender equality in marriage. Some families will continue to be patriarchal and some matriarchal; possibly an increasing proportion will achieve in practice, as well as in attitude, a semblance of equal sharing of roles, responsibilities, and decision making.

In the 1989 survey an attempt was made to assess church members' gender role attitudes; this was not done in 1972. Table 5-5 gives the response distributions for seven of the items that pertain to gender role identity and the career development of married women.

Table 5-5. Responses to the Items on Gender Role Identity

	Responses*				
	SA	A	U	D	SD
			(Percent)		
Role identity:					
1. In respect to the family's relationship with agencies and matters outside the household, the husband-father should carry more responsibility than the wife-mother	10	43	14	26	7
2. Whenever the wife and husband cannot agree on a matter, the husband's decision should be followed	7	25	25	31	12
3. On all matters pertaining to the household (furnishings, food, care of the children, etc.) the wife-mother's wishes are more important than the husband-father's	4	26	12	47	11
Wife's career development:					
1. In a marriage, the woman's career development should be given as high a priority as the man's	17	39	18	22	4
2. Household tasks should be shared nearly equally between husband and wife	17	45	15	21	2
3. Women today are neglecting their family responsibilities by going outside the home to work on a full-time, career basis	13	39	19	23	7
4. The demands associated with child-rearing and homemaking should not prevent a wife-mother from pursuing a professional career or other employment	9	30	20	33	9

*SA=strongly agree; A=agree; U=uncertain; D=disagree; SD=strongly disagree

The table indicates that attitudes differ from one extreme to the other, with many respondents adhering to traditional views and others taking strong equalitarian attitudes. Responses to the three role identity items were combined to construct a role identity scale. Scale scores ranged from most traditional to most equalitarian limits.[5] As measured by this scale, traditionalists opt for more role segregation; equalitarians believe in more role sharing or overlap.

The last four items in Table 5-5 were used to construct a married women's career scale, with item codes of one to five. Scores ranged from 4 to 20, the possible limits, once again demonstrating the wide range of views on these issues currently found among Mennonites and Brethren in Christ. A high score represents views favorable toward the woman's career development.

The construction of these scales made it possible to correlate gender role attitudes with the modernization concepts developed in previous chapters. Table 5-6 reports the Pearsonian correlation coefficients between these two scales and four demographic variables and the four concomitants of modernization.

Table 5-6. Correlations Between Modernization and Gender Roles

Modernization items	Equalitarian role identity	Women's career development
Demographic items:		
Age	–.32	–.16
Residence (urban)	.17	.20
Education	.29	.19
Socioeconomic status	.29	.20
Concomitant items:		
Secularism	.10	.29
Individualism	.02	.22
Personal independence	.03	.20
Materialism	–.07	.11

The negative correlations between age and the scores in the gender role scale indicate that older persons were less favorable than younger persons toward equalitarian roles and married women's career development, a finding that is not surprising. The positive correlations between the other demographic variables and the gender role scales mean that persons with urban residence, more education, and greater socioeconomic status had (at least on the average) more favorable attitudes toward equalitarian roles and the career development of married women.

The correlations between the role identity scale and the concomitants of modernization are very low (-.07 to .10) and therefore quite insignificant, meaning that traditionalists and equalitarians were quite similar with respect to secularism, individualism, and materialism. However, the findings are different for the married women's career scale. The respondents who were more favorable to the career development of married women held more secular, more individualistic, and more materialistic attitudes than did those with less favorable attitudes toward women's career development. These findings clearly indicate that equalitarianism in marriage and the development of married women's careers are associated with the modernization of Mennonites.

A finding not reported in the table is that church members who were more favorable to equalitarian roles and women's career development scored lower on orthodoxy of beliefs, Anabaptism, and devotional practices. They scored higher on several measures that will be developed in later chapters: pacifism, political activism, race relations, and favorable attitudes toward expanded roles for women in the church.

Distribution of Authority

As noted early in this chapter, the decline of patriarchy is assumed to be one aspect of the modernization of family patterns. Presumably, a significant factor in this trend has been the movement toward gender equality in the past two decades (Dyer, 1979:271). The increased employment of married women is another factor favoring gender equality, since it enhances the bargaining power of women in their family's financial management (Reiss, 1980:76-79).

To test the hypothesis of declining patriarchy, one needs comparable data for two points in time for the same, or similar, populations of married persons. Such concrete data are rare indeed, and most assumptions of declining patriarchy have been based on circumstantial evidence, such as the increased overlapping of husbands and wives in income-earning and housekeeping roles and the trend toward identifying the wife by her own given name rather than by her husband's name (e.g., Mary Jones rather than Mrs. John Jones).

One item in the 1989 questionnaire probed the distribution of authority between husband and wife: "In general, who is dominant (that is, takes the lead) in the marriage relationship?" The (married) respondents selected one of these five responses: husband definitely, husband slightly, equal, wife slightly, wife definitely. Kauffman (1960:106) used this item and its responses in his 1956 survey of 149 midwestern Mennonite families (MC only), thus affording rough comparability to the current study.[6] Table 5-7 gives the results obtained in the two studies.

In both surveys, considerably more wives than husbands responded that the "husband definitely" was dominant. Not surprisingly the wives perceived spouse dominance as greater than the husbands perceived their own dominance. The degree of husband dominance has diminished somewhat, with a shift from 26 to 17 percent of the husbands, and from 47 to 27 percent of the wives, regarding the husbands as definitely dominant. This decline in definite dominance of the husband was balanced by small increases in the equal and wife dominant categories.

Table 5-7. Percentage Distribution of Midwestern Mennonite Spouses, 1956, and CMP II (MC) Spouses, 1989

Item	1956		1989	
	husbands N=148	wives N=148	husbands N=343	wives N=353
In general, who is dominant (that is, takes the lead) in the marriage relationship?				
husband definitely	26	47	17	27
husband slightly	30	20	38	22
equal	41	30	37	42
wife slightly	3	3	6	7
wife definitely	0	0	2	2
Total	100	100	100	100

These two studies of MC families give limited support to the assumption that patriarchy has been declining through the years. If one can judge from these limited data, about half of all Mennonite marriages still show husband dominance or leadership. Equalitarian marriages and those led by the wife show small increases when compared with the marriages of a generation earlier. The current emphasis on equality between the sexes, both within and outside of marriage, is still some distance away from becoming a reality.

Denominational differences in the responses on the dominance item were small, with MB and EMC respondents showing somewhat higher proportions of husband dominance than did the other groups. The fact that these were the most urbanized denominations in the study may suggest that urbanization does not diminish husband dominance. Conservative religion may be a more potent factor than urbanization in determining the distribution of authority in marriage. We suggest that personality factors are actually the most potent, but our survey did not probe this dimension.

If declining patriarchy is associated with modernization, we would expect urbanization and higher educational achievement among Mennonites to result in more equalitarian marriages. Urban residents were only slightly less patriarchal; the variation between residence categories was not statistically significant. Education has an opposite effect from what was assumed. Respondents who attended college and graduate school showed somewhat higher husband dominance, and somewhat less equalitarian marriages, than did those who attended only elementary and high school. Do the more educated males, who tend to assume leadership roles outside the family, tend to exert leadership within marriage as well? Or perhaps the more educated females are more aware of, and therefore report, more gender inequalities. Schulz (1982:49-53) points out that husband dominance is characteristic of families of high socioeconomic status.

No significant differences in patterns of authority were found when respondents were compared on the basis of nation (Canada and the United States), region, Swiss/Dutch origin, and socioeconomic status. This suggests that the distribution of authority in marriages is more dependent on personality factors than on cultural origins or social circumstances.

Marital Relationships

Burgess and Wallin (1953:470-506), in their pioneering work on measuring success in marriage, concluded that a single criterion is not adequate to measure success in marriage. They developed a composite index measuring nine criteria of success: permanence of the union; happiness with the marriage; general satisfaction; specific satisfactions; consensus (as indicated by agreement and absence of disagreement; love and affection; sexual adjustment; companionship, confiding, and common interests; and compatibility of personality and temperament of husband and wife. The lengthiness of their marriage success index led other scholars to develop shorter versions. For his 1956 survey, Kauffman (1961) validated 28 items, half of which probed areas of agreement and disagreement in the marriage.

Thirteen of these items were included in the 1989 CMP II questionnaire in an attempt to assess the quality of contemporary Mennonite and BIC marriages. Married respondents were asked to indicate the degree of their agreement or disagreement on the handling of family finances, recreation, religious matters, personal habits, demonstration of affection, the wife's working outside the home, disciplining the children, sharing household tasks, sexual intercourse, and the number of children wanted. Scores on these ten items were combined to form a marriage agreements scale.

In addition, three items probed the respondents' happiness with their marriages, how easy or difficult they found it to talk over marriage problems, and whether they would marry the same persons if they had their lives to live over. Table 5-8 gives the response distributions for these latter three items, for the 1956 spouses and the 1989 married respondents (MC only).[7]

Table 5-8. Percentage Distribution of Responses to Selected Items on Marital Success (MC only), 1956 and 1989

	1956		1989	
Marital success items	Husbands	Wives	Husbands	Wives
How easy or difficult is it to talk over marriage problems with your mate?				
very easy	42	36	17	19
easy	29	27	27	20
fairly easy	22	26	30	31
somewhat difficult	7	10	21	21
difficult	0	1	4	6
very difficult	1	0	2	2
If you had your life to live over, do you think you would marry the same person?				
yes, definitely	60	74	56	56
yes, probably	27	19	31	30
possibly	8	5	9	11
would marry a different person	4	1	3	3
would not marry at all	1	1	1	*
Everything considered, how happy has your marriage been for you?				
extraordinarily happy	24	19	26	20
decidedly happy	29	32	36	40
happy	31	32	26	23
somewhat happy	1	2	4	5
average	13	15	5	7
unhappy	1	0	4	5

*Less than one-half percent.
Source: 1956 data reported in Kauffman (1960).

A large majority of the respondents felt that it was easy to talk over problems with their mates, they would definitely marry the same persons again, and they rated their marriages as very happy. In 1956 approximately 10 percent indicated difficulty in talking over problems and questioned marrying the same persons if life were to be relived. In 1989 somewhat more (nearly 30%) admitted difficulty in discussing problems, and the wives in somewhat larger proportions than in 1972 (14 vs. 7%) questioned marrying the same person again. Nevertheless their judgment on happiness in marriage was similar in both generations and between husbands and wives in both surveys.

A close examination of the response distributions gives the impression that the 1989 respondents did not fare quite as well in their marriages as those in 1956. If this is a trend related to modernization, it begs further study that would take us beyond the scope of this survey.

Response values for the three items in Table 5-8 were summed to form a spousal relationships scale. Male and female scores on the scale were only slightly different, barely enough to be statistically significant. However, there was a tendency for females to rate their marriages slightly lower than did males.

When the scores in the spousal relationships scale were correlated with those of other scales, most of the correlation coefficients proved to be small and statistically insignificant. There was no significant variance in spousal relationships between the categories of age, residence, and socioeconomic status. Only one scale, devotionalism, had a substantial correlation (.20) with spousal relationships, indicating that people who regularly practice the disciplines of prayer, Bible study, and group worship tend to have, on the average, somewhat happier relationships with their spouses.

How does the quality of marital relationships vary according to spouse dominance patterns? Scores on the spousal relationships scale (and also on the marriage agreement scale) did not vary significantly between husband dominance and equalitarian patterns, but were substantially lower for families in which the wives took the lead. These negative findings for wife-dominated marriages were also obtained in 1956, and confirm the results of other studies (Kauffman, 1960). Because we found little difference in 1989 between equalitarian and husband-dominated marriages as to the quality of marital relationships, we conclude that marital success depends on other factors. Equalitarian marriages may have advantages not covered in this study.

Summary

We began this chapter by noting different views on the impact of modernization on family patterns. Changes in family life are abundantly evident. Each generation of families must adapt to new social and economic conditions and to shifts in prevailing ideologies. Whether people view these adaptations as positive or negative depends heavily on what values they have in mind when they make their judgments. Conservatives are more likely to hold to traditional values and deplore many of the changes that are occurring. People with more liberal views tend to focus on individual freedoms gained and give less attention to growing problems.

In this chapter we scrutinized the 1972 and 1989 surveys to determine what changes are occurring in Mennonite and Brethren in Christ families and what direction the changes are taking. Few aspects of family life appear stable. We found virtually no change in age at marriage and in attitudes toward premarital and extramarital intercourse. We found significant increases in exogamy (marriage outside the group), in the proportion of women who are widows, in the divorce rate, and especially in the rate of employment of married women. There was a decline in the birthrate and in the average number of persons living in households.

There were slight shifts away from patriarchy toward more equalitarian marriages. Greater acceptance of divorce and divorced and remarried persons within the congregations is evident.

Urbanization was associated with increased rates of employment of married women, higher divorce rates, and a slight decline in patriarchy. Urban residents had fewer children and smaller households. They were more accepting of divorced persons. The rates of exogamy for rural and urban residents were similar.

Increased education was associated with lower birthrates and higher rates of exogamy and divorce. Respondents with more education showed more liberal attitudes toward divorce and greater favorableness toward equalitarian marriages. However, male leadership in the marriage relationship seemed to increase at higher educational levels.

Compared to national populations, Mennonites have a very low rate of marriage breakup. Despite urbanization Mennonites seem to preserve most of the positive values in family life. Modernization may be chipping away at the edges of some traditional family values, but some gains are being made and losses are being kept at a low level.

CHAPTER 6

Emerging Institutions

SOCIAL INSTITUTIONS are the principal components of any society, providing structure and organization for the benefit of its members. Mennonites also have their in-group institutions and organizations. Indeed, they have come to be highly organized in recent decades, causing some members to charge that the conferences have become "over-organized" and "top heavy" (Schlabach, 1980:83-108).

Eisenstadt (1968:410) defined institutions as "regulative principles which organize most of the activities of individuals in a society" and which help meet "some of the perennial, basic problems" of a society. Examples of "regulative principles" or "social practices" include marriage, parenthood, insurance, worshiping, and voting. In order to regulate these institutions, groups and organizations emerge. These organizations (such as church congregations, schools, and government bodies) also come to be called institutions.

Berger (1975:73) defined institutions as "regulatory patterns, that is, as programs imposed by society upon the conduct of individuals. . . . In common usage the term means organizations that somehow 'contain' people—such as a hospital, a prison, or, for that matter, a university." Following Berger and many other sociologists, we prefer a definition of institutions that includes both principles (or patterns) *and* organizations, so the terms *institution* and *organization* will be used interchangeably.

Institutions or organizations are ways of getting things done, of meeting perceived needs. In previous chapters three institutions were considered: religion, family, and community. In this chapter we look at several other institutions, particularly educational and political institutions. We are interested in the extent to which Mennonites have developed institutions and whether these church-related institutions are serving their intended purposes. To the extent that they help to develop and maintain a Mennonite identity, they are additional stakes in holding up the Mennonite "sacred canopy."

Mennonite Institutions

Congregations have been the most prevalent organizations among Mennonites since their 16th-century beginnings. In North America they were almost the **only** type of organization until conferences began to emerge in the latter part of the 19th century. It is only in the past century that other types of church-related institutions have developed, with proliferation in the past 50 years. During these years Mennonites have perceived many new needs and have correspondingly formed a host of agencies and programs for "getting things done."

Juhnke (1989:186) documented the emergence of Mennonite institutions from 1890 to 1930: "From the founding and flourishing of new institutions such as mission boards, colleges, hospitals, orphanages, mutual aid societies, and retirement homes, Mennonite peoplehood took on a new appearance." Many of these organizations can be viewed as devices for boundary maintenance, providing a guarded in-group environment for the education and service of members. Others, such as mission boards and social service agencies, were formed for the purpose of serving other populations at home and abroad.

The emergence of large scale organizations and "bureaucracies" are frequently cited as evidence of modernization. While admitting that bureaucracies may be rigid and inefficient, Max Weber argued that in large scale industrial societies the bureaucratic form of administration is necessary to gain efficiency, flexibility, and competency in regulating affairs under the rule of law (Turner, 1981:237). Noting differences between small sects and large denominations, Yinger (1970:261) viewed the emergence of bureaucratic structures as a concomitant of increasing complexity in church organizations. Berger (1975:205) regarded bureaucracy as "processing" individuals, frequently stifling individual initiative. Hence the debates over the question of whether the disadvantages outweigh the advantages of large-scale bureaucracy.

Thus, in becoming highly organized, Mennonites simply reflect the spirit of the times. Modern means of transportation and communication greatly facilitate the formation and functioning of organizations. Above all, the economic affluence of our age makes possible the large sums of money needed to support the staffs and activities of agencies. Whereas in former times the special needs of individuals were met primarily by family, kin, and neighbors, it has now become the function of churches, governments, and many types of voluntary organizations to help meet people's needs, particularly in times of crisis. Will the increasing complexity of Mennonite organizational structures, noted below, promote or retard the achievement of spiritual values?

A Variety of Church Institutions

The *Mennonite Yearbook & Directory, 1990-91* contains a comprehensive list of Mennonite denominational and inter-Mennonite agencies and projects. The following summary will provide the reader with an idea of the great number and complexity of current Mennonite institutions.

Church administration and extension. This category includes denominational and district conference organizations, foreign and domestic mission boards and committees, Mennonite World Conference, councils of urban congregations in 17 major cities, 59 church camps and conference centers, and many coordinating councils. Already in 1974 Paul Kraybill (1974) identified 72 inter-Mennonite organizations and projects that combine the work of two or more Mennonite denominations. Only three of those predated 1940; many have been added since 1974.

Congregational organization. Most congregations conduct their affairs via a variety of boards, commissions, and committees. Congregational programs and groups include Sunday schools, youth organizations, women's organizations, and men's fellowships. In some communities, congregations sponsor athletic teams and leagues.

Educational institutions. The *Yearbook* lists four biblical seminaries; 15 colleges; 10 Bible institutes; 27 high schools and academies; 72 elementary schools; 36 historical societies, libraries, and archives; nine publishing houses with bookstore outlets; over 100 church periodicals, magazines, newspapers, and newsletters; several museums; and several radio programs.

Service agencies. The largest of these is the Mennonite Central Committee, which organizes many relief and service units throughout the world; sponsors Mennonite Disaster Service, peace organizations, Mennonite health services; and receives contributions from 37 Mennonite relief sales held in communities throughout Canada and the United States. In addition to the inter-Mennonite MCC, there are denominational and district conference voluntary service programs, child welfare agencies, developmental disabilities services, and deaf ministries. Mennonites administer 16 general hospitals, 10 mental health hospitals, and 108 retirement communities and nursing homes.

Financial institutions. District and local Mennonite property insurance associations began to develop more than 100 years ago. The current listing of financial agencies includes seven credit unions and 29 insurance organizations, the largest of which is Mennonite Mutual Aid, Inc., with programs of hospital and surgical insurance, life insurance, retirement pension funds, and investment programs. Mennonite Economic Development Associates provides funding for worldwide development projects. Finally, although not operated as church enterprises, many commercial and industrial firms are owned and/or operated by Mennonite church members. Though in one sense they are Mennonite institutions, these firms are integrated into the production and marketing structures of the larger economy and do not operate to serve only Mennonite interests.

Professional organizations. As Mennonites became urbanized they formed Mennonite associations that bring together those in specialized occupational categories. There is no "Mennonite Farmers Association," but the list includes the Mennonite Medical Association, Mennonite Nurses Association, and similar organizations for Mennonite lawyers, chaplains, historians, sociologists, psychologists, artists, airplane pilots, computer users, and others. Teachers in Mennonite elementary and secondary schools also gather periodically for fellowship and study.

Rationale for Institutional Development

This array of Mennonite institutions gives the church a very different character from its earliest Anabaptist beginnings, when there were almost no organizations at all and congregations met secretly in caves and other hiding places. Institutional functions were limited mostly to worship, fellowship, Bible study, and informal mutual aid.

Churches face a "being-doing" dilemma—to borrow an expression from Redekop (1976:139). In their beginnings (as in the times of the New Testament church, the early Anabaptists, and contemporary charismatic movements), congregations focus on their "new being"; worship and fellowship are central, with emphasis on the grace and gifts of God. But the Christian message is also purposive and process-oriented, calling for witness and service to those beyond the immediate fellowship. Thus emerges the "doing" phase, with rudimentary organizations to carry out the "mission" of the church. While the early disciples were practicing fellowship, prayer, and breaking of bread together, their "widows were being neglected" (Acts 6:1). So the beginnings of church organization took place in the appointment of deacons to look after the widows.

As the above lists indicate, Mennonites in recent decades have greatly elaborated the "doing" phase. In part this phase is a concomitant of Mennonite urbanization and educational advancement, as well as the affluence which affords the capital necessary to establish and operate institutions. The rural community setting afforded relative cultural isolation for Mennonites, and their educational levels did not provide the technical skills necessary to function in industrial and professional settings.

As they lost their cultural isolation in the city, new strategies were needed to prevent loss of identity. Driedger (1988:124, 176) argues that a degree of "institutional completeness" (schools, colleges, a hospital, service agencies, credit unions, retirement homes, newspapers, and many Mennonite-operated businesses) provides for Mennonites in Winnipeg the possibility of maintaining a Mennonite identity in the face of urban diversity. "The rationale for institutional completeness is that when an urban minority can develop a social system of its own with control over its institutions . . . their position should result in . . . less influence of outgroups." Lacking such institutional development, Mennonite churches in Chicago have experienced less growth.

Despite the successes of Mennonite institution building, the being-doing dilemma still exists today, shown in the debate over the "bureaucratization of the church." Some fear that the elaboration of service organizations will overwhelm the "preaching of the gospel," the witness of the Word. As Redekop (1976) notes, the institutionalization of the church carries the risk that unequal power allocation (leaders have more power) may result in unchristian use of power. Noting that institutions and power are necessary so that churches can get things done, Redekop (1976:148) concluded that "religious movements must use power and create institutions—it is *how* they are used that makes the difference." Balancing individual "freedom in Christ" with institutional structuring is a continuing agenda for those in church administration.

Within the limitations of this survey, it was not possible to test member loyalties and support of all these church institutions. We have been selective, giving attention mainly to congregation, family, community, schools, and some service institutions, the last to be covered in chapter 8. In this chapter we will limit our attention primarily to educational and political institutions, with some attention to "stewardship," the financial support that church members give to their institutions.

Educational Institutions

Objectives of Church Schools

As noted above, Mennonites in Canada and the United States currently operate 72 elementary schools, 27 high schools, 10 Bible institutes, 15 colleges, and four seminaries, most of which have been established since World War II. Why all the expense of operating private schools when public education without extra cost is readily available? Speaking about the colleges, Redekop (1989:180) offers three answers to this ques-

tion: (1) to keep Mennonite young people from learning strange doctrines and beliefs elsewhere, (2) to carry on and preserve the religious
heritage, and (3) to prepare people for certain vocations within the context of a particular view of the Christian life. Perhaps these answers
would also be given by those who administer elementary and high
schools.

Writing primarily for the Mennonite Church, Hertzler (1971:18)
suggested that education within the context of the people of God should
(1) make their history and identity clear, (2) counteract the influence of
the larger society, (3) train themselves to serve as God's reconciling people, and (4) educate others as a form of service and opportunity for witness.

Attitudes Toward Church Schools

The 1989 survey provides some indication of member support for
church-related schools. To the question "Do you think the benefits derived from our present church colleges justify the costs of maintaining
them?" 58 percent of the respondents answered "yes," 7 percent "no,"
and 34 percent "uncertain." This response compares to 45, 10, and 44
percent respectively in 1972, indicating a 13 percent shift in greater support of church colleges. Favorable responses in 1989 ranged from 68 percent for the Mennonite Brethren to 54 percent for the Evangelical Mennonites.

A similar question probed support of church high schools, with 49
percent favorable in 1989, 9 percent unfavorable, and 42 percent uncertain. Percentages in 1972 were 33, 15, and 52, respectively. Thus, favorableness toward church high schools has also increased, although members are still considerably divided on the issue. If church members live
within commuting distance of a church high school, their attitudes tend
to be more favorable. Fifty-five percent of the respondents living within
25 miles of such a school reacted favorably on the high school question;
only 41 percent of those living farther away did so. Positive responses
varied from a high of 54 percent for the Mennonite Brethren to a low of
35 percent for the Evangelical Mennonites.

We conclude that favorable attitudes toward church schools are increasing and are somewhat stronger for colleges than for high schools.
However, about one-half of the respondents were still not convinced that
church schools at these levels are worth their cost.

The Impact of Church Schools

Do people who attended their church schools turn out to be more
accepting of their church's values than those who did not? This question

has been widely debated, often with inconclusive results, depending on the values preferred. Rossi and Greeley (1964) surprised Catholics and others when they published the results of their surveys on the impact of Catholic schools. They concluded (1964:48):

> Parochial school Catholics are "better" Catholics than those who attend public schools, but the differences . . . are so slight that we might raise the question whether the investment is worth the return if the main purpose of the investment is to produce better religious practice.

These authors assumed that a selective factor may determine who attends parochial schools. Since the church requires its parishes to provide parochial schools and expects its children to attend them, attendance itself is a measure of church loyalty. Therefore,

> to compare parochial and public school Catholics is in part to compare persons with different levels of adherence to the teachings and rules of the church, a factor which may affect the outcome of parochial schooling as much as the fact of schooling itself [*ibid.*:36].

Would conclusions about the impact of Mennonite schools on Mennonites be any different from these conclusions for Catholics? One main difference is that Mennonites have never made attendance at Mennonite schools a requirement, although in some communities the sentiment favoring attendance is strong.

The Schludermanns (1990) surveyed juniors and seniors attending Mennonite and Catholic high schools in Winnipeg, focusing on the question of whether family influence or attendance at church schools has the greater impact on the religious beliefs of the students. The respondents included Mennonites, Catholics, evangelicals, and "unchurched" students. Although the commitment to traditional Christian beliefs was significantly related to the church attendance of the respondent's parents, the researchers found no significant relation of beliefs to the number of years the respondent had attended church schools. The study did not compare students at church schools with students attending public schools.

Using the data from the Kauffman-Harder survey of 1972 and four other studies, Kraybill (1978) summarized the differences between those Mennonites who attended church schools and those who did not. Whereas the 1972 data included respondents of all ages who had attended Mennonite schools at any level, the other surveys covered only current students or recent graduates of Mennonite and public high schools. Moreover, the Kauffman-Harder survey included Mennonites of five denominations, whereas the other studies were based exclusively on persons attending MC-sponsored schools. Kraybill's careful review of these studies attempted a definitive answer to the question of whether church school attendance "makes a difference."

Kraybill (1978) concluded that church-related schooling does make a positive difference on some religious variables but not on others. Where differences were evident they tended to favor church schooling, but, with a few exceptions, the differences were small and not statistically significant. Kraybill's review showed that youth attending church schools did not differ from public school students on orthodoxy of Christian beliefs, religious practices (prayer, Bible reading, church attendance), and attraction to the Mennonite Church. However, the Kauffman-Harder study (1975) found that those attending Mennonite schools (at all levels) had a greater attraction to the Mennonite churches than did others. This could be due to the "college level effect," since in that survey church-related college education had a greater effect than did other levels.

Kraybill (1978) also concluded that "Mennonite schooling has a positive effect on the acceptance of Anabaptist beliefs." Some of the high school studies were less conclusive on this point. College education probably does have a greater effect than high schools do on Anabaptist beliefs, as demonstrated in the 1972 survey. Kraybill cautioned that the differences may be due to a selective factor in who attends church schools. As reported for the Catholic schools, students at Mennonite church schools may also have come from homes somewhat more committed to the church than other homes.

Church-related schooling may have effects not covered in the aforementioned studies. One possibility is that attendance at church high schools and colleges may result in a greater proportion of in-group marriages and lifetime friendships. Also, in the 1972 survey (Kauffman and Harder, 1975:230) those who had attended church schools showed somewhat greater support of church educational institutions.

Attendance at Church Schools

The proportion of Mennonites and Brethren in Christ who have attended one or more levels of church-related schools, elementary through seminary, has not changed since 1972. As noted in Table 6-1, 44 percent of the 1989 respondents attended a church school; 45 percent in 1972. Attendance rates varied from a high of 55 percent for the MBs to a low of 5 percent for the EMCs. Some EMC members attended church-related colleges, but not Mennonite or BIC schools. By denominations, the attendance rates in 1989 were virtually the same as in 1972, except that the BIC dropped from 38 to 25 percent.

Table 6-1. Attendance at Church Schools by Denomination, 1972 and 1989

	1989					Totals	
	MC	GC	MB	BIC	EMC	1972	1989
Percent attended a Mennonite or BIC school:	46	43	55	25	5	45	44
Elementary school	10	4	3	4	2	8	6
Secondary school	19	15	21	9	1	18	17
Bible school or institute	7	10	23	2	0	12	10
Bible college	2	7	10	2	1	2	5
Liberal arts college	24	17	14	13	2	19	19
Seminary (graduate level)	6	6	5	*	0	3	5
Percent attended non-Mennonite colleges or universities	36	49	53	40	54	21	43

*Less than 0.5 percent.

With respect to levels of schooling, the last two columns of the table show little change between 1972 and 1989. The shift from 3 to 5 percent of members having attended seminary is the only noteworthy change. With the emergence of more precollege schools since 1950, bringing more individuals within commuting distance, one would expect an increase in the proportion having attended church schools at precollege levels.

A breakdown of the respondents into age-groups shows that this is indeed the case. The oldest group (age 70 and over) had the lowest attendance rates at all levels of schooling. The 50-69 age-group had the highest attendance rate (6%) at Bible colleges. The 30-49 age-group rated highest in attendance at liberal arts colleges (24%) and seminaries (8%). The 20-29 age-group had the highest attendance rates for secondary schools (24%) and Bible schools and institutes (12%). The teenagers (aged 13 to 19) had by far the highest attendance rate at church-related elementary schools (21%), but this is due mainly to increased attendance in schools of the Mennonite Church, offset by declines in attendance at church-related elementary schools in the other denominations.

To summarize, attendance at church-related elementary schools is growing only in the Mennonite Church, with secondary school attendance declining among the Brethren in Christ and stable among the other churches. At higher levels of schooling Mennonites may have reached a plateau in church school attendance (all age-groups taken together).

Attendance at non-Mennonite colleges and universities has grown from 21 to 43 percent in 17 years. Thus, as many Mennonites and Brethren in Christ have attended other colleges as have attended their own church colleges. This shift probably reflects increased urbanization and a greater need for professional training in fields (e.g., agriculture, engineering, law, medicine) not offered in Mennonite colleges.

Table 6-2 shows national differences in church school attendance. In 1989 Canadians had higher attendance rates than Americans at the secondary level (20 vs. 16%) while at the elementary level Americans had higher rates than Canadians (8 vs. 4%). At the college level 25 percent of Americans, but only 6 percent of Canadians, attended church-related institutions. Rates in 1972 and 1989 were essentially the same in both nations, except for a slight decline at the college level in Canada and a slight increase at that level in the United States. The increase in non-Mennonite college attendance in Canada from 18 to 48 percent was even greater than the increase in the United States (from 22 to 41%). This reflects, in part, the tendency of Canadian Mennonites to prefer the provincial universities over church colleges.

Table 6-2. Trends in Church School Attendance by Nation

	Canada		United States		Totals	
	1972	1989	1972	1989	1972	1989
Percent attended a Mennonite or BIC school:						
Elementary	4	4	9	8	8	6
Secondary	21	20	17	16	18	17
College	8	6	22	25	19	19
Graduate seminary	3	6	3	5	3	5
Attended a non-Mennonite college or university	18	48	22	41	21	43

Regional differences were also significant (not shown in Table 6-2). Attendance at elementary schools in 1989 was greatest in the eastern United States (12%, compared to 5% in the western United States, 2% in Ontario, and 4% in western Canada).[1] Attendance at Mennonite secondary schools was greatest in Ontario (24%). Mennonite college attendance was greatest (29%) in the western part of the United States (from Ohio westward), and eastern Canada (Ont.) had the largest seminary attendance rate (7%). Attendance at non-Mennonite colleges and universities was greatest in western Canada.

Does Attendance Make a Difference?

The first comparisons (not shown in tables) are between those who ever attended a Mennonite school at any level (attenders) and those who never attended (nonattenders). On scales developed in previous chapters, the attenders ranked higher on the following: Bible knowledge, Anabaptism, pacifism, church participation, devotionalism, and support of church colleges. They were slightly higher on measures of communalism and separatism. They were lower than nonattenders on the two orthodoxy scales. All these differences were in the same direction as those in the 1972 findings, although the *degree* of difference between the two surveys varied somewhat. These data do not reveal whether the differences were due to the impact of the Mennonite schooling or to selective factors in the decision to attend a church school.

In Table 6-3, which shows the differences in greater detail, the respondents are grouped into three categories: (1) those who attended non-Mennonite colleges and universities and did not attend any Mennonite or BIC school, (2) those who attended Mennonite or BIC high schools, and (3) those who attended Mennonite or BIC colleges.[2]

Respondents who attended Mennonite high schools and colleges scored lower on the general orthodoxy and fundamentalism scales, as in 1972. As suggested in the Kauffman-Harder study (1975:225), we hypothesize that the lower scores on these measures were not due specifically to church-school attendance, but to the liberalizing impact of education per se. This hypothesis is supported particularly in respect to fundamentalist beliefs. Among those who did not attend college at all nor any Mennonite elementary or high school (cases not included in Table 6-3), 35 percent scored "high" on fundamentalism, compared to only 20 percent (see table) among those who attended non-Mennonite colleges only. Thus college education lowers fundamentalism scores, whether at Mennonite schools or elsewhere. Not all of those in the "non-Mennonite college" column attended secular colleges; an undetermined number attended colleges sponsored by other religious bodies, some of them emphasizing fundamentalist beliefs—which may explain why as many as 20 percent scored high on fundamentalism.

On nearly all other variables, respondents who attended Mennonite and BIC schools showed stronger adherence to Mennonite values: Anabaptism, Bible knowledge, pacifism, church participation, communalism, women in church leadership, and support of church colleges.[3] Those who attended only non-Mennonite colleges scored highest on the political variables. On the concomitants of modernization, Mennonite school attenders scored slightly lower, but the differences were not statistically significant.

Table 6-1 reported six levels of schooling in Mennonite schools (elementary through seminary). Does the number of levels of Mennonite schooling attended show any relation to adherence to Mennonite values? The answer is "yes."

One respondent reported attending five levels of Mennonite or BIC schools; 22, four levels; 88, three; 321, two; and 924 attended only one level. Correlation of scales with number of levels showed positive and statistically significant correlation coefficients for nearly all scales. There were negative correlations with the orthodoxy scales and the four concomitants of modernization. Low and nonsignificant correlations were obtained for the two political scales (discussed later in this chapter) and the number of levels attended. These findings show that the larger the number of levels attended the greater the adherence to Mennonite values.

Table 6-3. Comparisons by Schools Attended, 1989

	Attended:		
Scale	Non-Menn. college N=603	Church high school N=531	Church college N=581
	(Percent scoring "high" on scale)		
Beliefs and Bible knowledge:			
General orthodoxy	75	72	60
Fundamentalism	20	13	7
Bible knowledge	35	51	62
Anabaptism	14	27	31
Religious practice:			
Church participation	29	30	43
Devotionalism	18	21	23
Stewardship	23	31	33
Social ethics:			
Pacifism	15	23	36
Women in church leadership	39	28	63
Political participation	36	21	24
Political action	50	40	49
In-group identity:			
Communalism	9	30	37
Separatism	15	16	18
Support of church colleges	40	56	73
Concomitants of modernization:			
Secularism	17	16	16
Individualism	18	14	14
Personal independence	26	21	21
Materialism	16	15	14

*To be significant at the .05 level, differences between categories need to be at least 4 percent.

From these findings we conclude that church members who have attended Mennonite and BIC schools, with few exceptions, show higher acceptance of Mennonite values than those who have not attended. Our evidence does not reveal to what extent these differences are actually due to the effect of the schooling and to what extent they are due to the selectivity of students. To determine this would require more elaborate research, in which students would be tested before and after attendance, with similar testing of a control group attending elsewhere.

Political Institutions

Religion and politics are two topics that often generate heated discussions and disagreements. They can be particularly troublesome when they come together in the church. Power can be wielded in church councils as well as in secular governments. Redekop (1976:138) noted that "the Christian church itself has wrestled throughout its history with the problem of institutions and power."

Many Mennonites see a conflict between the use of power and the "suffering servant" motif that Jesus followed in his short ministry on earth. To perform a servant ministry, Mennonites have often shied away from using power within the church, and they have been doubly hesitant to become involved in the power politics of government (Schlabach, 1988:207-10). On the other hand, some Mennonites have entered politics in order to render a public service and to bring an ethical witness to public institutions.

Political Participation

Neither the 1972 nor the 1989 survey probed the complexities of the use of power within church organizations; this will remain the task of future research. We have attempted to discover the extent to which Mennonites have favored participation in government, and the extent to which they have voted, held office, and expressed their opinions to members of governmental institutions. Thus we are reporting not on Mennonite political institutions, but Mennonite participation in public institutions.

We presented some initial findings on the relationship of Mennonites to politics in chapters 1 and 2, in the discussion of rural-urban and regional variations. In this chapter we will report on the scales developed and their correlations with other variables.

We have conceptualized "political participation" as voting, holding office, and having attitudes favorable to contacting and communicating with government officials. Table 6-4 shows six items used in measuring political participation. The trend toward more participation is evident in the last two columns, comparing 1972 and 1989 responses. Voting in all or most elections increased from 46 to 65 percent, and officeholding from 3 to 4 percent. On the remaining (attitudinal) items, the proportion

Table 6-4. Political Participation of Mennonites by Denomination, 1972 and 1989

	1989					Totals	
	MC	GC	MB	BIC	EMC	1972	1989
Agree that members of our denomination should vote in public state, provincial, or national elections	72	88	94	95	96	76	84
Agree that members should witness directly to the state by writing to legislators, testifying before legislative committees, etc.	73	74	79	77	83	61	76
Disagree that it is not the business of the church to try to influence the actions of government on such issues as war and peace, race relations, poverty, etc.	64	68	75	74	68	56	70
Disagree that members of our denomination should *not* hold any local, state, provincial, or national government office	63	83	90	92	95	62	68
Voted in all or most elections in recent years	45	64	84	85	87	46	65
Held an elective or appointive office in a local, city, state, provincial, or national government	3	3	6	3	5	3	4

(Percent)

of respondents favorable toward political participation has increased from roughly two-thirds to three-fourths.

Mennonites in Canada were more favorable toward political participation than were those in the United States. The proportion who voted in all or most recent elections was 80 percent for Canadian respondents and 59 percent for U.S. respondents (47% in the eastern United States). The table shows that voting ranged from 45 percent in the Mennonite Church to 87 percent among Evangelical Mennonites.

Responses to the first four items in the table were combined to comprise a scale measuring political participation. Individual scores on the scale ranged between the possible low of 4 and the high of 20. Respondents were located along the entire range of views, from no participation to full participation. Kauffman and Harder (1975:152) suggested three categories to describe this range of views: nonparticipation, selective participation, and free participation. Members of the Mennonite Church were least involved in political participation, in both 1972 and 1989, with the largest proportion (a minority, however) favoring nonparticipation. Free participation was greatest among GCs in 1972, but by 1989 the EMCs and MBs favored political participation slightly more than the others. The proportion holding public office was greatest among the GCs.

Increased willingness to participate in politics seems to correlate with a greater openness to involvement in the larger Canadian and American societies, that is, a diminished separatism. This willingness may indicate a greater desire to encourage governments to work for peace and justice and to follow ethical principles in the conduct of governmental affairs. It may also reflect a greater tendency of conservative religious denominations to try to influence government on moral issues, such as abortion, pornography, poverty, and sexuality. A cross-tabulation of responses on several moral issues (introduced in chapter 9) with scores on the fundamentalism scale strongly supports this assumption. Those scoring high on fundamentalism, compared to those scoring low, revealed much more conservative attitudes on abortion, homosexual acts, premarital sexual intercourse, capital punishment, and prayer in the public schools.

Hunter (1983:115) noted the increased political activism of conservative groups in recent decades, stating that "Evangelical Protestants believe it is very important that religious organizations make public statements about spiritual and religious matters." Based on a national survey in 1979, his data indicate that evangelicals had a greater commitment to political activism than did all other groups (Catholics, mainline Protestants, and non-Christians). Among Mennonites, however, those higher on the fundamentalism scale tended to be *less* active politically than those low on the scale.

In a 1983 public opinion survey of the voting patterns of evangelicals and fundamentalists in the United States, Rothenberg and Newport (1984:148) probed attitudes on a number of political issues. They concluded that the political activism of these conservative groups translates into attention to particular candidates and issues, notably those which have high religious significance (abortion, prayer in public schools, dissemination of birth control information, etc.). This may describe Mennonites and Brethren in Christ of a more fundamentalist orientation, and may explain why the EMCs and MBs have emerged as the most favorable toward political activism. Other Mennonites may focus on such issues as antimilitarism, a nuclear freeze, public housing, environmental issues, and women's rights—which have ethical but less specifically religious content and which tend to be the concern of mainline Protestants (Roof and McKinney, 1987:186-209). On the basis of his analysis of the 1972 data and reports on voting in other church populations, Kauffman (1989:376) concluded that Mennonites vote in proportions similar to those of other Americans.

Political Action in the Congregation

It is one thing for church members to be personally active in the political realm; it is quite another thing for members to discuss politics within the program of the local congregation. The former involvement can be private; in the context of the congregation, however, the discussion of religion and politics becomes public and is likely to foment controversy.

We tested the degree to which church members favored consideration of political matters within the context of the congregation. The results are given in Table 6-5. Responses to these four items were combined to construct a political action scale.

Table 6-5. Political Action Within Congregations, 1972 and 1989

Items	Responses	
	1972	1989
Do you feel that it is proper for your congregation to:	(Percent "yes")	
1. Encourage its members to study political issues and candidates?	68	79
2. Encourage its members to engage in political action?	32	55
3. Endorse particular candidates for office?	25	39
4. Encourage the minister to discuss political issues from the pulpit?	16	28

The four items represent steps from least to most direct congregational involvement in the political process, so favorable attitudes diminish with these steps. Although a majority of the respondents favored encouraging the congregation to study issues and candidates and engage in political action, only a minority favored endorsement of candidates or preaching on political issues. These latter actions might appear to commit the congregation to a particular political stance, something on which the members might not be able to agree. As to trends, it is clear that Mennonites were increasingly ready to consider political issues within the framework of the congregation.

Respondents were asked to check whether they belonged to any "major political groups, such as Canadian political parties, Democratic or Republican clubs, political action groups such as voter's leagues, NAACP, Civil Liberties Association, etc." In 1989, 10 percent checked the item; in 1972, 7 percent. Thus an increasing minority reported entering the political process in this manner.

Political Party Preference

Canadian respondents were asked, "With which one of the following Canadian political party positions do you tend to be most in sympathy or agreement?" American respondents were asked a similar question regarding American political positions. Table 6-6 shows that the responses differed slightly in the two surveys.

Table 6-6. Political Preferences of Respondents, 1972 and 1989

Political preference	1972	1989
	(percent)	
Canadian respondents:		
Social Credit	15	6
Progressive Conservative	31	47
Liberal	25	19
New Democratic Party	6	12
Other parties	1	2
I take no position at all	23	14
American respondents:		
Republican Party conservatives	35	46
Republican Party liberals	9	8
Democratic Party conservatives	5	10
Democratic Party liberals	6	9
Independent, or some other party	9	3
I take no position at all	35	23

In Canada the Social Credit Party (the most conservative) lost Mennonite votes between 1972 (15%) and 1989 (6%), but large numbers shifted to the Progressive Conservatives (from 31 to 47%). Those left of center remained the same, with fewer in 1989 voting Liberal (19%) than in 1972 (25%). However, support of the NDP doubled from 6 to 12 percent. The Conservatives attracted additional Mennonite and BIC voters from those who in 1972 took no position.

If we deduct those who took no position at all, about 55 percent favored the Conservative Party; 22 percent, the Liberals; and 14 percent, the NDP. This puts Mennonites into line with the most conservative religious groups in Canada. According to Bibby's 1985 survey (1987:194) of Canadians, the Conservative Party was favored by 47 percent of United Church members, 48 percent of the Anglican Church, 32 percent of Lutherans, 25 percent of Presbyterians, and 56 percent of "Conservative Protestants"—a category combining smaller Protestant denominations including Baptists, Pentecostals, Nazarenes, and Mennonites.

Among American respondents, the 12 percent decrease in those taking no position at all and the 5 percent decrease in independents were apparently distributed among both Democrats and Republicans, but with the Republican Party conservatives receiving the lion's share of the shift. Among those expressing a preference (excluding the "no position at all"), 68 percent in 1972 and 70 percent in 1989 favored the Republican Party; 17 percent in 1972 and 25 percent in 1989 favored the Democratic Party. Although those favoring the Democratic Party increased, they were still only one-third the number favoring Republicans.

The overall 17-year shift was slightly in the conservative direction, probably reflecting the national trends toward conservatism in the 1980s. Clearly the identity of Mennonites in both countries increasingly includes getting involved in political affairs, but they do so as conservatively as any other religious groups for which we have data.

Finally, it is interesting to note how Mennonites and Brethren in Christ actually voted for their heads of government in the elections held in both countries in 1988 (see Table 6-7).

Table 6-7. Mennonite Voting for National Candidates, 1988

Canadians		Americans	
Brian Mulroney	51%	George Bush	49%
John Turner	16	Michael Dukakis	18
Edward Broadbent	10	Someone else	1
Someone else	8	I did not vote at all	24
I did not vote at all	10	I do not qualify to vote	8
I do not qualify to vote	5		
Total	100		100

At least two-thirds of Mennonite and BIC voters supported a conservative ticket, a larger proportion than for the national populations. In their 1983 survey of the political orientation of 1,000 American evangelicals, Rothenberg and Newport (1984:83) reported that 41 percent usually voted Democratic, while 32 percent generally voted Republican.[4]

Thus, Mennonites and BIC appeared to be much more conservative politically than American evangelicals, and more conservative than mainline Protestants whose voting behavior seemed to be closer to the outcome of the national election.

The Rothenberg and Newport findings were somewhat surprising since studies have generally indicated that conservative religion is correlated with conservative politics. In Hadden's survey (1969:88) of several thousand clergy in six major denominations, conservative religious views were associated with preference for the Republican Party, and liberal theological views with preference for the Democratic Party.

A report by Kauffman (1989:383) demonstrated the negative relationship between religiosity and political participation, not only among Mennonites but also among other denominations. Many may feel that this is unfortunate, believing that it is undesirable in public affairs to have politics without religious values and religion without political interest.

Scale intercorrelations

Table 6-8 gives the correlations of the political attitude scales with other scales. (The "giving" column is included for reference in the next section of this chapter.)

The data indicate that political participation did not vary with age, but increased with urbanization, more education, and higher socioeconomic status. Support for political action by the congregation diminished with greater age, but it increased with urbanization, education, and higher socioeconomic status.

Both political scales show low negative association with religious beliefs, church participation, devotionalism, communalism, and separatism. Political participation and action are clearly associated with modernization of Mennonites and BIC, but a significant relationship to the concomitants of modernization (individualism, materialism, and secularism) was not found.

Financing Church Institutions

Except for minor fluctuations generally associated with business cycles, financial contributions to Mennonite and Brethren in Christ institutions have shown steady growth since their beginnings. Current financing of church institutions is big business. On the basis of the most recent annual data available, a total of over $230,000,000 was contributed to the churches in the five participating denominations plus the Mennonite Central Committee.

Table 6-8. Correlations of Political and Stewardship Scales with Other Variables

Variable	Political partici- pation	Political action	Giving*
Age	.01	-.18	.18
Residence	.23	.17	-.07
Education	.30	.25	-.03
Socioeconomic status	.28	.20	-.11
Orthodoxy	-.08	-.16	.12
Fundamentalism	-.15	-.21	.12
Anabaptism	-.23	-.21	.17
Church participation	-.03	-.02	.20
Devotionalism	-.06	-.14	.25
Communalism	-.19	-.14	.10
Separatism	-.11	-.12	.10
Individualism	-.02	.01	-.15
Materialism	.05	.08	-.09
Secularism	-.10	.03	-.14

*Proportion of household income given to church and charity.

As reported in their current yearbooks, total giving for the most recent year (monies contributed for local congregations, district conferences and general conferences) was as follows: Brethren in Christ, $17,124,000 (1987); Evangelical Mennonite, $3,879,000 (1987-88); General Conference Mennonite, $36,119,000 (1986); Mennonite Brethren, $50,733,000 (1989); Mennonite Church, $85,500,000 (1988); Mennonite Central Committee (U.S. and Canada), $40,000,000 (1989). It goes without saying that much good was accomplished at home and abroad with these resources.

Household Giving Patterns

Respondents were asked to estimate the amount of money given to church and charitable causes by the members of their household in 1988. These amounts varied from zero to the highest category offered, "10,000 and over." To determine the percentage of income given to church and charity, the amount contributed by each household was divided by the reported household income. These household percentages constitute the "giving" scale.

Following is the percentage of households in each denomination whose computed giving was 5 percent or more, for 1972 and 1989.[5]

	Percent	
	1972	**1989**
Mennonite Brethren	79	70
Evangelical Mennonites	77	66
Mennonite Church	66	65
Brethren in Christ	77	61
General Conference Mennonites	63	55
All denominations	68	63

The percentage given to church and charity appears to have declined over the 17 years, maximally (16%) for the BIC and minimally (1%) for the MC. The amount of giving in absolute dollars increased through the years. Why did the percentage go down? As affluence increases, should not the percentage go up instead of down?

Referring back to Table 6-8, we note that the "giving" variable was positively correlated with all religious beliefs and practices, with in-group variables, and with age. However, modernization does not bode well for proportional giving to church and charity, since giving had negative correlations with urbanization (-.07), education (-.03) and SES (-.11). While we can expect contributions to increase, an emphasis on tithing or other emphases on giving will be necessary to prevent further decline in proportional giving.

Summary

A major facet of modernization is the extraordinary proliferation of social institutions, which help society get things done. Mennonite society is no exception. In recent decades hundreds of Mennonite and BIC organizations have emerged, either to meet the needs of in-group members and families or to serve people beyond Mennonite boundaries.

Forty-four percent of the respondents attended schools sponsored by Mennonite and Brethren in Christ churches, about the same proportion as in 1972. Except for slight regional variations, there has been little change in the proportion of members who have attended church schools. The attitude toward church colleges and high schools has become more favorable, but nearly half of the respondents were still not convinced that these schools are worth their extra cost.

Those who attended church schools scored somewhat higher than nonattenders on most scales measuring Mennonite values. It is not certain how much of this difference is due to Mennonite schooling itself and how much to the factors that determine which school a student attends.

Mennonites and Brethren in Christ increasingly participate in national political institutions through voting, officeholding, and expressing opinions to government agencies and leaders. Attitudes toward political participation and action have become more favorable. The Mennonites in the 1989 survey seemed to be voting in proportions similar to those of other denominations, especially the conservative ones. Increased political participation by Mennonites was significantly correlated with urbanization, educational achievement, and higher socioeconomic status, earmarks of modernization, but there were negative correlations with the religiosity scales.

With respect to political party preferences, Mennonites and Brethren in Christ in 1989 appeared to favor conservative parties more heavily than did evangelical and mainline Protestants. The 17-year trend indicated a very slight shift toward greater political conservatism.

Although there has been a substantial increase in Mennonite's financial support of church institutions, the proportion of household incomes contributed to church and charity has diminished somewhat. Institutional growth could be stronger if church members would increase rather than decrease their proportional giving to church causes.

CHAPTER 7

Changing Consciousness of Peoplehood

WE BEGAN PART TWO of this volume with Peter Berger's (1967) metaphor of a sacred canopy. In chapters 3-6 we discussed four different "stakes"—the sacred, community, family, and institutions—that work together to hold up the Mennonite canopy as a shelter against outside forces. In the security of this sacred canopy, amid the flux of modernization, individual self-identity and in-group identity can be fostered. To be sure, the various parts of the canopy must be adjusted and sometimes replaced in order to be most effective as times and places change. Thus, in-group identity is constantly changing. Individuals should not abandon their canopy, but continually help to modify it as they live under it. Changes result in modified identity; abandonment of the canopy means assimilation or loss of identity.

Driedger (1980:341-56; 1988:37-48) has applied Berger's metaphor of a sacred canopy to three Canadian prairie groups (Indian, Hutterite, Jewish). He observes that while construction of supportive canopies can occur under very different circumstances and in different places, the task of canopy-building may involve reconstruction, transferral, or transformation—depending on the specific circumstances. Driedger (1980) suggests that the prairie Indians faced their situation with reconstruction, the Hutterites with transferral, and the Jews with transformation. Although not relevant to our discussion of Mennonites here, reconstruction for the Indians meant the complete change—with its political, social, and religious implications—from a food-gathering to an agricultural economy and way of life. The Hutterites uprooted their way of life—their economic, religious, political, and social structures—and transplanted it in another place, keeping the basic structures intact. Transformation for the Jews involved the change from an agricultural way of life to urban life; spatial, economic, and political changes took place, and religious, family, community, and institutional structures were modified, but not completely changed.

Transformation of the Mennonite Canopy

In this chapter we want to focus on the modifications in the Mennonite canopy as they relate to a sense of "peoplehood." To what extent have Mennonites retained a sense of personal and group identity during the process of modernization (Yoder, 1984)?

Transferral of the Mennonite Canopy

As Driedger (1980; 1988) points out, the Hutterites exhibit a type of canopy which developed in Europe. As agriculturalists in Europe, the Hutterites developed communal living, and they brought their integrated sense of peoplehood and a consciousness of kind with them to North America. They transplanted their ideology, life patterns, communal structures, and economic system onto the North American prairies with relatively minor modifications. While migration required some adaptation, their basic canopy was unfolded and set up again in North America—limiting social shock (Driedger, 1980:341-56).

Richard MacMaster (1985) has traced the establishment of Mennonite communities in Pennsylvania, beginning in 1683; he calls these earliest immigrants "aliens in ferment." Mostly of Swiss and South German background, these immigrants developed Mennonite communities in Lancaster County and surrounding counties; they were known as the "Old" Mennonite Church, today called the Mennonite Church (MacMaster, 1985:80; Schlabach, 1988). Their transferral was not as complete as that of the Hutterite communities, but their basic religious, agricultural, organizational, and cultural features did not change much in the new environment. Interestingly, they often chose wooded, hilly areas in which to settle—not so unlike the Swiss and South German countryside from which they came.

These earliest South European Mennonites came primarily from rural areas and were inclined to focus their community-building on cultural features of traditional dress, grooming, and resistance to technology in order to reinforce their separate identitiy. The Amish, who emerged in Europe as very conservative culturally, produced a variety of versions and many schisms as a result of their emphasis on preserving traditional cultural boundaries to maintain separation from outsiders (Schlabach, 1988). "Tradition" became a major stake in the sacred canopy of the Amish. The Anabaptist world became increasingly sectarian.

A wide range of Amish and Mennonite groups emerged, with the Old Order Amish at the most traditional end of the continuum ("identity ladder"), and moving along the ladder, other versions of the Amish, conservative Mennonites, and "Old" Mennonites, to the more "progressive" General Conference Mennonites at the other end (Driedger, 1977:278-91). The continual influx of Amish into the Mennonite Church, the largest group in this study, has added to that denomination's greater emphasis on features of traditional ethnic culture. The Brethren in Christ and the Evangelical Mennonites are smaller versions that split away from the "Old" Mennonites in the past. The schismatic groups always had to begin afresh, modifying their own identities, their own canopies. Thus, both migration and schism have added to the need for modification of the sacred canopies of Mennonite groups.

To a large extent, transferral also occurred when the Russian Mennonites came to Canada and the United States. Especially in Canada, the more conservative Russian Mennonites who came in the 1870s transferred their village plans and architecture (house-barn combinations) onto Mennonite land reserves; they were again segregated from others in solidly Mennonite agricultural communities similar to those they left in Russia. Although the settlement of Mennonites on the American prairies in Kansas was somewhat less segregated, solidly Mennonite communities were established between Newton and Hillsboro, Kansas (Juhnke, 1989:80-105).

A second wave of North European (Dutch-Prussian-Russian) Mennonites came mostly to the Canadian prairies in the 1920s, taking up the land and ready-built residences vacated by Mennonites who had left for Mexico. These Russian Mennonites participated in a form of transferral that could be called "circulation of the saints," which modified the need for extensive reconstruction. These North European Mennonites are the ancestors of today's General Conference Mennonites and Mennonite Brethren.

Transformation of the Mennonite Canopy

Driedger (1980) suggests that the Jews who came from the shtetls of eastern Europe, with their experience in small-town trade, were forced to transform their canopy when they arrived in Canada. Their sense of peoplehood, buoyed by their religion during the pogroms in Europe, was nurtured through solid, cohesive communities; and their emphasis on education prepared them to participate in the larger, urban society. The educational and mutual aid organizations that they had developed became a more dependable focus than did language and cultural distinctiveness. These religious and economic institutions were more compatible with urban life and could more easily be adjusted and transformed to become functional supports in the city (Driedger, 1989:90-110). Earlier experiences with adjustment and transformation of their canopy was a key to their success in the transfer from rural to urban life.

As immigrants and minorities in the United States and Canada moved from rural areas into the city, they were faced with major adjustments. Mennonites had usually been segregated in rural areas—living in villages, or on reserves or in closed communities on the prairies. When they moved to the city, it was more difficult to live in spatially segregated communities. They participated less exclusively in their own schools and more in organizations over which they had little control. Culturally, they were more exposed to the fads and fashions of the surrounding society. The most dramatic adjustment was change of occupation—from agricultural work to a variety of professions and industrial jobs. Thus the religious, family, community, and institutional stakes in the Mennonite canopy all needed to be adapted to the new social structures and values.

The more progressive Russian Mennonites who came from exclusively Mennonite villages and regions in the 1870s settled in the American West. Since they had earlier developed institutions, such as schools, they naturally soon founded schools in their new home; Bethel College was the first Mennonite college in North America. This was a boost to John Oberholtzer's efforts—in the General Conference Mennonite Church—at promoting education and mission outreach (Schlabach, 1988; Juhnke, 1989). The Mennonites who left Russia in the 1920s and settled mostly on the Canadian prairies also developed schools, businesses, and various communal aid societies. They had been considerably involved in institutional life in Russia, and their involvement continued on the Canadian prairies (Toews, 1981; 1982).

Like the Jews, the Russian Mennonite immigrants of the 1920s, reinforced by more immigrants in the 1950s, have led the move into the city (Driedger, 1980; 1986a; 1989; Driedger and Kauffman, 1982). The largest urban concentration of Mennonites—in Winnipeg, with its 47 churches—is comprised mostly of these immigrants, who either settled in the city immediately or lived for a while in rural or town settings on the Canadian prairies and moved to Winnipeg later (Driedger, 1990). Again colleges, various other institutions, and businesses were established in the process of the urban transformation of the Mennonite canopy.

Having reviewed these two versions of preserving the Mennonite canopy (transferral and transformation), we now summarize part two, to see (1) how modernization and change have affected the Mennonite canopy, (2) how the sense of "peoplehood" (a consciousness of kind) has been adjusted and maintained, and (3) what combination of religious, family, community, and institutional stakes have held up the canopy protecting Mennonite identity from the onslaughts of modern life (Driedger, 1988:44-48).

In-group Identification

To investigate the various forms of in-group identity and solidarity discussed in chapters 3-6, we asked respondents a series of questions about identification with Mennonite organizations and schools, ethnic language, in-group friends, and family. The responses revealed significant variations among the Mennonite denominations.

Table 7-1 presents our questionnaire's 10 items on in-group identification—which, when factor-analyzed, ordered themselves into three general categories (communications, social relations, and organizations).[1]

Table 7-1. In-group Identification in Communications, Social Relations, and Organizations

In-group identification	Percent Agreeing					Total
	MC	GC	BIC	MB	EMC	
Communications						
Should subscribe to a Mennonite newspaper	63	64	54	63	36	62
Should perpetuate Mennonite life through schools	48	49	39	42	23	46
Education in a Mennonite school is very important	43	38	28	33	14	38
Should learn own ethnic language if they have one	28	35	32	24	15	29
Social relations						
Parents should discourage dating with non-Mennonites	39	30	29	28	25	34
Should have mostly Mennonite friends	19	13	13	9	8	15
Should not marry a non-Mennonite	18	11	11	9	4	14
Parents are less favorable to non-Mennonite friends	9	6	7	8	4	8
Organizations						
Mennonite organizations help me be active in my group	62	62	60	53	48	59
Mennonite organizations are relevant—not too ingrown	47	43	44	43	38	45

In regard to communications, almost two-thirds (62%) of the respondents agreed that every Mennonite family should subscribe to at least one Mennonite newspaper or magazine. Between one-third and almost half (38 and 46%) favored maintenance of Mennonite identity through church-related schools, regarding Mennonite education as one of the best gifts that parents can give to their children. More than one-fourth (29%) felt that Mennonites should make an honest attempt to learn their ethnic language (if they had one). There were significant differences among the five denominations in this respect, with GC and MC respondents usually scoring above the average and the Evangelical Mennonites consistently scoring considerably below the 50th percentile.

We designed four questions to determine whether Mennonites feel that social interaction should occur mostly within the in-group, or interact extensively with others. One-third (34%) of the respondents agreed that parents should discourage dating with non-Mennonites and felt that doing so was not a disservice to their children; an equal number disagreed. The Evangelical Mennonites were most open to relating to others and the members of the Mennonite Church were least willing. Generally, very few held restrictive views on social interaction with non-Mennonites.

Two questions probed attitudes toward involvement in Mennonite organizations. Over half (59%) of the respondents felt that such organizations are good because they enhance in-group participation, and almost half (45%) felt Mennonite organizations are relevant—not too ingrown or narrow on world issues. Generally, most Mennonites seem favorably inclined toward their institutions.

The 10 in-group identification questions were broken down further into five clusters—organizations, schools, language, friends, and family. Table 7-2 shows the percentage of respondents who scored "high" on each of the five clusters. Of the total sample, one-third identified strongly with Mennonite organizations, and almost one-third (30%) strongly agreed that attendance at Mennonite schools is important. Other respondents identified with Mennonite organizations and schools, but not strongly; still others were uninterested.

One-fourth (24%) of the respondents strongly affirmed the study of their ethnic language and subscription to Mennonite newspapers, and one-fourth (23%) felt that choosing friends and associates from the in-group is important. A basic core of one-third to one-fourth expressed very strong in-group identification. However, relatively few (17%) were willing to limit dating and marriage to Mennonites. This lack of support for keeping endogamy and the Mennonite family intact indicates that Mennonites will likely intermarry more readily in the future; and that trend will affect Mennonite identity.

Table 7-2. Distribution of Respondents by Aspects of In-group Identification and Denomination

Aspects of in-group identification	MC	GC	BIC	MB	EMC	Total
	(Percent scoring "high")					
Organizations	35	33	35	28	23	33
Schools	34	32	22	22	8	30
Language	24	29	23	21	10	24
Friends	27	21	21	16	11	23
Family	23	14	13	11	7	17

Denominational Identification

In his recent book exploring Mennonite Brethren ethnicity and identity, *A People Apart*, John Redekop (1987) suggests that the Mennonite Brethren might want to change their name, omitting the designation *Mennonite*. In the 1989 survey three out of four respondents (76%) disagreed that the term *Mennonite* or *Brethren in Christ* should be deleted from the names of their local congregations. Although the Mennonite Brethren respondents were among those who showed less preference for the name *Mennonite*, two-thirds preferred to retain its use. The Brethren in Christ (82%) and General Conference Mennonites (80%) had the strongest preference for keeping their names.

Seventy percent of the respondents felt that their denomination taught the Word of God most accurately, and well over half (56%) felt much satisfaction in being known as a Mennonite (or Brethren in Christ). Almost half (48%) indicated that they knew at least half of their congregation's members intimately (congregation size being a factor), although only 37 percent of the Mennonite Brethren could make that claim. Only one in four (28%) indicated that they "will certainly always want to remain in their denomination and could never feel right about being a member of another denomination." Another 50 percent said that "although I prefer my own denomination, there are some other denominations that I would not hesitate to join if the occasion arose."

These results show a fairly high religious identification. Members of the Mennonite Church tended to show the highest in-group identification, but not on all items. John Redekop's concerns, noted above, seem to be warranted since the Mennonite Brethren ranked fourth or fifth on these five items, and never first, while all the other groups can claim to have ranked highest at least once. Only 16 percent of the Mennonite Brethren and Evangelical Mennonite respondents could say that they would always remain a member of their denominations. In the discussion which follows we will explore some of the possible factors related to religious identification, or the lack thereof.

Table 7-3. Responses to Items on In-group Identification

In-group identification	Percent in 1989					Totals	
	MC	GC	BIC	MB	EMC	1972	1989
Prefer the name *Mennonite* (BIC) in name of congregation	78	80	82	67	64	*	76
My denomination teaches the Word of God most accurately	76	62	70	69	73	74	70
Satisfied in being known as a Mennonite (BIC)	55	60	59	52	50	52	56
Know over half of the members of my congregation	52	48	46	37	52	*	48
Will always remain a member of my denomination	34	26	27	16	16	26	28

*Not included in the 1972 survey

Identity Amid Modernization

In chapter 1 we outlined the challenge of modernization to religious and in-group identities and suggested that demographic factors of modernization could adversely affect identity and result in fragmentation. As Mennonites move to the city, they leave their stable, somewhat segregated communities for a more pluralistic environment, where change is more difficult to control. As Mennonites become more highly educated, as their earnings increase, as they enter a multiplicity of occupations, they become more differentiated and stratified. Many business and professional occupations require travel, and promotions often require moving to different locations. Thus, we proposed, these three forms of modernization lead to greater change.

In-group Identity and Demographic Modernization

To what extent do increased urbanization, stratification, and mobility correlate with the maintenance or reformulation of Mennonite identity (Driedger and Harder, 1990)? Does the Mennonite canopy need to be reconstructed? To what extent can it be transferred? How much of it is transformed to adjust to the modern urban environment?

To test the relationship of in-group identity with these three modernization factors, we developed a composite in-group identity scale using the 10 items listed in Table 7-1.[2] Figure 7-1 presents the associations of this composite scale with the modernization factors—urbanization, so-

cioeconomic status, and mobility.[3] As indicated in chapter 1, urbanization, higher socioeconomic status, and mobility all correlated with each
other at a fairly high positive level (rs=.20 or higher). As Mennonites
move to the city, get more education, find higher-status jobs, earn more
income, and travel more, they become part of the larger society, and this
integration tends to distract from in-group concentration.

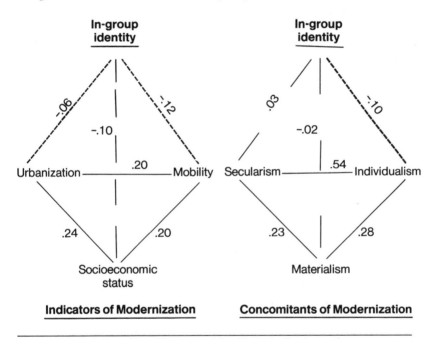

**Figure 7-1. Relationship of In-group Identity to Indicators of
Modernization and the Concomitants of Modernization**

As shown in Figure 1, each of the three demographic indicators of
modernization was slightly and negatively related to in-group identity
(rs ranging from -.06 to -.12). These findings suggest that modernization
makes it more difficult to retain Mennonite identity, although the negative influence is very small. Is there a trade-off, whereby giving up some
in-group solidarity in the modern fray has its compensations? As Mennonites move out of more boundaried, rural enclaves, are there opportunities which open up in the process to form new networks of both strong
and weak ties (Driedger, 1984:374-86)?

Identity and Concomitants of Modernization
In the past, rural Mennonites feared that the city and the influence of
the larger society would lead to greater materialism and individualism.

Thus they often segregated themselves from "the world," both spatially and socially. Mennonites tended to view identity in "two-kingdom" terms; they often saw these two kingdoms as complete opposites, and believed that members in the kingdom of God are to keep themselves separated from the world (Juhnke, 1975).

In chapters 3-6 we examined the religious, community, family, and institutional stakes of the Mennonite canopy; also the concomitants of modernization—secularism, individualism, and materialism—which undermine these stakes. The right half of Figure 7-1 shows the relationship of in-group identity to these three concomitants. Interestingly, neither the relationship between in-group identity and materialism (r=.02) nor that between in-group identity and secularism (.03) was statistically significant; a low negative association was found with individualism (-.10). These data suggest that when there is strong in-group identity in communications, social relations, and in-group organizations, the concomitants of modernization are not influential. Mennonites who identify strongly with their in-group are no different from others in respect to materialism and secularism, and have slightly less individualism. Strength of in-group identity seems to be the crucial criterion in the extent to which Mennonites resist negative modern influences.

Association Between Identity and Modernization

By breaking the in-group identity scale into its component parts—organizations, schools, language, friends, family—we can have a somewhat closer look at these five indicators of Mennonite and BIC identity. This reveals some interesting variations. Identification with Mennonite organizations in 1989 was not affected by modernization in the form of urbanization (r=.01) and mobility (.01), but was somewhat positively related to higher socioeconomic status (.08). As indicated in Table 7-4, identification with Mennonite schools and ethnic language showed a similar pattern, except that mobility tended to affect these in-group segments negatively (rs of -.05 and -.09). Possibly it is more difficult to send children to Mennonite schools and to learn the ethnic language when the family is highly mobile. However, those members who have higher SES—more education, greater income, and higher occupational rank—tend to support ethnic language learning and Mennonite organizations to a slightly greater extent (rs=.06 and .08 respectively).

As shown in Table 7-4, identification with family and in-group friends was somewhat negatively related to all three indicators of modernization. It is more difficult to influence friendships and dating patterns of children in the city (rs= -.12 and -.10). Mennonites with higher SES have more difficulty controlling the friends and intermarriage of their children (-.14 and -.17), and mobility (-.11 and -.10) does not help either.

Table 7-4. Relationship of Indicators of Modernization and Concomitants of Modernization to In-group Identity

In-group identity	Indicators of modernization			Concomitants of modernization		
	Urban-ization	SES	Mobility	Secu-larism	Materi-alism	Individ-ualism
Organizations	.01	.08	.01	-.13	-.08	-.15
Schools	.03	.01	-.05	.07	.04	-.04
Language	.02	.06	-.09	.07	.05	-.03
Friends	-.10	-.14	-.11	.11	.06	.00
Family	-.12	-.17	-.10	-.04	-.01	-.11

The correlations between in-group identities and the concomitants of modernization are weak and in some cases not statistically significant. In-group attitudes toward organizations and family relate negatively to secularism, materialism, and individualism. In-group attitudes toward schools, language, and friends relate to secularism and materialism with very small positive correlations; the relation of these elements to individualism is insignificant.

Shaping Consciousness of Kind

In chapter 3 we suggested that Anabaptist beliefs could be seen as the center pole in the Mennonite canopy, with family, community, and institutional stakes supporting that center pole in the shelter against the onslaughts of modernization. Let us examine five factors of religiosity (beliefs, devotionalism, religious experience, church participation, and Bible knowledge) for the extent to which in-group identity and religiosity are related.

Identity and Religion

Critics of the Kauffman and Harder (1975) discussion of Mennonite religiosity suggest that the Stark and Glock (1968) indicators of general religious orthodoxy do not capture the Anabaptist concept of people-hood as it should (Driedger and Harder, 1990). The concept of in-group identity is much broader and may be more useful in a discussion of Mennonite identity.

In the discussion of in-group identity and modernization, we noted that the indicators of modernization—urbanization, SES, and mobility— were moderately correlated with each other, but that in-group identity was somewhat negatively (although only weakly) related to these indica-

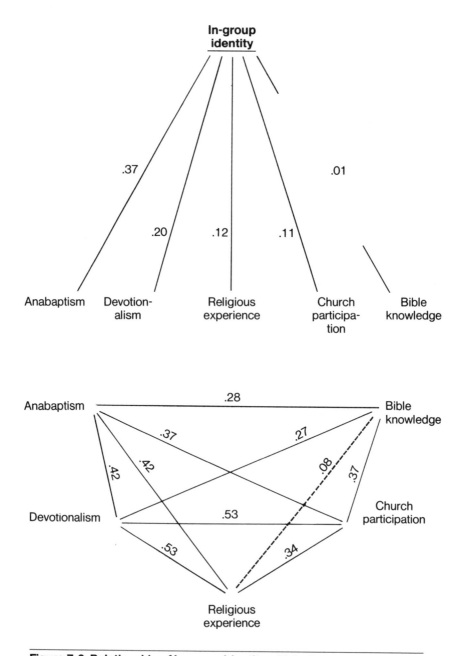

Figure 7-2. Relationship of In-group Identity with Indicators of Religiosity

tors. Figure 7-2 shows that the indicators of religiosity introduced in chapter 3 were consistently and strongly interrelated. Most of the coefficients were higher than .30. Thus, religiosity, like modernization, is a substantial and cohesive network of interrelated factors that have a major influence on other variables.

How is this substantial force of religiosity related to group identity among Mennonites and Brethren in Christ? While in-group identity was negatively related to the indicators of modernization, it was positively related to the indicators of religiosity. Anabaptist beliefs were fairly strongly related (r=.37) to in-group identity, while fundamentalism (.08) and general orthodoxy (.10) were only weakly associated with in-group identity. For this reason we have come to believe that Anabaptist beliefs are more amenable to a sense of peoplehood in a mobile, stratified, urban society.

With correlations as indicated, devotionalism (.20), religious experience (.12), and church participation (.11) were positively related to in-group identity, while Bible knowledge (at .01) was not. Anabaptism related as strongly to devotionalism (.42) and church participation (.37) as it did to in-group identity (.37). Anabaptist beliefs seem to link the more inward-looking devotional and experiential aspects of religiosity with the associational (participation) and in-group aspects. While modernization was negatively related to in-group identity, religiosity was positively related. In chapters 8-12 we plan to pursue further some of these important relationships.

Identity and National Regions

In chapter 2 we identified seven regions of Mennonite populations in Canada and the United States, which we then collapsed into four regions—east and west in each country. Do Mennonite identity and consciousness of kind vary by regions and by country?

Some variations by region occur in the demographic factors of modernization. Table 7-5 reminds us that urbanization is lowest (30%) in the American East and highest (75%) in the Canadian West; the other two regions are in between. The regions vary very little in regard to SES and mobility, except for the Canadian East which has a higher SES than the other regions. If demographic modernization is a negative influence, we would expect Canadians, with higher rates of urbanization (especially in the Canadian West) to show higher rates on secularism, materialism, and individualism, and consequently show lower rates on in-group identity. This did not turn out to be true. The rates of secularism, materialism, and individualism were not higher in the regions of greater Mennonite urbanization, but were similar in all regions.

Table 7-5. Demographic Modernization, Concomitants of Modernization, and Mennonite Identity by Region

| Variables | Region | | | | |
	American East	American West	Canadian East	Canadian West	Totals
	(Percent scoring "high")				
Urbanization	30	42	48	75	48
SES	22	25	33	28	26
Mobility	18	13	16	18	16
Secularism	22	19	24	16	19
Materialism	18	18	17	16	17
Individualism	14	20	20	13	17
In-group identity	25	22	21	24	23
Anabaptism	25	21	21	26	23
Communalism	21	23	29	18	22

How do Mennonites in the various regions compare in regard to the stakes in their sacred canopies? The percentage scoring high on in-group identity, Anabaptism, and communalism did not vary significantly between regions, except that the Canadian East was higher (with 29%) than other regions. It would be difficult to account for these small variations between regions. Further explorations of regional differences will be made in part three of this volume where programs of Mennonite outreach will be discussed.

Identity and European Origins

Let us look now at the effect of differences in European origin—Swiss or Dutch—on Mennonite identity. Table 7-6 shows that the respondents of Dutch background were almost twice as urban (63%) as those of Swiss background (37%). If modernization through urbanization has an impact, then the Dutch should show more of the identities associated with urbanism. With respect to the other two indicators of modernization—SES and mobility—there were no differences between the Swiss and the Dutch. Thus the respondents of Dutch and Swiss background differ with respect to urbanization, but not on the basis of SES and mobility.

Regardless of origin, few of the respondents scored high on any of the concomitants of modernization. The Dutch Mennonites scored slightly higher than the Swiss on secularism (19 vs. 16%), materialism (18 vs. 14%), and individualism (18 vs. 13%). Perhaps this slight difference relates to the greater urbanization among the Mennonites of Dutch origin.

Table 7-6. Modernization, Concomitants of Modernization, and In-group Identity by European Origin

Variable	Origin		Totals
	Swiss	Dutch	
	(Percent scoring "high")		
Urbanization	37	63	49
Socioeconomic status	27	27	27
Mobility	53	54	54
Secularism	16	19	17
Materialism	14	18	16
Individualism	13	18	15
In-group identity	27	24	26
Anabaptism	29	23	26
Communalism	28	22	26

Likewise, on indicators of in-group identity the differences between the Swiss and the Dutch were very small. The Swiss scored somewhat higher on in-group identity (27 vs. 24%), Anabaptism (29 vs. 23%), and communalism (28 vs. 22%). The small size of these differences makes it risky to generalize, but such differences as did exist seem to consistently relate to the greater urbanization of the Dutch.

Summary

In many ways this chapter, with its focus on changes in the identity and the sacred canopy of the Mennonites, is a summary of part two of this volume. In chapters 3-6 we examined Mennonite religion, community, family, and institutions as stakes holding up the canopy which protects the Mennonites from the onslaughts of modernization. How have these stakes been adjusted to accommodate modernization?

Using Driedger's model of transferral and transformation, we examined the early beginnings of Mennonites in North America. Many of the Swiss who came in the first wave of Mennonite immigration to North America, as well as later immigrants, especially the Russian Mennonites who came in the 1920s, simply *transferred* their rural-based communities to the New World. However, like the Jews, Mennonites moving to the city were faced with the task of *transforming* their sacred canopy to make it more relevant, competitive, and viable.

In the construction of canopies, some of the five denominations in the study identified more strongly with the in-group than did others. In communications, social relations, and in-group organizations, members of the Mennonite Church had the strongest in-group attitudes, while Evangelical Mennonites had the least. The same pattern prevailed in regard to the aspects of in-group identity—organizations and schools, ethnic language, in-group friends, and family.

Probing denominational identification, the desire to retain the name *Mennonite* was slightly lower among the Mennonite Brethren and Evangelical Mennonites than among others. Over half of the sample found much satisfaction in being known as Mennonite. Members of the Mennonite Church identified most with their denomination, while the Mennonite Brethren seemed to struggle with their in-group identity.

In-group identity was negatively correlated with all three indicators of modernization—urbanization, socioeconomic status, and mobility—but these correlations were weak, suggesting that effects of modernization can be moderated by a stronger in-group identity. Indeed, in-group identity was associated positively with four of the five indicators of religiosity, especially with Anabaptist beliefs and devotionalism. Also, while in-group identity was not significantly related to measures of secularism and materialism, it was negatively related to individualism.

In sorting out the elements of Mennonite identity affected by modernization, we found that urbanization was not important in identification with Mennonite organizations and schools and ethnic language, but that higher socioeconomic status had a mildly positive influence, and mobility a mildly negative influence. However, in-group social relations—choosing in-group friends and keeping the family intact—were somewhat negatively associated with all three forms of modernization (urbanization, SES, and mobility). The correlations between the in-group factors and the concomitants of modernization were very small and not consistently positive or negative.

In shaping consciousness of kind, identification with the in-group correlated moderately with the religiosity variables of Anabaptism and devotionalism, and weakly with religious experience and church participation. But there was no correlation with Bible knowledge. In-group identity tends to support religiosity, especially Anabaptist beliefs.

Regional differences proved to be relatively insignificant. There were no significant differences among regions with regard to secularism, materialism, and individualism; nor did the strength of Mennonite in-group identity, Anabaptism, and communalism vary much by region. The findings were similar in regard to European origin, although Mennonites of Swiss origin showed slightly stronger in-group identity, Anabaptist beliefs, and communalism than did the Dutch. On secularism, materialism, and individualism the differences between Swiss and Dutch were very slight, with the Swiss scoring slightly lower.

As they increasingly move to the city, Mennonites can no longer simply transfer their identities and canopies from one location to another. They must transform their canopy so that a sense of peoplehood can be sustained; otherwise their in-group identity will gradually erode. Mennonite peoplehood is shifting from spatially segregated ethnic enclaves to more open, urban networks. This transformation is still very much in the testing stages.

PART III

Consequences for Mennonite Life

CHAPTER 8

Finding Networks of Service

Having explored sources of Mennonite identity, we now turn to an examination of Mennonite ties with the larger society. The Mennonite canopy described in chapters 3-7 suggests that in-group identity, solidarity, and cultural boundaries are facing the pressures of modernization—urbanization, increasing social status, and mobility. In part three of this volume we want to look at the consequences of modernization for Mennonite identity. While the influences of modernization press identity toward secularization, individualism, independence, and materialism, these pressures can also force Mennonites to change and adjust so that their canopy remains relevant and in touch with the larger, changing society. Historical circumstances have forced Mennonites into various forms of service. Mennonites have become involved in many forms of social participation and action, leading to diversity, new social patterns, and changed identity. All of this we want to explore in chapters 8-12.

Part two of this volume dealt with internal, primary ties referred to by Granovetter (1973:1373) as "strong social ties." Granovetter also stressed the importance of "weak ties" with the larger, secondary society. In fact, he emphasizes "the strength of weak ties," which we want to explore in our discussion of Mennonite ties with the larger society (Driedger, 1986b:247-69). Orrin Klapp (1975:251-57) suggests that communities must develop mechanisms of opening and closing in order to control change, and Barry Wellman (1979:1201-31) suggests that communities become "lost," "saved," or "liberated" depending on how changes are integrated. Chapter 8 begins with finding Mennonite networks of service.

From Enclaves to Outreach

The early Christians of 2,000 years ago used their Jewish enclaves as a launching pad for outreach with the new message of Jesus. The Anabaptists of the 16th century were in the forefront of leavening the entrenched Catholic world of the Holy Roman Empire with a new, evangelical message. After centuries of building their own rural enclaves, Mennonites have again entered the cities and new lands, reaching out to people beyond the perimeters of their sacred canopy. At least three important forms of outreach (evangelical missions, alternative service, and MCC relief service) have emerged during the past century and led Mennonites again into the world rather than away from it. Let us briefly trace the beginnings of Mennonite outreach.

The Missionary Movement

"The Mennonite missionary thrust was at the heart of progressive Mennonites' new, wide-ranging denominational activity in the years between 1890 and 1930"—best chronicled and celebrated in Edmund Kaufman's (1931) *The Development of the Missionary and Philanthropic Interest Among the Mennonites of North America* (Juhnke, 1989:139). "His data showed that in the fifty years between 1880 and 1930 American Mennonites founded sixteen foreign mission programs (including those for Native Americans) and sent out more than four hundred missionaries" (Juhnke, 1989:139). Missionary activities brought changes in style and pace as well as change in the meaning and message of Mennonite community. Although insulated, the Mennonite communities could not contain the ferment, and many individuals signed up with nondenominational missions. Soon, however, Mennonites too began to prepare for the larger task, although cautiously.

The General Conference Mennonite Church originated in 1860, with missions as one item on its agenda. By 1880 mission work with American Indians in Arizona and Montana had begun with the help of European-trained Mennonites. The Mennonite Brethren Church was born in Russia in 1860 as a missionary church. "The missions movement generated a host of new activities and rituals which in the late 19th and early 20th centuries sent surges of energy through Mennonite congregations and communities" (Juhnke, 1989:156). The missionaries returned to tell stories about new cultures. Large crowds gathered to hear these missionary messages, new kinds of singing emerged, the status of women missionaries changed, and schools were established to train personnel. Theron Schlabach (1980) suggests that two distinct gospels emerged, the biblical Anabaptist-Mennonite community tradition and a missionary gospel that grew out of American pietism in which the salvation of souls was paramount. James Juhnke (1979:2) suggests that evangelism and outreach were twice-born among Mennonites, first in the 16th century among the Anabaptists, and then near the end of the 19th century, when Mennonites adopted aspects of the pietistic Great Awakening.

Alternative Service

The second great opening of Mennonite communities in North America occurred with the coming of the two world wars in the twentieth century (Hostetler, 1990:49-73). American Mennonites were hard-pressed to exercise their nonresistance during the American Revolution two centuries ago and the American Civil War from 1861 to 1865, especially since some of the war activities occurred in their own backyard (Schlabach, 1988:173-200). World War I (1914-18) severely tested the Mennonite peace position, and World War II (1939-45) brought about extensive alternative-service programs, which scattered Mennonites from their rural home communities (Juhnke, 1989:208-42; Toews, 1975:342-60).

During World War I the Mennonites were unprepared for the military draft. Alternative service options were not yet available, and many young men suffered; some even endured imprisonment (Epp, 1975:365-414; Toews, 1975:347-49). During World War II alternative-service options were developed and almost half (46%) of the 9,809 Mennonites, Amish, and Hutterites who were drafted chose alternative service over going to war; the remainder accepted military service (Toews, 1975:349-53; Klippenstein, 1979:1-104). The 4,500 who engaged in alternative service returned to their home communities having been exposed to forestry work, service in mental hospitals, and the like (Klippenstein, 1979).

Immediately after the war it was clear to Mennonite leaders and alternative service alumni that the peace teaching of the church had been badly neglected and that major educational and service programs were needed to involve the constituency (Epp, 1982:543-92). Thus, new conference peace committees and special MCC peace efforts were implemented (Dyck, 1980:9-79; Hostetler, 1990:49-67), including a major thrust in linking peacemaking with missions (Ramseyer, 1979). Special study conferences on peacemaking were held (Kaufman, 1979; Friesen, 1986; Toews, 1981). Out of the war experiences and postwar peace emphasis grew a larger concern encompassing other social issues (Hostetler, 1990:58-67), to be discussed in chapter 9. In this chapter we wish to explore the extent to which nonresistance and peacemaking, one of the major original Anabaptist tenets of faith, is still a part of constituency concern and conviction.

Relief and MCC Service

Russia's defeat by Germany in 1917, during World War I, profoundly affected the Mennonites in Russia; at the same time, the Mennonites were caught in the communist revolution. When this upheaval left many helpless and facing starvation, the North American Mennonites responded with a major relief effort (Dyck, 1980:9-39; Kreider and Goossen, 1988:19-41). This effort to save Mennonites in Russia and the later effort of helping them emigrate to North America were a response to the needs of their own people, but again Mennonites were exposed to the larger world beyond their own enclaves. In the Mennonite Central Committee, formed in 1920, Mennonites and Brethren in Christ banded together to coordinate their relief efforts.

When the relief and emigration needs of the Russian Mennonites subsided, MCC work became less urgent for a while. After World War II the needs in Europe again became urgent. MCC experienced a great surge of growth after the war, when its work was expanded to cover other needs; domestic programs—such as mental hospital service, Mennonite Voluntary Service, and Mennonite Disaster Service—began to involve all age-groups, both genders, and many in the larger constituency (Dyck, 1980).

Overseas relief work continued and has since expanded to a steady program that now has 1,000 MCC workers serving in 50 countries of the world, with a budget in the tens of millions of dollars annually (Kreider and Goossen, 1988; Epp, 1983; Dyck, 1980). Over the past 70 years since MCC was founded, thousands of Mennonites have served at home and abroad. Tens of thousands have participated at home by providing funds and serving as volunteers in thrift shops, at auction sales, and in various social services.

During the past century Mennonites in North America have moved out of their communities into the larger society, exposing themselves to modern influences. The evangelical missionary movement attracted many to the Great Awakening near the end of the 19th century, which challenged Mennonites to think through their theological commitments. The two world wars compelled Mennonites to take a serious look at the issue of nonresistance and their peace position. The needs created by the revolution in Russia and later regional and national revolutions beckoned many to serve. Distraught because of these disasters, Mennonites were moved to serve. These external events fanned the embers of their emphasis on peace and love into flames of service "In the Name of Christ" (MCC's motto). Has this service and outreach momentum faded or increased?

Mennonite Recruitment and Outreach

Let us examine—using the 1972 and 1989 surveys to document trends—four forms of Christian outreach that Mennonites have been engaged in: evangelism and church planting, peacemaking and alternative service, relief and MCC service, and local church outreach.

Evangelism and Church Planting

Table 8-1 reports the responses to questions concerning evangelism and church planting. The respondents were asked whether the members of their congregation felt it was more important "to work for a more just and equitable world" or "to help individuals find a personal saving faith." Three-fourths (73%) of the 1989 respondents said they believed that helping others find a personal saving faith was more important than working for a more just and equitable world (27%).

Table 8-1. Responses to Items on Evangelism and Church Planting

Evangelism items	Percent in 1989					Totals	
	GC	MC	BIC	MB	EMC	1972	1989
Members of my church feel it is more important to help others find personal salvation	60	71	87	88	93	*	73
Sometimes (several times a year or more) witness orally about faith to others	62	63	66	70	63	66	64
Tried to lead someone to faith in Christ at least a few times	43	42	53	55	55	48	46
Regularly or occasionally invite non-Christians to church or Sunday school	36	39	51	51	52	42	41
Am willing to help start a new church (at home or elsewhere)	31	42	37	45	39	*	39
Members of my church feel it is more important to work for a more just and equitable world	40	29	14	12	7	*	27

*Not included in the 1972 survey.

When asked how often they witnessed orally about their faith, two-thirds (64%) of the 1989 respondents said they did so several times a year (24% monthly or more often); in 1972 nearly the same percentage (66%) had said they witnessed several times a year. In both years about half (46% in 1989 and 48% in 1972) said they personally had tried to lead someone to Christ (35%, a few times; 11%, often). Thus about one-half to two-thirds had been involved in personal evangelism, and this proportion had changed little since 1972.

Somewhat fewer than half (41%; 42% in 1972) indicated that they "occasionally" invited non-Christians to church or Sunday school (3% of these did so "often"). More than one-third (39%) said they would be willing to help start a new church; 12 percent of the respondents said they would be willing to move to another community to do so.

According to these findings "personal salvation" was of highest priority for a large majority of the respondents, about one-half were actually involved in such evangelical recruitment, and more than one-third were willing to get involved in church planting. About one-fourth of the Mennonite Brethren, Evangelical Mennonites, and Brethren in Christ scored high on evangelism, and about one-sixth of the Mennonite Church members and General Conference Mennonites did so.[1] While members of the two largest denominations participated in evangelism somewhat less than did those of the smaller denominations, more of their members thought that working for social justice is more important than outreach.

As shown in Table 8-2, Mennonites in both the city and the country favored and were involved in evangelism. However, urbanization as one form of modernization seems to facilitate outreach; this was also the case among the early Christians and the Anabaptists. Modernization offers opportunities for church growth as well as threats to Christian commitment. Mennonites of higher socioeconomic status were also more involved in evangelism and church planting. Higher education, income, and occupational status seemed to facilitate rather than retard Christian outreach.

Peacemaking and Alternative Service

Since their European beginnings Mennonites have held to a belief in nonresistance and peacemaking, and this position has taken many forms. What is the state of peacemaking today and how is this expressed?

Table 8-3 shows that in 1972 around three-fourths (73%) of the respondents said that Christians should not take part in war; 71 percent indicated they would choose alternative service if faced with the military draft. Eighty percent said that MCC programs (I-W, VS, PAX, TAP) were acceptable alternatives to military service. When the same questions were asked in 1989, these figures had dropped somewhat—in each case to about two-thirds (66, 61, and 74% respectively). Clearly an erosion of

Table 8-2. Involvement in Evangelism and Church Planting by Rural-Urban Residence

Evangelism items	Percent in 1989				Totals	
	Rural farm	Rural non- farm	Small city	Large city	1972	1989
Members of my church feel it is more important to help others find salvation	78	77	71	66	*	73
Sometimes (several times a year or more) witness orally about faith to others	63	65	66	63	66	64
Tried to lead someone to faith in Christ at least a few times	40	46	51	46	48	46
Regularly or occasionally invite non-Christians to church or Sunday school	37	45	44	41	42	41
Am willing to help start a new church (at home or elsewhere)	40	35	41	42	*	39
Members of my church feel it is more important to work for a more just and equitable world	22	23	29	34	*	27

*Not included in the 1972 survey.

the traditional nonresistance occurred between 1972 and 1989.

On the other hand, Table 8-3 shows that other aspects of peacemaking have increased. Respondents agreeing that youth may register but should refuse induction went from 29 percent in 1972 to 37 percent in 1989. Those agreeing that Mennonites should actively promote the peace position and win others to it went from 56 percent in 1972 to 65 percent in 1989. These figures seem to demonstrate progress toward more active peace promotion instead of just doing a term of service when obligated, although recently, in contrast to 1972, Mennonites have not had to make decisions about alternative service.

Half (49%) of the respondents in 1989 said that noncombantant service is acceptable (39% in 1972). Quite a few more were willing to refuse to register for the draft (15% in 1989 vs. 3% in 1972). In 1989 only 13 percent said they themselves would do noncombatant service and only 6 percent said they would join the military service if drafted. Eighteen percent of the respondents reported that they had actually done one year or more of service under MCC.

Table 8-3. Responses to Items on War, Alternative Service, and Peacemaking

War and peace items	Percent in 1989					Totals	
	MC	GC	MB	BIC	EMC	1972	1989
Previous service programs (I-W, VS, PAX, TAP) are acceptable alternatives to the military	83	74	59	65	54	80	74
The Christian should take no part in war	78	65	56	39	11	73	66
We should actively promote the peace position and win others to it	68	75	53	55	42	56	65
It is all right to accept noncombatant service within the military	33	53	69	68	91	39	49
It is all right to register, but should refuse induction	48	33	21	24	6	29	37
Youth should refuse to register with the draft	12	21	15	8	1	3	15
Which of the following positions would you take if faced with a military draft?							
Alternative service	73	59	50	43	17	71	61
Noncombatant military service	7	14	20	21	38	10	13
Regular military service	3	6	8	16	32	5	6
Register, but refuse induction or service	5	3	3	1	0	2	4
Refuse to register	3	5	3	2	1	1	3
Quite uncertain	10	14	16	17	12	11	13

Table 8-3 also shows great differences between Mennonite denominations with respect to pacifist views. While the EMC and BIC respondents scored higher on evangelism, they were much lower than the other denominations in their support of the peace position. Three-fourths (73%) of the members of the Mennonite Church said they would do alternative service if faced with the draft, while only 17 percent of the Evangelical Mennonites took that position. The EMC respondents were more willing to enter noncombatant service. One-third (32%) of the Evangelical Mennonite respondents said they would enter regular military service if drafted while only 3 percent of the MC respondents said they would do so. The percentage of those who would register but refuse induction (4%) and those who would even refuse to register (3%) was small, and more of these were found among the larger MC and GC denominations. It is clearly the Mennonites in the larger denominations who are continuing to spearhead nonresistance and peacemaking.

Table 8-4 presents the responses to peacemaking items according to socioeconomic status categories. We found that the respondents varied more according to SES categories (which combine education, occupation, and income levels) than they did according to rural-urban differences.

Table 8-4. Responses to Items on War, Alternative Service, and Peacemaking by Socioeconomic Status

Peacemaking items	Percent in 1989 by status				Totals	
	Lower	Lower middle	Upper middle	Upper	1972	1989
Previous service programs (I-W, VS, PAX, TAP) are acceptable alternatives to the military	73	75	81	80	80	74
The Christian should take no part in war	65	64	65	74	73	66
We should actively promote the peace position and win other to it	64	65	65	74	56	65
It is all right to accept noncombatant service within the military	47	51	54	42	39	49
It is all right to register, but should refuse induction	39	39	34	38	29	37
Have done one year or more of MCC-related service*	22	23	25	24	—	18
Youth should refuse to register with the draft	12	13	11	18	3	15
Which of the following positions would you take if faced with a military draft?						
Alternative service	58	64	66	67	71	61
Noncombatant military service	15	15	10	12	10	13
Regular military service	7	5	10	6	5	6
Percent scoring "high" on the peace scale	12	16	19	33	—	20

*The figures in this row are slightly inflated, since some persons are counted more than once, having served in more than one program.

Support of the peace position was slightly stronger among the respondents of higher SES in regards to not taking part in war, promoting the peace position, and in choosing the alternative service position if drafted. On a composite peacemaking (pacifism) scale, 33 percent of the respondents in the upper category scored "high," while only 12 percent in the lower category did so.[2]

MCC Service: Attitudes and Action

In the first years after its founding in 1920, the Mennonite Central Committee served mostly Mennonites, but this situation has changed more recently. Mennonites and Brethren in Christ strongly support MCC. Table 8-5 shows that two-thirds (68%) of the 1989 respondents were satisfied with MCC's program and emphasis; only 16 percent were dissatisfied. The respondents were even more satisfied with Mennonite Disaster Service (79%). The strong support for MCC work in the Washington and Ottawa offices (72%) is striking because of the considerable resistance against establishing such offices in the early 1960s (Dyck, 1980). Many people were afraid that doing so might lead to too much political action. The steady and sensitive performance of Delton Franz and William Janzen over many years in their respective Washington and Ottawa offices has persuaded a large majority to accept this MCC presence in the capitals of the two nations. This support was somewhat higher among the larger Mennonite denominations.

To what extent have members of Mennonite and Brethren in Christ churches been involved in service programs? More than one-third of the respondents in 1989 had been involved in service programs conducted by MCC and other church-related agencies.[3] Eleven percent had served one year or more in MCC overseas or long-term Voluntary Service. In the United States 9 percent had done alternative service in World War II or I-W service in the period between 1950 and 1980. About one in five Mennonites had served in an alternative-service program during a war; their peace position had cost them something.

MCC services have reached far beyond compulsory alternative service, as demonstrated in Table 8-5. Six percent of the 1989 respondents had participated in short-term voluntary service, and 14 percent in Mennonite Disaster Service; although short-term, these two programs involve many with the larger community. Another 4 percent had served in other, non-MCC service programs. The large numbers of Mennonites who have participated in some form of MCC service illustrate the extent to which these multiple programs have pervaded Mennonite congregational life. Thousands more have served voluntarily in MCC thrift and gift stores, relief sales, mediation services, prison visitation, sewing circles, contributing to the Food Bank, and many other types of activity. This lay service movement, especially through the work of MCC, has become an important and widely known arm of the Mennonite churches.

Table 8-5. Responses to Items on Mennonites in MCC-Related Services

MCC items	Percent in 1989					Totals	
	MC	GC	MB	BIC	EMC	1972	1989
Satisfied with the program and emphases of MCC	67	71	69	63	53	66	68
Satisfied with the program of Mennonite Disaster Service	82	81	75	66	61	75	79
Favor the work of the MCC offices in Washington and Ottawa	71	75	72	69	61	55	72
Served in Mennonite Disaster Service	18	15	10	4	5	*	14
Served in alternative service	12	8	7	9	4	*	10
Served in VS or MCC overseas one year or more	11	9	6	5	2	*	9
Served in short-term VS	6	8	2	3	1	*	6

*Not included in the 1972 survey.

The larger Mennonite groups supported MCC work strongly, with 67 percent of the Mennonite Church respondents being satisfied with MCC in general—82 percent with Mennonite Disaster Service and 71 percent with the work in the Washington and Ottawa offices. Well over half (53%) of the Evangelical Mennonites indicated satisfaction with MCC, 61 percent with MDS, and 61 percent with the work in the capital offices. These figures are significantly lower than those for the larger denominations. The denominational differences are especially noteworthy in actual voluntary service, overseas relief service, alternative service, and disaster service, with members of the larger denominations being much more active. No doubt, volunteers who return from such services make members at home more aware of the needs of the world and encourage others to enter service programs.

Satisfaction with MCC work has increased since 1972 in both MDS (from 75 to 79%) and the work of the national offices (from 67 to 76%). Table 8-6 shows that the percentage of those who gave MCC a high rating, increased with higher socioeconomic status. Also (not shown in the table) respondents with higher education and urban residence were more favorable to the work of MCC. The modernizing influences of urbanization and higher socioeconomic status add to MCC support rather than detract from it. MCC seems to be a boon not only to others but also to the Mennonites themselves. They responded when others were in need in 1920, and now this faithfulness has translated into a multimillion dollar program serving 50 countries and using the skills of all members—manual laborers, professionals, and business people (Kreider and Goossen, 1988). Few church programs filter down to the grassroots this extensively.

Table 8-6. Responses to Items on Mennonites in MCC-Related Services by Socioeconomic Status

	Percent in 1989 by status				Totals	
		Lower	Upper			
MCC items	Lower	middle	middle	Upper	1972	1989
Satisfied with the program and emphases of MCC	69	64	70	75	66	68
Satisfied with the program of Mennonite Disaster Service	83	79	79	83	75	79
Favor the work of the MCC offices in Washington and Ottawa	67	71	77	86	55	72
Served in Mennonite Disaster Service	20	16	12	15	*	14
Served in alternative service	15	14	14	10	*	10
Served in VS or MCC overseas one year or more	7	9	11	14	*	9
Served in short-term VS	4	5	6	10	*	6

*Not included in the 1972 survey.

Local Church Outreach

While service has reached far and wide, such outreach is also carried on in the local communities (see Table 8-7). Three out of four (77%) of the 1989 respondents had done volunteer work for church and community agencies, in hundreds of settings—some individuals serving one or more days per week without remuneration. Almost as many respondents (72%) had visited nonrelatives who were sick or confined to their homes. These are only a few indicators of extensive involvement at the local level.

Table 8-7. Responses to Items Regarding Contributions

Contributions	Percent in 1989					Total
	MC	GC	MB	BIC	EMC	
Frequently or occasionally did volunteer work for church or community agencies	74	79	82	71	79	77
Frequently or occasionally visited a nonrelative who was sick or shut-in	72	74	69	73	72	72
Gave a planned amount to church regularly	67	63	70	73	80	67
Gave $5,000 or more to church and charity	14	10	18	10	15	13
Contributed money to religious television programs at least once or twice a year	11	13	15	15	15	12

Two-thirds (67%) of the respondents also gave regularly a planned amount of their incomes to their churches; others gave, but not a planned amount. In 1988 nearly half (44%) gave $2,000 or more to the church and charity; 13 percent gave $5,000 or more. Twelve percent gave to religious television programs at least once or twice a year, but only 4 percent gave at least several times a year. A very large majority regularly contributed to the church; a few gave additional amounts to outside programs, such as religious television programs. Contributions to local outreach activities did not vary greatly by socioeconomic status, residence, or denomination.

Involvement in Community Organizations

So far in this chapter we have explored the extent of Mennonite outreach through church activities. We now examine the general involvement of Mennonites in everyday community life—membership and activity in community organizations.

In chapter 4 (Table 4-3) the types of community organizations in which Mennonites hold membership were listed, together with the distribution of frequencies by denomination. The types of organization are listed in Table 8-8, but the breakdown is by socioeconomic status, showing that membership in organizations varies significantly by status levels.

Outside of the church, primary relations in the school were most popular. Parent-Teacher Associations, and Hi-Y and Y-teens clubs involve children in school, and education has always been a priority for Mennonites. Table 8-8 shows that 17 percent of the Mennonite respondents were involved in school service clubs in 1989 and 17 percent belonged to youth groups. As explained in chapter 4, the decline in these percentages since 1972 is due to the smaller proportion of youth in the 1989 sample. The percentage of youth currently involved in organizations is as great as it was earlier.

Table 8-8. Participation in Community Organizations by Socioeconomic Status

	Percent in 1989 by status				Totals	
Types of organizations	Lower	Lower middle	Upper middle	Upper	1972	1989
School service clubs (PTA, Hi-Y, Y-Teens, etc.)	8	15	21	33	24	17
Youth groups (boy scouts, girl scouts, 4-H, church youth)	14	15	16	18	23	17
Professional or academic societies	2	9	25	56	11	18
Farm organizations	15	14	8	5	12	9
Business corporations	3	7	15	17	5	8
Hobby or garden clubs	5	7	7	9	6	7
Labor unions	9	9	6	9	5	6
Literary, art, discussion, or study clubs	1	5	6	10	6	5
Service clubs (Rotary, etc.)	3	4	10	8	3	5
Fraternal groups (Elks, Masons, women's auxiliaries, etc.)	1	3	2	3	2	2
Veterans groups	2	2	1	1	1	1

Interesting changes had taken place in participation in occupational organizations. The proportion of respondents that are members of farm organizations has declined from 12 percent in 1972 to 9 percent in 1989. This reflects the decrease in the number of farmers, from 11 percent of the respondents in 1972 to 7 percent in 1989. The increase in the number of professionals (from 16% in 1972 to 28% in 1989) was reflected in a greater number of memberships in professional and academic societies, from 11 percent in 1972 to 18 percent in 1989. Almost twice as many belonged to professional societies in 1989 as did a generation earlier. Likewise, the increased proportion in business ownership and management occupations, from 5 percent in 1972 to 9 percent in 1989, was reflected in more respondents belonging to boards of directors and other corporate business organizations (from 5% in 1972 to 8% in 1989). This economic and occupational trend will likely continue as Mennonites further modernize, becoming more educated and urban. Memberships are shifting from more primary, gemeinschaft-like organizations to larger, more secondary economic organizations.

Mennonite membership in other clubs—hobby, garden, literary, art, service, and fraternal clubs—has not changed much since 1972. In both years no more than about one in twenty (5 to 7%) of the respondents belonged to any of these clubs, and about as many belonged to labor unions. While Mennonites joined these clubs in 1989 about as much as in 1972, the shift toward professional and business involvement has accelerated. Mennonites are more and more joining groups with economic power; their influence will be more widely felt.

The shift from the more isolated farm location to greater occupational ties with other people is well underway, and this will be reflected in more and more memberships in economic and political power groups. Later we will see that modernization is having important effects in greater ties and involvement with others. For example, 39 percent of those in higher status groups joined four or more of these organizations, while only 6 percent of the lower socioeconomic status Mennonites did so—a ratio of more than six to one. Education is an important factor; only 5 percent of the respondents who did not go beyond elementary school joined four or more organizations; six times as many with graduate education (32%) did so. Modernization has a great effect on involvement in community organizations.

Shaping the Range of Mennonite Outreach

Having looked at five forms of Mennonite outreach and participation in the larger society (evangelism, peacemaking, MCC work, serving others, and community organizations) we seek now to create some order out of this range of involvement.

Networks of Service and Outreach

Socioeconomic status differentiated among Mennonites in the extent of their outreach (see Table 8-9). Higher education, occupational status, and income—which combine to form higher socioeconomic status—correlated with greater involvement with others in service and community activities.

As shown in Table 8-9, twice as many of upper-status respondents (27%) as the lower-status respondents (15%) scored high on evangelism; this difference is significant (r=.08 between SES and evangelism). The correlation was even greater between socioeconomic status and peacemaking (r =.14), between SES and support for MCC (r =.13), and between SES and serving others (r =.16).

Table 8-9. Outreach and Involvement in Community Organizations by Socioeconomic Status

Scales	Socioeconomic status				Correlation coefficients*	
	Lower	Lower middle	Upper middle	Upper	SES	Urban-ization
	(Percent scoring "high")					
Evangelism	15	17	22	27	.08	.04
Peacemaking	12	16	19	33	.14	.09
MCC service	16	17	22	32	.13	.05
Serving others	22	25	32	39	.16	.02
Memberships in community organizations**	6	14	20	39	.35	.01

*Pearson's r above .045 or below -.045 is significant at the .01 level.
**Four or more memberships.

The socioeconomic differences were still greater with respect to community involvement. Six times as many upper status respondents (39%) scored high on membership in community clubs and organizations (r=.35). One-fourth to one-half of the upper-status Mennonites participated in all five of these outreach activities, while relatively few of the lower-status group did.

Socioeconomic status, one indicator of modernization, was highly correlated with greater involvement in evangelism, peacemaking, MCC service, service to others, and memberships in community organizations. Urbanization, another indicator of modernization, also had positive correlations with these outreach variables, but the coefficients were very low. Those who live in the city were slightly more active in peacemaking (r =.09) and MCC service (.05), but the correlations between urbanization and evangelism (.04), service to others (.02), and community memberships (.01) were not statistically significant. In general, modernization related positively to greater outreach and participation in the larger society.

Dialectic of Modernity, Identity, and Outreach

Clearly, modernity, Mennonite identity and outreach are associated in complex ways. We will attempt now to bring together the influences of modernization, identity, and outreach (discussed in parts one, two, and three, respectively, of this volume).

In Table 8-10 we report correlations between outreach variables (evangelism, peacemaking, serving others, MCC service) and three indicators of Mennonite identity (Anabaptism, peoplehood, and communalism) and the four concomitants of modernization. These variables were all significantly correlated except for evangelism and communalism (r=.04). Anabaptist beliefs were most strongly correlated with most of the outreach scales, especially peacemaking (.48), serving others (.29), and evangelism (.26). This strong correlation of four of the types of outreach with Anabaptism, peoplehood, and communalism scales represents a bulwark which Mennonites and Brethren in Christ might do well to build upon if they wish to become a dynamic witness and grow.

Table 8-10. Correlation of Outreach Variables with Indicators of Identity and Concomitants of Modernization

Outreach variables	Mennonite identity		
	Anabaptism	Peoplehood	Communalism
Evangelism	.26	.10	.04
Peacemaking	.48	.33	.35
Serving others	.29	.13	.15
MCC service	.16	.21	.22
Membership in organizations	–.17	–.12	–.09

	Concomitants of modernization			
	Secularism	Individualism	Independence	Materialism
Evangelism	–.33	–.31	–.18	–.11
Peacemaking	.02	–.15	–.20	–.08
Serving others	–.35	–.31	–.18	–.01
MCC service	–.10	–.02	–.13	–.09
Membership in organizations	.08	.06	.08	.06

Note: Pearson's rs above .045 and below –.045 are statistically significant at the .01 level.

It is interesting to note that the concomitants of modernization (secularism, individualism, personal independence, materialism) related negatively to four of the five types of outreach (see the lower part of Table 8-10). While urbanization, higher socioeconomic status, and mobility related positively to the outreach variables, there remains the risk of erosion of the Mennonite faith, family, community, and institutions. Secularism, individualism, personal independence, and materialism can seriously undermine Mennonite identity in the process of reaching out to others.

Summary

As an introduction to part three, this chapter focused on the networks of service in which North American Mennonites are engaged. We traced three major forms of outreach in this century: the evangelical missionary movement, alternative service in World War II, and the relief and service work of the Mennonite Central Committee, begun after World War I.

Among North American Mennonites and Brethren in Christ, concern for personal evangelism was strong in 1972 and remained strong in 1989. Many were at least occasionally involved in recruiting new members for the church and were willing to help start new congregations. A large majority believed that Christians should take no part in war, that they should actively promote peace, and that they themselves would do alternative service if faced by war and the draft. Many had actually served in alternative service. The strength of some of these convictions has declined since 1972, but that of others has increased somewhat. A vast majority of the respondents approved of the work of the Mennonite Central Committee—of MDS and the work in the MCC offices in our national capitals. They were highly involved in local volunteer work, visitation, and the support of churches and charity through monetary contributions. Most of these involvements increased with higher socioeconomic status and urbanization. The number of memberships in community organizations also increased with higher socioeconomic status and urbanization.

In summary, the modernization factors of greater urbanization and higher socioeconomic status have resulted in greater involvement in outreach of many kinds. Mennonite identity factors—such as Anabaptism, a sense of peoplehood, and communalism—correlated positively with evangelism, peacemaking, serving others, and MCC service, but there were low negative correlations with the number of memberships that respondents held in community organizations. The concomitants of modernization—secularism, individualism, personal independence, and materialism—were negatively associated with evangelism, peacemaking, serving others, and MCC service, and somewhat positively related to membership in community organizations.

CHAPTER 9

Probing Moral and Ethical Issues

THIS CHAPTER CONTINUES our examination of the consequences of modernization for Mennonite identity. The focus is on Mennonite adherence to certain moral and ethical principles and the degree of similarity and difference between Mennonites and other religious traditions in North America. Some of these issues (pacifism, service outreach) were discussed in the previous chapter. At this point we turn our attention to matters of personal morality and some additional ethical issues in the relationship of Mennonites to the larger society. In understanding the Mennonite sacred canopy, these issues are probably as important as matters of doctrinal orthodoxy.

Changing Social Norms

In the history of humankind much rational thought has been given to the determination of how persons should or should not act, either alone or in the company of others. Each generation inherits the distilled wisdom of the past, including its definitions of right and wrong. Each generation will either accept the inherited definitions or alter them in some way. We live in an age when the wisdom of the past is rigorously examined and the traditions are often suspect simply because they are old. The new is in and the old is out, whether it be in technology, theology, clothing, music, or social values.

Morality and Social Ethics

Religion has much to do with definitions of good and evil. Within the Judeo-Christian context, basic standards of morality were set down by divine revelation, through the Ten Commandments and the words of the prophets. Jesus and the apostles added many definitions. Beyond this, people are given great latitude to determine what is moral or ethical, either by a rational extension of the basic definitions or through the process of social experimentation.

In an age that stresses personal freedom and individualism, people often perceive moral precepts as limiting personal behavior. Chafing under the prescriptions or proscriptions of parents, the church, or even the law, some persons go so far as to declare, "No one can tell me what to do. I'll decide for myself." Insofar as this declaration has to do with what is right and what is wrong, each individual becomes, in effect, his or her own god.

As noted in chapter 4, there is an inevitable tension between individual freedom and social order. Social philosophers and sociologists have argued that a set of shared values is necessary for any society to exist and endure. It would be difficult for a legal system to develop without substantial agreement among the members of the society as to what is right and wrong. If wrongdoing is to be identified and punished, there must be agreement on what is a crime or misdemeanor.

Bellah (1985:139) is particularly helpful in clarifying the relationship between morality and social order:

> It is the moral content of relationships that allows marriages, families, and communities to persist with some certainty that there are agreed-upon standards of right and wrong that one can count on and that are not subject to incessant renegotiation.

Bellah adds that a "common commitment to the good" allows traditional relationships to persist coherently. Thus the "social mores," those inherited principles regarding what is right and good, are a necessary ingredient of any successful society or subgroup thereof. On the other hand, Bellah is not blind to the hazards of a heavy-handed administration of social rules that leads to rigidity, closed-mindedness, and negative criticism. Mennonites can benefit by paying attention to the following comment by Bellah:

> Where standards of right and wrong are asserted with dogmatic certainty and are not open to discussion, and, even worse, where these standards merely express the interests of the stronger party in a relationship, while clothing those interests in moralistic language, then the criticism is indeed justified.

For Christians seeking consensus on moral issues (such as abortion, drinking alcoholic beverages, and the ordination of women), a clear dilemma is posed. The rational approach, more likely to be followed by those with higher education, seeks to retain a degree of "open-mindedness" on issues, being willing to hear all sides of the argument and deferring judgment or closure until all arguments are heard. Some might even prefer never coming to full closure, for fear that the future might bring forth new arguments that would negate a previous decision. On the other hand, consensus can never be reached if closure is indefinitely postponed. Hence many church members, impatient with those who would debate issues endlessly, seek a "word from the Lord" or from church leaders that will end the arguments and provide a solid basis from which there can be forward movement in Christian education and righteous living.

Roof and McKinney (1987:30) noted that recently "moral and religious attitudes have crystallized around one of two camps: moral traditionalists versus those advocating a more libertarian, freewill position." On many issues religious conservatives tend to clash with what they call "secular humanism." On the other hand, mainline church leaders often deplore the rigidities and seeming intolerance of the religious right-wingers. Although the press coverage of issues may suggest the polarization of church members, we suspect that the extremists of both right and left comprise only small groups. The "moral majority" is probably in the middle and comprises both the more liberal members of the fundamentalist and evangelical camps and the conservatives in the Catholic and mainline Protestant denominations.

In the 1980s issues of morality became headline topics in the public press as well as in church publications. Among these issues were abortion, homosexuality, pornography, sexual standards, sex education in the schools, and a variety of issues related to women's rights. Advances in medical science highlighted the health and crime implications of the use of alcohol, tobacco, and mind-altering drugs. Heavy debates raged over the increasing volume of crime, violence, pornography, and profanity appearing in the movies. States and provinces faced public dissension over the legalization of gambling and public lotteries.

Roof and McKinney (1987:186) believe that the emphasis on morality in American religion stems from the separation of church and state and the role which is subsequently required of churches as guardians of public virtue in a free society. Although Christian churches share a common morality, there is much disagreement on particulars.

Hunter (1983:104) notes that from the perspective of evangelicals, modernization has posed a serious threat to traditional morality, particularly since the 1960s. Evangelicals strive to maintain such principles as premarital chastity, marital fidelity, sacredness of life (in opposition to abortion and euthanasia), prayer in the public schools, the undesirability of divorce, and other matters of public and private morality.

In times of confusion and rapid social change, Christians commonly seek to reemphasize biblical standards and traditional social mores. Those of a more liberal orientation are likely to tolerate, or even seek, new definitions of right and wrong, while those of a conservative bent will dig in their heels and resist changes in church standards and practices. Those open to modernization, steeped in the tenets of individualism, tend to resist steps by church hierarchies to codify and promote well-defined statements of right and wrong. Others, accepting a more collectivist or communal approach to the determination of moral standards, are happy to have a conference or synod undertake studies and arrive at conclusions as to what paths church members should follow for righteous living.

It is not surprising that the locus of movements for changing churchly defined standards of morality is found in college and university settings, where those imbued with the rational approach to value determination are most open to redefinitions of right and wrong. We would expect the least educated and most rural to adhere more strongly to traditional definitions. These assumptions will be tested later.

The Mennonite Heritage

From their beginnings Mennonites have concerned themselves with a wide range of issues regarding personal morality and social ethics. There is evidence that at times they have concerned themselves more with moral and ethical questions than with doctrinal issues. Minutes of the meetings of the district conferences during the past century reveal extensive deliberations on a wide range of questions about how Christians should or should not act.

As Kauffman and Harder (1975:118f.) noted in their report of the 1972 survey, the early Anabaptists demanded a disciplined church that admitted and retained as members only those who gave evidence of being "called out" of the world to a life of holiness and love patterned after the life of Christ. They were not satisfied with the easy tolerance of Reformation leaders for the continuing immoral practices of many church members. They demanded a moral nonconformity that became visible in loving their enemies, feeding the hungry, telling the truth, and working for reconciliation between conflicting groups (Yoder, 1969:263).

Even their enemies admitted that the moral achievements of the Anabaptists were generally superior to those of the members of the state churches. An enemy of the Anabaptists as head of the Reformed Church in Zurich, Heinrich Bullinger (Hershberger, 1957:44) testified that:

Those who unite with them will by their ministers be received into the church by rebaptism and repentance and newness of life. They henceforth lead their lives under a semblance of a quite spiritual conduct. They denounce covetousness, pride, profanity, and lewd conversation and immorality of the world, drinking and gluttony.

Although Anabaptists were often persecuted for their rejection of infant baptism (which, incidentally, circumvented the state's tax on church members), they were also opposed because of some of their ethical principles, notably their insistence on the separation of church and state and their refusal to perform military service. The tensions created by their more rigorous ethical and moral standards caused Anabaptists to be persecuted more or less continuously throughout the 16th and 17th centuries. In Holland, however, there was greater religious toleration, and, freed from overt persecution, the Dutch Anabaptists gradually accommodated to the larger society and became increasingly wealthy. As a result, many of the Dutch followers of Menno Simons gradually lost their ethical and moral distinctiveness, including their opposition to military service. Others among the Dutch Mennonites, holding onto greater distinctiveness, migrated eastward through north Germany, Poland, and ultimately Russia to find new land and the opportunity to establish communities that were, except for economic trade, largely separate from the surrounding cultures.

Thus, through 400 years Mennonites have vacillated in respect to their definitions of nonconformity to the world, particularly with reference to their definitions of right and wrong. Adherence to rigorous ethical standards varied greatly from country to country and locality to locality. At times and in some places Mennonites apparently lost their unique principles and simply mirrored the ethical norms of the larger society. At other times and places, Mennonites developed long lists of prescriptions and proscriptions to define nonconformity to the world around them. This became particularly true of conservative groups in North America from the mid-19th to the mid-20th century.

In a chapter entitled "Keeping the Old Order," Schlabach (1988) chronicles the gradual emergence of the Old Order Amish and the Old Order Mennonites as their leaders resisted 19th-century modernization. Less conservative Mennonites and "Amish Mennonites" more readily adapted to new patterns of dress, new styles of worship, use of the English language in worship, participation in community organizations, participation in political affairs, education beyond the eighth grade, etc. By the end of the 19th century the more progressive Mennonites adopted Sunday schools, four-part singing, revival meetings, conference organization, church-operated high schools and colleges, foreign missions, and church periodicals, none of which have been accepted by the Old Orders to this day. To resist the forces of modernization, the Old Orders have not accepted ownership of telephones, electricity, automobiles, radios, television, and other technological devices, although they do use telephones and automobiles owned by others.

Impatient with the slowness of change, some Mennonite leaders moved faster than others. This resulted in the emergence of several new groups that became disconnected from the larger body of Mennonites. Among these was the Oberholtzer division, led by John H. Oberholtzer, who was interested in forming a General Conference that would bring together the disunited local and regional groups. In 1847 Oberholtzer and his followers adopted a constitution that was a first step in the later formation of the General Conference Mennonites (Schlabach, 1988:121). Another was the "Stucky group" which formed what came to be the Central Conference of Mennonites, but later—in 1947—joined the General Conference Mennonite Church. Another group was the "Egly Amish," who formed the Defenseless Mennonite Church, which later became the Evangelical Mennonite Church.

Thus the 19th century contributed significantly to the emerging pluralism of North American Mennonites, a widening of the spectrum from the most conservative to the most progressive groups. Redekop (1989:30) refers to the spectrum as a Mennonite "rainbow." His chart (pp. 32-33) traces the growth of the "Anabaptist-Mennonite Family Tree," which currently includes some 33 independent conferences or clusters of congregations deriving from European sources. Not included are the many groups that have sprung from mission activities in third-world countries.

In his survey of Canadian Mennonites, Driedger (1988) contrasts "Dualists" with "Wholists," the former emphasizing a strong church-world dichotomy and the latter being more involved in this-worldly processes. He (p. 165) found that the Dualists favored greater control over personal morality than did the Wholists, and also expressed stronger ethnic identity. This finding supports the assumption that those of more conservative orientation tend to insist on more restrictive codes of personal behavior.

The five Mennonite and Brethren in Christ churches included in the 1972 and 1989 surveys are only part of a larger North American mosaic that includes some 15 additional bodies. At the conservative end of the continuum are the Old Order Amish, Old Order Mennonites, and Old Colony Mennonites. At the "liberal" end are the five groups in the two surveys. Between these clusters are several other groups: Beachy Amish, Conservative Mennonite, Church of God in Christ Mennonite, and Sommerfeld Mennonites.

When individuals modernize or liberalize their views, they tend to transfer their memberships to more liberal groups, what Driedger (1988:170-74) calls traveling up the "identification ladder." Members of the Old Orders wanting to own automobiles and other proscribed technological devices (which the Old Orders define as wrong) can shift to a Beachy Amish or Conservative Mennonite congregation. From these latter groups, members who want to avoid the required distinctive dress can move to a Mennonite Church congregation. Until recently, Mennonite Church women wanting to wear jewelry would have felt more comfortable among the General Conference Mennonites. Those men who entered military service would be most accepted among the Evangelical Mennonites. In respect to the orthodoxy of Christian beliefs, the whole spectrum of Mennonite groups is more conservative than the mainline Protestant denominations, except perhaps for the Southern Baptists (Kauffman and Harder, 1975:107).

Any treatment of Mennonite emphases on personal morality must take into account the developments in Mennonite polity and conference authority as well, particularly among the MC and BIC groups from about 1910 to 1950. Juhnke (1989) has effectively chronicled the efforts of conference leaders in the Mennonite Church to resist "modernism" and to emphasize "nonconformity to the world," some aspects of which led to unfortunate broken relationships—to defections of individuals and whole congregations from the Mennonite Church to the less conservative General Conference Mennonite Church.

Under the growing power of district conferences, local congregations were subjected to a whole series of legalistic regulations, the purpose of which was "to control the church's drift in many areas—dress, amusements, secret societies, insurance, paid ministry, school problems, and more" (Juhnke, 1989:301). At various times the more conservative MC district conferences legislated against smoking, drinking (buttressed by the national Prohibition from 1918 to 1933), dancing, card playing, gambling, radios, television, movie attendance, carnivals, and other "worldly" activities.

With the decline of conference authority since the 1950s, *congregations* have been expected to deal with issues of morality. Increasingly education (study conferences, workshops, Sunday school classes, church schools, and Christian literature) has displaced legislation as the way to deal with issues of morality and ethics. Consequently proscriptions have weakened, radio and television are accepted and used to promote the church's mission, and discrimination is suggested with respect to movies and other forms of amusement.

Trends in Personal Morality

The questionnaires in both 1972 and 1989 probed church members' attitudes on a list of moral and ethical issues. Rather than attempting all-inclusiveness, we restricted the list to issues under debate at the time. For each item the respondents were asked to choose between three responses: "always wrong" (under all conditions), "sometimes wrong" (under *some* conditions, whether few or many), or "never wrong." An "uncertain" response was the fourth alternative.

Table 9-1 reports the totals from both surveys, with a breakdown by denomination for the 1989 data.[1] For the purpose of simplification, the table gives only the percentage responding "always wrong." The percentages responding "never wrong" and "uncertain" differed very little between the two surveys; most of the shifts in attitudes were between "always wrong" and "sometimes wrong."

Table 9-1. Responses on Issues of Personal Morality

	Percent "always wrong" 1989					Totals	
	MC	GC	MB	BIC	EMC	1972	1989
Increasing opposition							
Smoking tobacco	72	60	72	74	70	64	69
Smoking marijuana	92	90	95	98	97	87	92
Homosexual acts	90	90	98	99	99	86	92
Increasing acceptance							
Drinking alcoholic beverages (moderately)	50	31	37	52	47	50	43
Social dancing	24	14	25	26	18	43	21
Gambling (betting, gambling machines)	65	55	56	72	68	75	61
Masturbation	35	29	34	36	39	46	34
No significant change							
Attending movies rated for adults only	49	42	44	64	63	48	47
Owning stock in companies that produce war goods	51	45	36	27	11	44	44
Income tax evasion	88	88	95	93	95	90	90
Not included in 1972							
Profanity (swearing)	84	83	89	91	93	*	85
Buying state (government) lottery tickets	51	35	36	56	53	*	45

*Not included in 1972.

Denominational variations were mixed. In most cases the GC members were less likely to view the behavior as always wrong; MC members were next in order. The MB, BIC, and EMC members were most opposed, except on the item of owning stock in companies that produce war goods.

The columns showing totals indicate that opposition to smoking tobacco and marijuana increased somewhat between 1972 and 1989, no doubt reflecting the increased public awareness of the health hazards of smoking. The increased percentage of respondents rejecting homosexual acts (from 86 to 92% who answered "always wrong") resulted primarily from a shift from 7 to 2 percent responding "uncertain." It should be noted that the item asked for opinion regarding "homosexual acts" rather than "homosexual orientation."

Use of Alcohol and Tobacco

Table 9-1 also indicates that opposition to drinking, dancing, gambling, and masturbation has diminished. After the end of Prohibition in 1933 in the United States, most Mennonite congregations continued to openly discourage the use of alcohol by members at least until the 1960s, the most conservative congregations until the present. Although church members still strongly oppose drunkenness (94% of respondents in 1972 regarded "becoming drunken" as "always wrong"), few congregations any longer make alcohol use a disciplinary matter. Mennonite colleges have policies opposing drinking on campus, but they no longer attempt to regulate student use of alcohol off campus.

Early in the twentieth century Mennonite and Brethren in Christ congregations shifted from wine to grape juice for communion services—a practice which continues. Our data indicate that attitudes toward alcohol use are somewhat more accepting in Canada than in the United States, and Mennonites in some Canadian communities commonly serve wine at weddings and other celebrations (Currie, Driedger, and Linden, 1979).

Our findings indicate that fewer Mennonites smoked in 1989, but a larger number used alcohol. The percentage that regularly used tobacco dropped from 6 percent in 1972 to 4 percent in 1989. Those who "drink occasionally or regularly now" rose from 13 to 22 percent. The increased use of alcohol was totally among those under the age of 50. There was no change among those over 50. Use rates were 36 percent for those in the 20-29 age-group and 31 percent for those in the 30-49 group, but only 5 percent for those over the age of 70.

What of the future? Will Mennonites simply assimilate the mores of the larger society? Or will an increasing public awareness of the hazards to mental and physical functioning (especially evident in automobile and other accidents) resulting from even a moderate use of alcohol help to reverse the trend? Medical experts and public officials are increasingly calling alcohol the nation's number one drug problem. As in the case of smoking, perhaps a watershed will be reached when alcohol use, even moderate use, will diminish for health reasons. Mennonite interest in morality and stewardship of the human body causes many to promote abstinence or limits on alcohol use.

Social Dancing

Under constant pressures from young people, many congregational and church college leaders have modified past policies against social dancing. Most Mennonite colleges now permit dancing on their campuses, within institutional policies and with appropriate supervision. Few congregations would sponsor dances, but there is currently little effort to discourage attendance at local school or other community events that feature dancing. Nevertheless, some members regard dances as "worldly" and do not participate. In 1989, 9 percent of the respondents indicated that they take part in social dancing "regularly"; 24 percent, "occasionally." A considerable increase in social dancing has occurred since 1972, when the figures were 4 percent "regularly" and 12 percent "occasionally." Again the increase has occurred mostly among persons under the age of 50.

Attitudes Versus Behavior

What is the relationship between attitudes and behavior? Do those who use tobacco or alcoholic beverages think that it is never wrong to actually smoke and drink? Do those who never dance feel that it is wrong to do so, or are there other reasons for not dancing? Our data provide partial answers to these interesting questions.

A cross-tabulation of the frequency of use of alcohol with attitudes toward its use shows that only 3 percent of occasional or regular users think that moderate drinking is always wrong, while 79 percent of those that have never drunk any alcohol believe that it is always wrong. Thus a strong relationship exists between attitude and use. Sixty-five percent of the users saw moderate use as wrong under some conditions, and 5 percent were "uncertain." Reasons were not solicited, but one suspects that these respondents were thinking of use by pregnant women or previous to driving.

A correlation coefficient is an efficient device for showing the relationship between responses to attitude items and responses to behavior items. The following correlations were obtained from the 1989 responses: use of alcoholic beverages, .49; smoking tobacco, .27; social dancing, .50; and attending X-rated movies, .26.

The positive correlations were expected, but they were far from perfect (1.0). Social scientists do not agree on whether attitudes precede behavior, or vice versa. Likely the effect is interactive, that is, in both directions. Since changes in attitudes are likely to have some effect on changes in behavior, any Christian education program designed to discourage these behaviors must focus on education that will change attitudes. In a climate of individualism, churches will not likely be able directly to effect changes in behavior.

Abortion

In view of the current heated debates in state and provincial legislatures and in the press, it is important to note where Mennonites stand on the issue of abortion. Attitudes toward abortion vary according to the circumstances precipitating abortion cases. Both the 1972 and 1989 questionnaires asked the respondents whether they thought "it should be possible for a pregnant woman to obtain a *legal* abortion" under each of six circumstances. The three possible responses were "yes," "no," and "uncertain."[2] Table 9-2 provides the distribution of "no" responses for both surveys.

Table 9-2. Percentage Opposed to Legal Abortion

| | Percent opposed | | | | | | |
| | 1989 | | | | | Totals | |
Circumstance	MC	GC	MB	BIC	EMC	1972	1989
If the woman's health is seriously endangered	17	11	14	15	16	8	15
If pregnant as a result of rape	42	34	46	47	52	23	41
If strong chance of serious defect in the baby	50	37	53	56	66	19	48
If the family cannot afford more children	87	82	94	91	96	66	87
If not married and does not want to marry the man	88	80	94	93	96	69	87
If she does not want the baby	89	82	95	92	96	74	88

In 1989, 15 percent opposed legal abortion rights in cases of danger to the woman's health, and 41 percent were opposed if the pregnancy was a result of rape. Nearly half opposed abortion if there was a strong chance of a serious defect in the baby, while nearly nine out of ten opposed abortion for less compelling reasons.

A 1988 national survey in the United States by the Gallup organization probed attitudes on the same question of legalized abortion (Gallup and Jones, 1989:122). The proportions disapproving legalized abortion were as follows: if the woman's life is endangered, 2 percent; if the pregnancy was a result of rape or incest, 11 percent; if the woman may suffer severe physical health damage, 11 percent; if there is a chance that the baby will be born deformed, 29 percent; if the family cannot afford to have the baby, 75 percent. A comparison of these percentages with those in Table 9-2 shows that Mennonites were much more opposed to legalized abortion than was the general American public.

The usual pattern of denominational differences was evident, with least opposition to abortion expressed by GC members and most opposition indicated by EMC members. Between these extremes ranged the MC, BIC, and MB members—in order from less to more opposition to abortion. However, the differences were small.

As indicated in the last two columns of Table 9-2, for all circumstances the opposition to legalized abortion increased between 1972 and 1989. The proportions answering "yes" correspondingly decreased. With one exception (in the case of the woman's own health), the proportions answering "uncertain" decreased, suggesting that public discussion of the issues may have resulted in clarification of attitudes.

These results clearly show that changes can occur in both directions. Liberalization of views on controversial issues cannot be assumed. Mennonites, conservatively oriented regarding moral and ethical issues in general, have apparently moved further in the conservative direction under the impact of the public airing of the abortion issue.

An abortion scale was constructed by totaling the codes for the six items, with "yes" coded 1, "uncertain" 2, and "no" 3. A high score on the scale represents the conservative position of opposing legalized abortion. Positive correlations were obtained with the separatism scale (.28) and the moral attitudes scale (.47). Negative correlations resulted with the political action and political participation scales (-.17 in both cases), the welfare attitudes Scale (-.13) and the role of women scale (-.36). Thus, as expected, church members who favored political action, more welfare aid, and larger roles for women in the church tended to be more accepting of abortion.

Homosexual Acts

Space does not permit an adequate review of the nature of, and factors associated with, homosexuality. It is important to distinguish between homosexual orientation (preference for same-sex partners) and homosexual acts (the practice of homosexual relations). Since we did not probe attitudes toward homosexual orientation, a presentation of the findings on how Mennonites view homosexual acts must suffice.

Table 9-1 indicated that 92 percent of the 1989 respondents regarded homosexual acts as always wrong (86% in 1972). The survey of members of the Lutheran Church of America reported by Johnson (1983:235) indicated that 66 percent of the laity and 50 percent of the pastors viewed "homosexual relations" as always wrong. According to the 1989 General Social Survey (National Opinion Research Center, 1989), 74 percent of the American population regarded "sexual relations between two adults of the same sex" as always wrong. In a 1985 survey of the Canadian national population, 84 percent of the respondents who were "religiously committed" viewed homosexual relations as always wrong, as did 60 percent of those who were "not devout" (Bibby, 1987:155). By denomination the range was from 89 percent for the "Conservative Protestant" groups (Nazarenes, Pentecostals, Baptists, Mennonites, Salvation Army, etc.) to 67 percent for the Anglican Church. Thus the Mennonite and Brethren in Christ in 1989 were somewhat more opposed to homosexual practice than were any of the other groups for which data are available.

One critical issue is whether a homosexual may be a member of a Mennonite or Brethren in Christ congregation. Our data show that attitudes vary widely on this issue. Two questions introduced in the 1989 survey reveal members' attitudes. The items were not included in the 1972 study, since their significance had not yet clearly emerged.

The first item, "In your opinion, if a person has a homosexual orientation but does not practice homosexual acts, which of the following can be permitted?" generated the response distribution given in Table 9-3. To probe attitudes toward practicing homosexuals, a second question was asked: "If a person has a homosexual orientation and *does* engage in homosexual acts, which would you allow?" The answers are given in the lower half of Table 9-3.

All but one-third (32%) of the respondents would accept non-practicing homosexuals as members, and 20 percent would accept such persons in leadership positions. About four out of five respondents (78%) would oppose membership for a practicing homosexual, reflecting the attitude that homosexual acts are "always wrong." On this item males and females did not differ significantly. On the first item, females were more willing than males to accept a nonpracticing homosexual as a member of the congregation (53% vs. 43%).

Table 9-3. Attitudes Toward Church Membership for Homosexuals

| | Percent in 1989 | | | | | |
	MC	GC	MB	BIC	EMC	Total
If *not* engaging in homosexual acts:						
May be a member of						
congregation	48	51	48	44	47	48
Could serve as a leader	8	8	5	6	3	8
Could be ordained	13	13	9	8	5	12
Permit none of the above	30	28	38	42	44	32
	100	100	100	100	100	100
If engaging in homosexual acts:						
May be a member of						
congregation	19	26	10	13	11	19
May serve as a leader	1	3	0	0	0	1
Could be ordained	2	3	1	0	0	2
Permit none of the above	78	69	89	87	88	78
	100	100	100	100	100	100

Within each of the denominations the whole range of responses was represented. However, there were some significant differences in the aggregate. The proportion who would bar nonpracticing homosexuals from membership varied from 28 percent among the GCs to 44 percent for the EMC members. The proportions who would oppose membership for practicing homosexuals ranged from 69 percent for the GCs to 89 percent for the MBs. Opposition to membership was also highly associated with lower educational achievement and older age levels.

Although pastors and laity did not differ significantly with respect to membership for practicing homosexuals, they did differ on membership for nonpracticing persons. The proportions who would bar them from membership were 9 percent for ordained persons, 30 percent for congregational lay leaders, and 40 percent for nonleaders.

Comparable data for other church bodies are not easy to obtain. Roof and McKinney (1987:203-13)), analyzing data gathered by the General Social Survey, reported findings on attitudes toward abortion, homosexuality, premarital sex, extramarital sex, use of marijuana, and other issues. They broke their data down by major religious groups and the largest Protestant denominations, Mennonites not included. Some of their data are not directly comparable with the Mennonite findings, due to somewhat different wording of items and responses.

Three items are comparable, however, and these are given in Table 9-4. According to Roof and McKinney's categories, "liberal Protestants" included Episcopalians, Presbyterians, and the United Church of Christ. "Moderate Protestants" included Methodists, Lutherans, Northern Baptists, Reformed, and Disciples of Christ. The "conservative Protestant" group was comprised of Southern Baptists, Churches of Christ, Nazarenes, Adventists, and several Pentecostal bodies.

Table 9-4. Comparisons Between Mennonites and Major American Religious Bodies

Categories	Percent of respondents		
	Favor abortion in case of rape	Homosexual acts not always wrong	Premarital sex not always wrong
National population	83	27	35
Liberal Protestants	95	36	35
Moderate Protestants	88	23	29
Conservative Protestants	78	11	19
Catholics	79	31	36
No religious preference	93	60	66
Mennonites and BIC	31	8	15

Source: Roof and McKinney, *American Mainline Religion*, 1987: 206-213

Mennonites had more conservative attitudes than did any of the other categories listed in the table. Only 31 percent of the Mennonites approved legalized abortion in case of rape, while other categories approved at the rate of 78 percent (for conservative Protestants) and greater. Eleven percent of conservative Protestants and 8 percent of Mennonites did not regard homosexual acts as always wrong; those feeling premarital sex was not always wrong were 19 percent of conservative Protestants and 15 percent of Mennonites. All other groups had much higher percentages. Not surprisingly, those with no religious preference held the most liberal attitudes on homosexuality and premarital sex. They were second most liberal (at 93%) on the abortion item, with liberal Protestants even higher (95%).

Morality and Other Dimensions

What relation, if any, is there between moral attitudes and other aspects of social and religious beliefs? To help answer this question we present two scales that are an attempt to summarize moral attitudes and behavior, so that these in turn can be correlated with other scales developed in this study.

A moral attitudes scale was developed by combining the responses assessing members' attitudes on the wrongness of nine items: moderate drinking, smoking tobacco, smoking marijuana, attending movies for adults only, premarital sexual intercourse, homosexual acts, masturbation, gambling, and social dancing. Respondent scores on the scale ranged from zero to 27, the full range of possible scores, thus indicating the wide range of Mennonite views. A high score on the scale represents the more conservative or restrictive attitudes, that is, the "always wrong" responses.

Second, a moral behavior scale was created by combining the three behavior items: frequency of alcohol use, use of tobacco, and social dancing. The scores ranged from one to ten, the possible limits, with a high score representing nonparticipation in these activities.[3]

Table 9-5 presents the correlations between the two scales mentioned above and other scales in the survey.

As one would expect, positive correlations (.28 and .31) were obtained between age and moral attitudes and behavior. This finding indicates that older age-groups more strongly support conservative moral standards.

The negative correlations with the modernization variables indicate that as Mennonites become more urbanized, educated, and upwardly mobile their moral attitudes and behavior tend to shift in a liberal direction. The isolation of a rural environment makes it easier for an in-group to retain its traditional values in the face of social changes in the national context. The urban environment, affording many more social contacts beyond the boundaries of the in-group, tests the traditional values, and when these values are found wanting they may decline or be abandoned altogether. The Hutterites, who avoid the city except for commercial purposes, are an extreme example of the effectiveness of rural isolation in maintaining a separate ethnic and religious identity (Hostetler, 1974:257).

Other observations: (1) The scales measuring moral attitudes and behavior tend to produce similar results when correlated with the other scales. (2) Conservatism in the morality scales yielded substantial positive correlations with other conservative scales: the Anabaptism and orthodoxy scales, the religious practice scales (church participation, devotionalism, and evangelism), and the in-group scales (ethnicity, separatism, and communalism). (3) The negative correlations with the liberal, social issues scales (particularly race relations and women's roles) and the "openness to the larger society" scales (ecumenism, memberships in

Table 9-5. Intercorrelations Between Morality Scales and Other Scales

Scales	Moral attitudes scale*	Moral behavior scale*
Age	.28	.31
Demographic modernization		
Urbanization	-.20	-.16
Education	-.21	-.18
Socioeconomic status	-.20	-.12
Beliefs		
Anabaptism	.41	.35
General orthodoxy	.45	.26
Fundamentalism	.54	.32
Religious practice		
Church participation	.34	.28
Devotionalism	.48	.41
Evangelism	.31	.18
Ethical issues		
Pacifism	-.03**	.06
Race relations	-.21	-.17
Welfare attitudes	-.12	-.04**
Role of women	-.38	-.26
Openness to the larger society		
Ecumenism	-.20	-.15
Membership in organizations	-.24	-.21
Political participation	-.19	-.24
Political action	-.23	-.22
In-group identity		
Ethnicity	.25	.22
Communalism	.14	.25
Separatism	.29	.16
Concomitants of modernization		
Secularism	-.34	-.19
Individualism	-.29	-.19
Personal independence	-.14	-.13
Materialism	-.10	-.07

*High scores on these scales represent greater restrictiveness.
**Not significant at the .01 level.

community organizations, and political activism) suggest that as Mennonites increasingly participated in the social world around them, there was a shift away from conservative moral restrictiveness. (4) The negative correlations with the concomitants of modernization (secularism, individualism, personal independence, and materialism) suggest that, as modernization has proceeded, a decline in moral restrictiveness has taken place.

Trends in Social Ethics

In this section we will give brief attention to a number of ethical issues that relate to the larger society: race relations, poverty and welfare, capital punishment, and membership in labor unions. If space in the questionnaire had permitted, it would have been interesting to probe many other social and economic issues (such as treatment of offenders, litigation, bankruptcy, and environmental pollution). We examined issues related to war and peace in the previous chapter.

Race Relations

In both the 1972 and 1989 surveys five questionnaire items tested attitudes toward other races. These items probed agreement or disagreement with statements on racial equality, separation or intermingling of the races, willingness to sell one's house to someone of a different race, and keeping members of other races out of one's own neighborhood. Table 9-6 gives the distribution of responses to these items. Scores on the items were combined to form a race relations scale.

The percentages in the table represent favorableness toward racial equality. Roughly one-fourth of the church members were not yet able to accept racial equality; if all were accepting, the percentages would be 100. All percentages for 1989 were higher than for 1972, indicating increased acceptance of racial equality since the original survey. Variations between the denominations were small, except that the EMCs rated consistently lower on all items.

An additional item probed attitudes toward marriage between the races. "Marriage between Christians of different races if otherwise compatible," yielded the following responses: always wrong, 6 percent; sometimes wrong, 34 percent; never wrong, 42 percent; and uncertain, 18 percent.[4] The percentage answering "never wrong" varied from 57 for the 20-29 age-group to 21 for the 70 and over group, indicating clearly that young people were much more accepting of people of other races than were older generations. Education also helps to explain considerable variation in attitudes, since only 19 percent of those with elementary education alone responded "never wrong," while 64 percent of those with graduate school education did so. Part of this variation was due to the age factor, since older members averaged fewer years of education.

Table 9-6. Responses to Items on Race Relations

| | 1989 | | | | | Totals | |
Item	MC	GC	MB	BIC	EMC	1972	1989
	(Percent agreeing)						
Human races all share equally in such human qualities as intelligence, physical capacities, and emotional makeup	72	74	73	68	64	68	72
If one's own house were up for sale, one should be willing to sell it to an interested family of another race regardless of possible neighborhood reaction	71	72	75	70	66	59	72
There is a valid biblical basis for the separation of the races	(Percent disagreeing)						
	55	47	47	44	44	40	50
Even if there is no essential difference between blacks and whites, it is preferable for them not to mingle socially	77	75	79	76	72	59	77
People (black, red, or white) have a right to keep others out of their neighborhood if they want to, and this right should be respected	79	74	82	80	76	59	78

In correlations of the race relations scale with scores on other scales, favorable attitudes toward other races were positively associated with other liberal variables: political participation (.16), ecumenism (.21), role of women (.33). Negative correlations were obtained with conservative beliefs: general orthodoxy (-.15), fundamentalism (-.31), and moral attitudes (-.21). This finding further illustrates the tension between those people who emphasize a gospel of salvation and those who emphasize a gospel of social witness. With Anabaptism, however, a very low positive correlation of .07 resulted, indicating that conservatism in respect to Anabaptist beliefs is supportive of, rather than opposed to, racial equality.

The national data reported by Roof and McKinney (1987:197) support the conclusion of a clash between religious conservatism and openness toward other races. Attitudes favoring equal treatment of people of other races were more evident among Catholics and liberal Protestants than among conservative Protestants. More favorable than all church-related respondents were those with no religious preference! Why does religion produce less favorable attitudes toward other races?

Substantial positive correlations were obtained between scores on the race relations scale and the indicators of modernization: urbanization (.19), education (.38) and SES (.34). Modernization yields improved attitudes toward racial equality.

Interestingly, the findings showed negative correlations between race relations and the concomitants of modernization: secularism (-.18), individualism (-.23), personal independence (-.08), and materialism (-.17). Those persons with warm feelings toward persons of other races likely are, at the same time, less secular and less given to individualism and materialism.

Poverty and Social Welfare

Three questionnaire items provided a test of Mennonite views regarding the causes of poverty and the efforts of governments to assist those who live in poverty. One might expect Mennonites, being conservative in many ways, to take conservative attitudes toward poverty and public programs to ameliorate the effects of poverty. On the other hand, the Mennonites' belief in service and sharing with those in need (noted in chapter 8) would seemingly motivate them to take liberal positions toward those in poverty. Which motivation does indeed have the greater effect?

Apparently, Mennonites and Brethren in Christ have very mixed attitudes toward poverty and its remedies. Table 9-7 shows a wide distribution of responses to the three relevant items.

On all three items the 1989 responses were slightly more accepting of the poor and programs to remedy poverty than were the responses in 1972. Nevertheless, 21 percent still believed that poverty results from lack of effort, and 24 percent were in favor of decreasing benefits to the poor. Thirty-eight percent opposed a guaranteed annual income for the poor. Those responding "uncertain" were 25 percent for the first item and 36 percent for the second. Thus, Mennonites vary all the way from hard-liners to hand-outers in the treatment of the poverty stricken. Mennonites were somewhat more favorable toward welfare benefits than were Lutherans in the Johnson report (1983:236); 6 percent of the Lutheran laity favored "spending more government money for people on welfare," while 75 percent opposed more aid.

Table 9-7. Attitudes Toward Poverty and Its Remedies

Items	Percent "agree" 1972	1989
For the most part, people are poor because they lack discipline and don't put forth the effort needed to rise above poverty	30	21
The government should guarantee a minimum annual income for all individuals and families who are unemployed or who receive incomes below the poverty line	26	28
With respect to national welfare programs . . . do you feel that your government should increase, decrease, or maintain current levels of welfare benefits? Increase the levels	17	20
Decrease them	51	24
Maintain current levels	32	56

Responses to the three items were combined to create a welfare attitudes scale. Those scoring high on the scale (those favoring the poor) tended to be more urban, more educated, and occupying higher socioeconomic status. Also, those higher on the welfare attitudes scale scored higher on pacifism (.39), race relations (.32), and expanded roles for women (.35). Other scale intercorrelations tended to be low and insignificant—for example, the age variable (-.03). The highest negative correlation was with those of fundamentalist beliefs (-.29). Anabaptism was positively correlated (.14) with welfare attitudes. A correlation of .21 was obtained with the scale measuring support of the programs of the Mennonite Central Committee; this finding is of interest since many of the MCC programs are designed to relieve poverty.

Expanding Roles for Women

The role of women in church and society is another social issue that has gained much public attention in recent years. In the past three decades significant advancements have been made toward a more equal sharing of male and female roles. Conservatives insist that women are not oppressed; that biological differences between males and females necessitate role differentiation, making it impossible for each sex to fill all the roles of the other. Liberal views insist that women cannot be liberated from sexual discrimination until women have access to all the social and occupational roles afforded to men (Jagger and Struhl, 1984).

Mennonites have also been moving in the direction of more equal sharing of gender roles, in the home, in the church, and in the community (Nyce, 1980). Perhaps the acid test of attitudes toward equal sharing of occupational roles is the ordination of women to the Christian ministry. A few women in the MC and GC denominations were ordained in recent years, and have served as pastors of a congregation and in other ministerial roles. Other women have obtained seminary training for the role of pastor.

Three questionnaire items, both in 1972 and 1989, provided a test of the attitudes of church members toward expanding roles for women. Table 9-8 reports the percentage of respondents that answered "yes" to the questions, which, when combined, form a role of women scale.

In 1989 one-third (32%) of the respondents believed that women in Canada and the United States suffer discrimination, up from 16 percent in 1972. Consciousness raising is taking place. Half (52%) of the respondents favored expanded leadership roles for women at local, district, and denominational levels; only 32 percent in 1972. A sharply increased minority of Mennonites favored the ordination of women in 1989—44 percent, compared to 17 percent in 1972.

General Conference Mennonites were most open to expanded roles for women, with 59 percent in favor of the ordination of women. Members of the BIC and EMC gave the most conservative responses to these items; only about one-sixth favored the ordination of women.

Male and female responses were similar on these items, except that the proportion of males that favored ordination (47%) was slightly higher than the female proportion (42%). Middle-aged respondents favored expanded roles for women in greater proportions than did the teenagers and the oldest respondents. Respondents with higher education and urban residence favored expanded roles more than those of lower education and rural residence.

Capital Punishment

Regarding the statement "Our national, provincial, and state governments should provide for capital punishment (the death penalty for a major crime)," 34 percent of the respondents agreed, 40 percent disagreed, and 26 percent were uncertain. Opposition to the death penalty varied little between age-groups, but there was a consistent increase in opposition with increased levels of education. Many Mennonites oppose the death penalty on the grounds that it is a violent and terminal act, out of harmony with sentiments of peace and the sanctity of life. Some people in the pews clearly do not share such opposition.[5]

Mennonites were only slightly less favorable toward the death penalty than were Lutherans. Johnson's report (1983:236) of the 1979 survey of members of the Lutheran Church in America indicated that 49 percent of the laity favored the death penalty, while 32 percent opposed it. Using a differently worded question, "Are you in favor of the death penalty for persons convicted of murder?" the General Social Survey (1989:128) reported that 56 percent answered "yes," a larger percentage than for either Lutherans or Mennonites.

Table 9-8. Responses to Items on Expanding Roles for Women

Item	1989					Totals	
	MC	GC	MB	BIC	EMC	1972	1989
			(Percent "yes")				
Do you believe that women in Canada and America are being discriminated against and denied certain basic rights?	31	36	32	21	16	16	32
Should larger numbers of qualified women be elected or appointed to church boards and committees?	50	58	53	50	38	32	52
Should the policy on ordinations in your denomination allow for the ordination of women to the ministry?	45	59	27	38	15	17	44

Labor Union Membership

Not many Mennonites lived in the large urban industrial centers until recently. Therefore, only a small minority of Mennonite workers have faced the question of joining a labor union. Some Mennonites have objected to union membership on the grounds that unions resort (or reserve the right to resort) to aggressive, sometimes violent methods to achieve the goals of collective bargaining—specifically strikes, boycotts, and picketing. Under the leadership of Guy F. Hershberger in the 1940s, signed agreements were obtained with some unions that would allow a Mennonite laborer to work in a union shop without joining the union or without paying union dues (Hershberger, 1958:309). Some agreements provided for money in lieu of union dues to be paid into an alternative fund to be contributed to worthy causes either within or outside the union.

The Mennonite Church's Committee on Economic and Social Relations pioneered these efforts on behalf of some MC and BIC members who desired the provisions that were worked out. These agreements never became widespread, and by the late 1950s the program had generally come to an end. Nevertheless, some church members still opposed union membership, achieving this goal mainly by seeking employment where union membership was not required. Doubtless other church members were in agreement with the union goals and programs of collective bargaining.

One 1989 item, repeated from the 1972 questionnaire, probed current attitudes toward union membership: "A church member should not join a union even if getting or holding a job depends on union membership." The statement elicited 18 percent agreement in 1972 and 14 percent agreement in 1989. Some members in all five denominations took this position, but the MC and BIC respondents had the largest minorities opposed to union membership—17 and 14 percent, respectively. With the general decline of unions in North America, and church leaders silent on the issue, opposition to union membership will likely continue to diminish.

Summary

In any society, observance of moral and ethical principles is vital to social order and congenial relationships between people. Each generation inherits past standards and alters them to fit new conditions.

Since their beginnings Mennonites have emphasized following Christ and, for the most part, not being conformed to the "kingdoms of this world." The history of Mennonites indicates considerable vacillation between laxness at some times and a too legalistic, authoritarian approach to morality at other times. Currently, educational strategies are displacing earlier conference regulations in dealing with moral and ethical issues.

The trend in recent decades has been toward greater acceptance of alcoholic beverages, dancing, and gambling among some members. On the other hand, opposition to abortion, smoking, and homosexual acts has increased. Favorable attitudes toward the poor and people of other races have slowly increased. However, religious conservatism seems to stand in the way of more accepting attitudes toward other races, while the more educated and urbanized members show greater racial acceptance. Higher scores on the Anabaptism scale showed a low but positive relationship to attitudes favoring racial equality and aid to the poor. There has been a substantial increase in Mennonite attitudes favoring expanded roles for women in church leadership.

On the average, liberal views were more typical of members who were young, urbanized, more highly educated, and more involved in community organizations. Those retaining the more conservative attitudes on personal morality and social ethics scored higher on scales measuring religious orthodoxy, personal piety, and church participation.

In general, the modernization of Mennonites means there is less difference than formerly between Mennonites and the larger society on some issues but not on others. The Mennonite mosaic is very evident in the wide range of views among members on moral and ethical issues. The sacred canopy covers views much more divergent *within* each Mennonite and Brethren in Christ denomination than between them, a matter to which we turn our attention in the next chapter.

CHAPTER 10

Comparing Mennonite Denominations

AT VARIOUS POINTS in previous chapters we presented data showing differences and similarities between the five Mennonite denominations that participated in the 1972 and 1989 member surveys. The purpose of this chapter is to focus on the main dimensions of these denominational differences and to present some evaluations and conclusions regarding the differences.[1] We will also check how the forces of modernization appear to be affecting the participating denominations in similar or different ways.

Comparing Christian Denominations

Before examining the variations among Mennonite denominations we need to locate Mennonites within the spectrum of North American Christianity as a whole. Various grounds for comparing Christian groups have been used, but none seems to be more prevalent in the literature than the conservative-liberal continuum. For some analytic purposes the continuum can be extended to include four positions: reactionary, conservative, liberal, and radical. Our purposes will be served adequately by referring to conservative and liberal positions only.

The Conservative-Liberal Continuum

Berger (1977:107) argued that the great majority of people in most human societies are conservative. Not all persons agree with that opinion, but for the conservative person the known status quo is less threatening than a vague or unknown alternative. The reactionary wants to return to an earlier state of affairs thought to be preferable. The liberal is dissatisfied with the status quo to a greater or lesser extent and promotes changes to bring about more desirable conditions. The radical tends to feel oppressed by existing conditions and wants to alter the system radically.

The tendency of individuals and groups to vary along conservative-liberal lines is just as true within the realm of religion as it is in politics, economics, and philosophy. In the first half of the twentieth century the conservative-liberal continuum was manifest in the heated fundamentalist-modernist controversy (Wuthnow, 1988:134). Since World War II the polarity has muted, but significant differences continue in a fundamentalist-evangelical-mainline Protestant pattern. In the United States in the 1980s, Jerry Falwell and the "Moral Majority" movement were openly fundamentalist in calling for a return to more traditional moral standards (Hadden and Shupe, 1988; Falwell, 1981). Billy Graham and the National Association of Evangelicals represent the middle group (Hunter, 1983), and the National Council of Churches—representing the largest cluster of Protestant denominations—is generally regarded as the liberal wing of Protestantism (Roof and McKinney, 1987).

As a by-product of the fundamentalist-modernist controversy in the 1920s and 1930s, several small fundamentalist groups split off from the Baptist and Presbyterian denominations. These and other strongly right-wing groups make up a small but sometimes vocal segment of North American Christianity today.

The rise of evangelicalism since World War II has focused on a less strident version of conservative Christianity, a version that has appealed to the middle class. Hunter (1983:46) argues that, in view of their declining membership, mainline Protestant denominations are showing "cognitive impotency," while conservative evangelicals have grown in numbers and are building strong and stable institutions. He quotes Martin Marty as saying that evangelicals have remained a cognitive minority but have emerged as a sociocultural majority. In Hunter's view evangelicals are based in the middle and lower socioeconomic echelons of American society, but not the very lowest levels.

As noted in chapter 9, Roof and McKinney (1987) posited three categories along the conservative-liberal continuum: Conservative Protestants (Southern Baptists, Churches of Christ, Nazarenes, Pentecostals, Assemblies of God, Churches of God, Adventists), Moderate Protestants (Methodists, Lutherans, Disciples of Christ, Northern Baptists, Reformed), and Liberal Protestants (Episcopalians, United Church of Christ, Presbyterians). Their analysis of data from the General Social Surveys validates these variations. However, survey data show that the views of members of a particular denomination vary greatly among themselves; each denomination is a composite of members whose views range from one end of the continuum to the other. Denominational differences reflect differences only in the averages for all members. Even the congregations within a denomination can be ranged along the continuum, and neither are the members of a particular congregation uniform in their religious views.

Wuthnow (1988:133) reported the results of a Gallup poll in which the American respondents were asked to identify themselves with reference to religious conservatism and liberalism. The results were 18 percent very conservative, 23 percent conservative, 24 percent liberal, and 19 percent very liberal. Another 16 percent could not identify themselves as either conservative or liberal. These data, obtained in 1984, show that most Americans think of themselves in terms of a conservative-liberal continuum, and they are evenly distributed among these categories. Wuthnow concluded (1988:138) that "the great divide between liberals and conservatives cuts directly through the middle of many of the established denominations." The recent theological controversies that emerged among the Missouri Synod Lutherans and Southern Baptists is testimony to the tendency of polarization to emerge *within* denominations.

Canadian religious surveys reveal denominational differences similar to those of the United States. Bibby (1987:109) concluded that conservative Protestants, and to a lesser degree Roman Catholics, exceed other groups (United Church, Anglicans, Lutherans, and Presbyterians) in their levels of commitment to traditional beliefs and the extent of their group involvement.

Mennonites Within the Christian Context

Where do Mennonites stand within the fundamentalist-evangelical-mainline Protestant continuum? Comparable data, though severely limited, are sufficient to provide a tentative answer to this question.

The measures of religious orthodoxy clearly place Mennonites at the conservative end of the general orthodoxy scale. The original survey by Stark and Glock (1968:30) included an item on belief in God. In their national sample 93 percent of the Southern Baptists chose the most conservative response ("I know God really exists and I have no doubts about it"). Other denominations ranged from 82 percent for American (northern) Baptists to 63 percent for the Congregational Church (now the United Church of Christ). Ninety percent of the Mennonites in the 1972 survey, and 88 percent in 1989, gave this response, putting them close to the Southern Baptists. The Stark and Glock surveys did not identify members of smaller conservative groups, like the Nazarenes and Adventists, whose responses might have been similar to those of the Southern Baptists.

On moral issues (abortion, homosexuality, premarital sex), as noted in chapter 9, Mennonites in 1989 were at least as conservative as other populations for which comparable data were available. Mennonites clearly do not fit the category of mainline Protestants.

Are Mennonites fundamentalists? Mennonite responses to doctrinal items in the fundamentalism scale (in chapter 3) were very conservative, probably not much different from responses a researcher might get from members of the small right-wing denominations. Hunter (1983:39) placed the Evangelical Mennonite Church among Protestant groups with strong fundamentalist leanings—for example, the Evangelical Free Church and the Christian Reformed. On issues of morality, Mennonites probably have much in common with fundamentalist and evangelical groups. On peace and social issues, however, Mennonites break company with fundamentalists, even with many evangelicals, and would be regarded as liberals within the Christian spectrum. Mennonites represent an unusual integration of highly conservative theological views with quite liberal social concerns, the latter growing out of their doctrine of love and nonresistance and their social activism manifested in their worldwide relief and service programs, noted in chapter 8.

Hunter (1983:7) placed Anabaptist groups within the evangelical category. He posited four major religious traditions in contemporary evangelicalism: (1) the Baptist tradition, (2) the Holiness-Pentecostal tradition, (3) the Anabaptist tradition, and (4) the Reformational-confessional tradition. Elaborating on the Anabaptist tradition, he noted that Anabaptist groups share with other evangelicals their concept of individual human salvation and their congregational polity, but they emphasize church community over the rights and privileges of individual believers more than do other evangelicals. Hunter noted also the Anabaptist distinctiveness in social activism, separation of church and state, and opposition to war and violence of any sort.

It is not easy to categorize Mennonites in terms of the conservative-liberal continuum. Although sharing some orthodox beliefs and moral codes with fundamentalists, Mennonites strongly disavow the stridency, nationalism, and militarism of fundamentalists. Although they share much with evangelicalism, Mennonites find more understanding and sympathy for their peace and social concerns among the more liberal mainline Protestant denominations.

How does the conservative-liberal continuum relate to the modernization variable? The survey reported on by Hunter (1983:52) showed that evangelicals are considerably more rural than the liberals. Hunter does not provide separate data for fundamentalists, but we hypothesize that they are even more rural, being strong in the rural South of the United States, in the Appalachian areas, and in the farming areas of the Midwest and the northern prairies.

Roof and McKinney (1987:134) reported that smaller proportions of liberal Protestants live in rural areas than do either the moderate or conservative Protestants. Denominations with the largest rural proportions are heavily located in the southern and midwestern portions of the United States and include Southern Baptists, Churches of Christ, Pentecostal-Holiness groups, and Churches of God, all of whom have large fundamentalist segments. Roof and McKinney's data also show that liberal Protestants have considerably higher socioeconomic status than do conservative Protestants.

On this basis we would expect the most modernized Mennonites to be the most liberal on scales measuring religiosity. There are some surprises ahead.

Variations in Mennonite Religiosity

Within the wider spectrum of North American Christianity, Mennonites would seem to occupy a narrow range more toward the conservative end of the continuum. Nevertheless, a considerable distance exists between the most and least conservative groups. At the conservative extreme are the Old Order Amish, Old Order Mennonite, and Old Colony Mennonites of Canada. Their Anabaptist cousins, the Hutterites, are also at the conservative end, characterized by a more complete ethnic identity than are all the other Canadian ethnoreligious groups described by Driedger (1989:149).

At the more liberal end of the Mennonite rainbow are the five groups that participated in the 1972 and 1989 surveys. Therefore our respondents represent only the more "liberal" portion of the Mennonite continuum. In the Mennonite context the term liberal is valid only in contrast to the more conservative segments. A "liberal" Mennonite is a conservative within the wider Christian spectrum.

In comparing these five Mennonite denominations we are dealing with relatively small differences. Previous chapters reported some important differences, but we do not wish to overemphasize these. Indeed, the similarities between these five Mennonite bodies are more significant than their differences. Their similarities have been the basis for the development of many interdenominational organizations and projects (Kraybill, 1974).

There are greater differences *within* the denominations than there are *between* them. This is evident from the range of scores on the scales that were developed from the questionnaire items. On all scales the members of each denomination ranged from one extreme to the other, with average scores not varying much among the denominations.

Figure 10-1, which shows the distribution of scores on the pacifism scale, illustrates the overlapping response distributions. The range of scores for the respondents of each denomination was similar to the ranges of the others, with the MC and GC curves somewhat more toward higher scores and the BIC and EMC curves more toward lower scores. Average (mean) scores were as follows: EMC, 13.7; BIC, 16.3; MB, 17.4; GC, 19.1; and MC, 19.3. Obviously the range of mean scores (5.6) *between* denominations was much smaller than the range of individual scores (roughly 20) *within* denominations.

On other scales the distribution curves generally were closer together than they were on the pacifism scale. For example, the distributions on the devotionalism scale had a range from 7 to 35 for MB and BIC respondents, 8 to 35 for MC and GC respondents, and 10 to 35 for the EMC respondents. The means ranged from 25.5 for the GCs to 27.3 for the MBs—a range of only 1.8 points. When comparable data were available in 1972, such as the Stark and Glock surveys of orthodoxy of beliefs in several Protestant denominations, the differences among Mennonite bodies proved much smaller than the differences between Mennonite bodies and other Protestant denominations (Kauffman and Harder, 1975:107).

This analysis raises the question of whether we are studying one Mennonite body or five. Within the broader spectrum of Christian denominations, Mennonite groups are sufficiently alike to be thought of as one body. Within the Mennonite spectrum, however, even within the "liberal" wing, there are enough differences to justify the comparisons drawn in this analysis.

We turn now to an analysis of the differences, however small, that do appear among the five groups. Our method for doing this is to utilize rankings on 37 scales that were either introduced in previous chapters or, in a few cases, will be introduced in this chapter. We use rankings as a summary device so that we do not simply repeat the comparisons made in earlier chapters on the basis of responses to individual questionnaire items.

In order to present summaries in as clear a form as possible, we have clustered the 37 scales into eight groups: demographic modernization, religious beliefs, religious practices, personal morality, social ethics, in-group identity, openness to the larger society, and concomitants of modernization. This shows the ranking on each of the 37 scales and also a *group* ranking, which facilitates generalization at a higher level—the

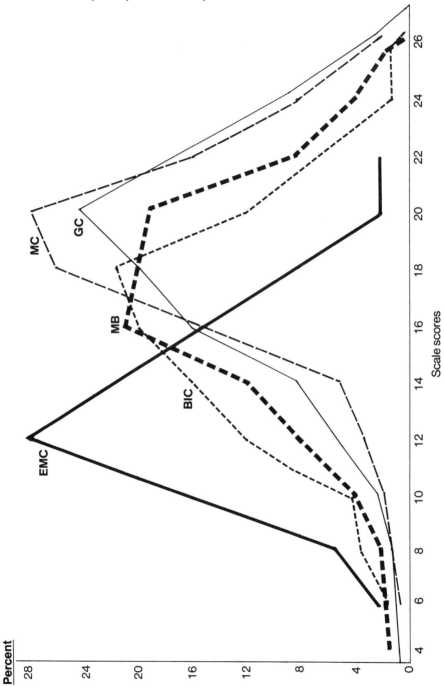

Figure 10-1. Distribution of Scores on the Pacifism Scale

major dimensions of our analysis (beliefs, practices, moral issues, ethical issues, in-group identity, and others).

Before introducing the specific measures of Mennonite religiosity, we need to recall the variations among the five denominations on the indicators of modernization. With that background to our analysis, we can then relate each of the major dimensions of religiosity to the modernization theme.

Indicators of Modernization

In chapter 1 five indicators of modernization were introduced: urbanization, education, occupational rank, income, and mobility. Table 10-1 indicates how the denominations ranked on each of these dimensions. The rankings are based on the mean scores computed for each dimension. The overall ranking for each denomination was obtained by totaling the individual ranks.

Table 10-1. Denominational Rankings* on Indicators of Modernization

Indicators	MC	GC	MB	BIC	EMC
Urbanization (residence)	4	2	1	5	3
Educational achievement	5	3	1	4	2
Income level	3	5	1	4	2
Occupational rank	3	4	1	5	2
Frequency of mobility	3	5	2	1	4
Totals of ranks	18	19	6	19	13
Overall ranking	3	4	1	4	2

*On these and subsequent tables, number 1 is the first or highest rank; 5 is the lowest rank.

On the basis of these measures, the Mennonite Brethren were the most modernized group in 1989, with the Evangelical Mennonites in second place. The General Conference Mennonites and the Brethren in Christ shared the position of least modernization, with the Mennonite Church close to their ranking. It will be interesting to see how these rankings on modernization are associated with rankings on the religiosity. We also need to explore the relationship of modernization rankings to the conservative-liberal continuum, insofar as it is possible to discern such a continuum among these five denominations.

Beliefs and Bible Knowledge

Measures of religious beliefs and Bible knowledge, major dimensions of Mennonite identity, were introduced in chapter 3. On the basis of scale means, Table 10-2 gives the rankings of the denominations on the scales measuring general orthodoxy, fundamentalist orthodoxy, Anabaptism, and Bible knowledge. Because the Anabaptism scale represents a different aspect of belief from that of the other belief scales, it is not included in the total rankings for the other three variables.

Table 10-2. Denominational Rankings on Beliefs

Scales	MC	GC	MB	BIC	EMC
General orthodoxy	4	5	2	3	1
Fundamentalist orthodoxy	4	5	3	2	1
Bible knowledge	4	3	1	5	2
Totals of ranks	12	13	6	10	4
Overall ranking	4	5	2	3	1
Anabaptism	1	3	2	4	5

On orthodoxy of doctrinal beliefs, the EMC, BIC, and MB members ranked higher, and the MC and GCM members lower. Combining Bible knowledge with the other two rankings placed the MBs second overall. The rankings on both orthodoxy scales were the same in 1989 as they were in 1972 (Kauffman and Harder, 1975:106-12). If the MB and EMC members ranked highest on dimensions of modernization, why did they also rank highest on orthodox beliefs? One would expect that the most modernized groups would evidence diminished strength of conservative beliefs and Bible knowledge. We will address this matter in a later section, with additional data.

Rankings on the Anabaptism scale were similar in both surveys, with MC and MB members ranking highest and EMC members lowest. This finding was in line with expectations, since acceptance of 16th-century Anabaptism represents an in-group viewpoint. As we shall see later in this chapter, the Mennonite Church was the most sectarian denomination (ranking highest on in-group identity, communalism, and separatism), and the Mennonite Brethren were either second or third on these scales. Acceptance of Anabaptist principles is likely related more to in-group loyalties than to modernization. Otherwise, the MBs, being the most modernized group, would rate lowest on Anabaptism. However, the Evangelical Mennonite Church, the second most modernized and the least sectarian group (as shown later), was consistently the lowest on Anabaptism.

Religious Practice

In this section we will summarize the denominational rankings on four variables that represent active church participation and personal piety. These measures reflect what church members *do* in the practice of their faith, rather than what they *believe*. To review, church participation constitutes attendance at church services, providing leadership in the congregation, and viewing participation in the church as very important. Devotionalism includes private prayer and Bible study, family worship, prayer at meals, and a sense of close relationship with God. Evangelism involves witnessing to the Christian faith, inviting non-Christians to attend church, and leading persons to faith in Christ. Stewardship is defined as the percentage of net household income given to church and charities and is included here as an additional facet of religious practice.[2] Table 10-3 reports the denominational rankings on these measures of religious practice.

Table 10-3. Rankings on Religious Practice

Scales	MC	GC	MB	BIC	EMC
Church participation	4	5	3	2	1
Devotionalism	4	5	1	3	2
Evangelism	4	5	1	3	2
Stewardship	3	4	2	5	1
Totals of ranks	15	19	7	13	6
Overall ranking	4	5	2	3	1

Once again the most modernized groups (MB and EMC) ranked highest, and the least urbanized (GC and MC) ranked lowest, in this case on measures of religious activity and personal piety. These findings do not support the hypothesis that modernization leads to diminished religious practice. One more set of findings will be added before we attempt an interpretation of these results.

Personal Morality

Findings on church members' attitudes and behavior with respect to moral issues were presented in chapter 9. Mennonite groups differ somewhat in the degree to which they have opposed such behaviors as smoking, drinking, dancing, gambling, attendance at X-rated movies, and premarital intercourse. The moral attitudes scale was constructed from nine items, in each case the respondents indicated whether they regarded the behavior as wrong. In 1972 the respondents were asked to report their actual behavior on only three such behaviors: smoking tobacco, drinking alcoholic beverages, and social dancing. From these three items a moral behavior scale was constructed.[3]

Another scale (not introduced earlier) was constructed to provide a more comprehensive measure of restrictive attitudes toward moral issues. This scale incorporated all 19 items on moral issues in the 1989 questionnaire, for which the possible responses were "always wrong," "sometimes wrong," and "never wrong." A respondent with the most re-strictive views would have checked "always wrong" on all 19 items.[4]

Finally, we introduce here a fourth scale measuring moral values and combining responses to four items. The respondents were asked to rate the importance of each of the following: "living a good moral life," "being obedient to the standards and teachings of my church," "keeping myself from being influenced by the world's values," and "living the sim-ple life."[5]

These four scales provide a fairly extensive assessment of Menno-nites' attitudes and behavior with respect to moral issues that the churches in recent decades have debated, and in some cases legislated on. Table 10-4 reports the denominational rankings on these scales.

Table 10-4. Rankings on Moral Issues

Scales	MC	GC	MB	BIC	EMC
Moral attitudes	5	2	4	1	3
Moral restrictiveness	3	5	4	1	2
Moral values	4	5	3	1	2
Moral behavior	1	5	2	4	3
Totals of ranks	13	17	13	7	10
Overall ranking	3	5	3	1	2

On these measures the Brethren in Christ had the highest ranking, with the Evangelical Mennonites second. The Mennonite Church and Mennonite Brethren tied for third rank, and the General Conference Mennonites were lowest. Thus, as in beliefs and religious practice, the MC and GC denominations were low, but the other three had shifted a bit in their ranking. Nevertheless, the more modernized groups ranked higher, as indicated earlier in this chapter.

It is now appropriate to attempt an explanation regarding the rejec-tion of the hypothesis that the more modernized groups would prove to hold more liberal views. We have found religiosity (measured in terms of beliefs, religious practice, and moral attitudes and behavior) to be greater rather than less in the more urbanized and modernized Mennonite bod-ies. Conservative religiosity still characterizes the most modernized groups, the Mennonite Brethren and the Evangelical Mennonites.

One possible explanation is that the differences between the more urbanized and less urbanized groups are so small that the observed rela-tionship between modernity and religiosity is due to chance. Another possibility is that our measures of modernity have questionable validity—an idea that the data do not really support. Would secularism, individualism, and materialism be better measures of modernity? We will have occasion to look into this possibility later in the chapter.

A third possible explanation is that countervailing religious forces offset the forces of modernization (urbanization, higher socioeconomic status, higher education), and that such forces are operating more strongly in the MB and EMC groups than within the others. This theory was introduced in chapter 1, in Figure 1-4 in particular, where secularization and sacralization were portrayed as dialectical forces operating between modernization and religiosity.

Peter Hamm (1987) has examined this theory. In his sociological analysis of Mennonite Brethren in Canada he (1987:248-49) argued that sacralizing forces offset the effects of secularization in the MB context. He wrote (1987:248-49):

> Empirically, almost all Mennonite Brethren witness to a conversion experience. Moreover, they continue to seek intense religious experiences subsequent to conversion and a rather active devotional life and personal witness. Sporadic renewals through revival have further brought vitality. . . . The overwhelming impact of these components of religiosity was integrating and helped to sacralize the identity of Canadian Mennonite Brethren.

Hamm's conclusions were based in part on the MB data in the 1972 survey. The 1989 data also appear to support these conclusions on the basis of comparisons between MBs and the other denominations in the survey. Although spiritual renewal emphases are found in all five denominations, general information indicates that the EMC, MB, and BIC groups are more intensively involved in evangelistic efforts than the others.

There is one other dimension of this issue that must be examined. *Within* the MB population, do the rural and urban segments differ in respect to religiosity? The MB data indicate a modest correlation between urbanization and educational achievement (r=.16), occupational rank (.16), and income (.11). These latter are the three elements in the socioeconomic status scale. Correlations between religiosity and urban residence and between religiosity and socioeconomic status help to answer the question. Table 10-5 gives the relevant data.

Both measures of modernization (urban residence and higher SES) had no significant effect on MB scores on Anabaptism, devotionalism, church participation, and evangelism, since the correlation coefficients were .08 or less with the exception of the association between SES and church participation (.19). Urban residence had small negative effects on the orthodoxy and morality scales, and SES had somewhat greater negative effects. Thus, modernization did have small negative effects on the

Table 10-5. Correlations Between Modernization and Religiosity, Mennonite Brethren Data Only

Scales	Urban residence	SES
General orthodoxy	-.10	-.15
Fundamentalist orthodoxy	-.15	-.37
Anabaptism	.02	-.05
Devotionalism	-.04	-.02
Church participation	-.01	.19
Evangelism	.05	.05
Moral attitudes	-.16	-.23
Moral behavior	-.11	-.18

Note: For MBs only, coefficients must be greater than .08 or less than -.08 to be significant at the .05 level.

MB population in respect to these religiosity variables.

The general hypothesis that modernization has negative effects on religiosity is supported, although very weakly, by the MB data. The data for the Evangelical Mennonites yielded similar results. We conclude, with Hamm, that the sacralizing forces among the MBs sufficiently offset forces of modernization so that, despite their greater modernization, the MBs rate highest on religiosity.

Perhaps this conclusion applies to all five of the Mennonite and BIC groups. If so, it is in line with Hunter's observations on the growth of evangelicalism in an age of modernization. According to Hunter (1983:134), modernity creates certain circumstances that evoke the bold reassertion of religious meanings, which, in turn, counter the impact of modernization. A revival or renewal of religious interest may occur among individuals and groups that feel threatened by modernization.

Social Ethics

We turn next to the cluster of variables that reveal Mennonite attitudes on ethical issues, namely, war and peace, welfare aid for the poor, and social equality for women and other races. All of the relevant scales were introduced in previous chapters. Table 10-6 indicates the denominational rankings for these variables.

GC and MC members rated highest in support of these social issues. These groups have given much more attention to social issues in their publications and in conference debates and resolutions, and support positions closer to those of the liberal, mainline Protestant denominations. The other groups, particularly the EMC, reflect their stronger orientation within the orbit of the National Association of Evangelicals where discussion of social issues is muted. As Kauffman reported (1989:372), *The Christian Century* and *Christianity and Crisis* have frequent articles on pacifism and peace movements, but these topics seem to be missing from the evangelical *Christianity Today*. The same can be said for the treatment of other social issues that the more conservative groups tend to sidestep for being too strongly identified with liberalism.

Table 10-6. Rankings on Ethical Issues

Scales	MC	GC	MB	BIC	EMC
Pacifism	1	2	3	4	5
Race relations	2	3	1	4	5
Welfare attitudes	2	1	3	4	5
Role of women	2	1	4	3	5
Women in congregational leadership	2	1	4	3	5
Totals of ranks	9	8	15	18	25
Overall ranking	2	1	3	4	5

We are faced with a real dilemma among Mennonites. The biblical literalism of Mennonites teaches that Christians should love their enemies, feed the hungry, clothe the naked, visit the sick and those in prison, and show love to all persons, whatever their race or sex. Why then did the groups that scored highest on dimensions of religiosity score lowest on pacifism and social concerns? The dilemma is not peculiar to Mennonites, but seems to be present within general Christendom. Why do the religiously conservative show the least interest in social causes? Do they feel that since the liberals promote these causes, they must avoid them? Do they see the liberals as "soft on sin" in respect to issues of morality (abortion, homosexual relations, divorce, etc.) and then refuse to get involved where the liberals are doing good? Do the conservatives dissociate themselves from the "sinners" (whom they may have excommunicated or failed to win) in order not to contaminate members within their own borders?

There is a good middle ground, and some Mennonite groups are working at finding it. While working to retain a strong evangelical religiosity, there can also be a strong concern to help the poor and oppressed as Christ taught his followers to do. This is current agenda for Mennonites and other Christian bodies.

Variations in Orientation

In this section we will review differences among Mennonite bodies regarding the degree to which they emphasize in-group sentiments.

Some groups are more open than others to interaction with people and organizations beyond the boundaries of the Mennonite family and community.

In-group Identity

As noted earlier, Mennonites in recent decades have shown evidence of a gradual accommodation to the mainstream of North American society, in terms of adopting the national language, food habits, commercial interests, and other practices. Nevertheless, many sectarian or in-group attitudes still exist, particularly among the more conservative groups. Of course, the most sectarian characteristics are found among groups not included in the survey, such as the Hutterites and the Old Order Amish.

The five participating denominations demonstrated considerable variation in their ethnocentrism and in-group attitudes. By their institutional completeness (their own schools, homes for the aged, mutual aid programs, etc.) some groups exhibited more concern for boundary maintenance than did others. This variation is evident in a summary of the rankings on a number of scales measuring in-group orientation, introduced in earlier chapters (see Table 10-7).

Table 10-7. Rankings on In-group Orientation

Scales	MC	GC	MB	BIC	EMC
In-group identity	1	2	4	3	5
Communalism	1	2	3	4	5
Separatism	2	5	1	4	3
Separation of church and state	3	5	4	2	1
Support of church colleges	2	3	1	4	5
Support of MCC	3	1	2	4	5
Totals of ranks	12	18	15	21	24
Overall ranking	1	3	2	4	5

Based on these measures, the Mennonite Church had the strongest in-group attitudes, followed by the Mennonite Brethren. The Evangelical Mennonites ranked lowest, demonstrating the most openness to the general society, as will be further noted in the next section of this chapter. Contrary to the general pattern, the Evangelical Mennonites evidenced most separatism on the scale measuring separation of church and state. This may be due to the specific content of the scale. Two of the three items in the scale have to do with the role of the church in trying to influence the government and society on moral and ethical issues, an area of less interest to the EMC. In the previous section we observed that the

EMC ranked lowest on concern for ethical issues. However, the EMC was the most favorable of the denominations on two items of government regulation, namely, capital punishment and allowing prayer in the public schools. This suggests that separation of church and state is favored more in some areas of regulation than in others.

The rankings on communalism were the same in 1989 as in 1972. The in-group identity and separatism scales were not used in 1972. On support of MCC, the GCs were highest and EMCs lowest in both surveys, but there was some shifting in middle rankings. Likewise, while there was no change in highest and lowest rankings on support of church colleges, there were shifts in middle rankings. Again, it must be emphasized that we are speaking of small rather than large differences between the denominations.

Openness to the Larger Society

The opposite of in-group separateness is integration or accommodation to the larger society. The Mennonite and Brethren in Christ groups varied somewhat in the degree to which their members interacted with agencies and organizations beyond their own church boundaries. We expected that the groups ranking highest on in-group identity would rank lowest on openness to the larger society. The findings, given in Table 10-8, support this expectation.

To review the content of the scales, ecumenism (detailed later in the chapter) measures favorableness toward cooperation and integration with other Mennonite groups and with non-Mennonite denominations. A respondent's score on the memberships scale is the number of community organizations in which he or she holds membership. Political participation represents favorableness toward voting, officeholding, and speaking to government. The political action scale indicates whether the respondents feel that it is proper for their local congregations to get involved in the political process. The number of mass media devices (TVs, VCRs, cable TV, satellite dishes, video cameras) in the respondent's home determines his or her score on the mass media scale. These are rough measures of the degree to which the church members are "networking" within the larger society, beyond the orbit of their churches.

In line with expectations, the Evangelical Mennonites, lowest on in-group identity, ranked highest on openness, despite a low ranking on ecumenism. MC members, who ranked first on in-group identity, were least open to the larger society. The other three denominations tied for middle rank, reminding us once again of the closeness of these groups to each other. There are much greater differences within the denominations than between them.

Table 10-8. Rankings on Openness to the Larger Society

Scales	MC	GC	MB	BIC	EMC
Ecumenism	2	1	3	4	5
Memberships in community organizations	4	3	5	2	1
Political participation	5	3	2	4	1
Political action	5	4	3	2	1
Mass media devices	5	4	2	3	1
Totals of ranks	21	15	15	15	9
Overall ranking	5	3	3	3	1

The 1989 rankings on ecumenism were similar to those of 1972. There was a shift in political rankings. In 1972 the GCs ranked highest on both political scales, but third and fourth in 1989, with the EMCs at the top. The MCs were lowest on the political scales in both years. The memberships and mass media scales were not included in the 1972 analysis.

Concomitants of Modernization

Denominational rankings on the demographic dimensions of modernization were reported earlier in this chapter. In this section we will report rankings on the four concomitants of modernization introduced in chapters 3 and 4, namely, secularization, individualism, materialism, and personal independence. The rankings are given in Table 10-9.

Table 10-9. Rankings on Concomitants of Modernization

Scales	MC	GC	MB	BIC	EMC
Secularism	2	1	4	3	5
Individualism	2	1	5	3	4
Personal independence	5	1	3	2	4
Materialism	5	4	3	1	2
Total of ranks	14	7	15	9	15
Overall ranking	3	1	4	2	4

The overall ranking on these variables is puzzling. Why were the MB and EMC groups lowest on these scales when they were highest on the demographic modernization scales? And why did the GC and BIC groups rank first and second on these measures when they ranked lowest on demographic modernization? These outcomes are surprising in view of the expectation that the more modernized groups would have had higher scores on the concomitants of modernization.

Given relatively small differences among the participating denominations, one might assume that the contradiction is merely a statistical aberration. Since this is not likely, a deeper explanation must be sought.[6]

In chapter 4 we noted that urban residence and income level were unrelated to secularism, individualism, and materialism. However, higher educational levels and occupational status were associated with *lower* scores on the concomitants of modernization. The data also revealed, as expected, a substantial negative correlation between measures of religiosity (beliefs, practice, and personal morality) and the concomitants of modernization. We conclude that the Mennonite Brethren and Evangelical Mennonites ranked low on the concomitants because they ranked high on the religiosity variables—a condition that overcame the expected relationship between the demographic indicators of modernization and the concomitants.

There remains yet the question of *why* higher educational and occupational status were *negatively* correlated with the concomitants of modernization. This finding may be peculiar to a Mennonite population and might not occur in other populations. Many Mennonites who received a higher education and entered professional occupations were products of Mennonite colleges and seminaries, which inculcate in-group values. As noted in chapter 6, the respondents who attended Mennonite institutions of higher education scored higher on most religiosity scales than did those who studied elsewhere. This finding suggests that in-group education has offset an expected positive correlation between higher education and other measures of modernization.

Mennonites and Ecumenism

Prior to 1940, efforts to bring separate Mennonite bodies into cooperative and joint programs represent a rather painful chapter in the history of North American Mennonites. From its beginning, the General Conference Mennonite Church has been the most active in trying to foster unity and cooperation among independent congregations and conferences—efforts that have often failed (Dyck, 1967; Schlabach, 1988). Schlabach (1980:79-80) has recorded the failure of an inter-Mennonite foreign mission attempt, and Ainlay (1990b) has reported the events leading to a breakdown in the efforts of certain GC and MC leaders to form a joint seminary. These are only two examples of the many spurned efforts to create joint programs. More recently the picture has changed.

In chapter 6 we noted that many inter-Mennonite agencies and institutions have emerged in recent decades. In 1974 Kraybill (1974) listed 72 organizations that had been formed jointly by two or more Mennonite denominations, and many more have emerged since that date. Currently the General Conference Mennonite Church and the Mennonite Church are exploring integration and possible merger. These movements are evidence of developing ecumenism among Mennonites. There are also indications that Mennonites are cooperating more extensively with other Christian denominations at local community levels and in wider contexts. In this section we will report on Mennonite attitudes toward greater cooperation among Mennonite bodies and between Mennonites and other Christian bodies.

Measuring Ecumenism

Three questionnaire items were used to explore ecumenical attitudes among Mennonites and to form an ecumenism scale. The first item probed respondents' attitudes toward cooperation among the various Mennonite denominations; the second, attitudes about cooperative activities among local congregations of different (Mennonite or non-Mennonite) denominations; the third, attitudes about the respondent's denomination uniting with another denomination. Table 10-10 records the percent of respondents favoring increased cooperation between denominations.

Table 10-10. Responses to Items on Ecumenism

Items	Percent in 1989					Totals	
	MC	GC	MB	BIC	EMC	1972	1989
Favor increased cooperation between Mennonite branches	64	72	65	50	42	70	64
Favor increased cooperation between local congregations of different denominations	61	73	65	63	50	57	65
Favor uniting with another Mennonite or BIC group	23	22	14	10	7	15	20

In 1989 about two-thirds of respondents favored increased cooperation at denominational and local levels. Between 1972 and 1989 there was a 6 percent drop in respondents favoring increased cooperation between Mennonite denominations, but an 8 percent increase favoring cooperation at the local level between congregations of different denominations. The General Conference Mennonites were most favorable and the Evangelical Mennonites least favorable toward increased cooperation. Only one-fifth of the respondents favored actual union of denominations, with MC and GC members showing the most interest.

Those who favored uniting with another denomination were asked which denomination they would prefer to unite with. Among all groups, the MC and GC members most frequently chose each other, thus indicating support for the current official exploration of integration between these two groups. However, in 1989 less than a fourth of the respondents in these two groups favored uniting with other denominations.

Variations in Ecumenical Attitudes

Scale intercorrelations showed a positive correlation between ecumenism and modernization, general openness to the larger society, and liberal attitudes on social issues. Ecumenism was negatively related to doctrinal orthodoxy and moral attitudes. Ecumenism had almost zero correlations with Anabaptism, religious practice, in-group identity, and the concomitants of modernization.

Younger and older respondents did not differ significantly in their ecumenical attitudes (for age, r= -.04). The relationship of ecumenism to modernization variables was positive but not strong: urban residence, .15; education, .17; and socioeconomic status, .14. Correlations with social ethics variables were as follows: pacifism, .22; race relations, .21; welfare attitudes, .24; and expanded roles for women, .33. The correlation was .16 with political participation and .19 with political action.

These findings suggest that church members who favor cooperation with other Christian churches are more ready to reach out to individuals and groups in the larger society. They are more concerned about the poor and members of other races. They are more ready to participate in the political process. In general, they are more modernized than those who are averse to ecumenical efforts.

The findings fit the model of the conservative-liberal continuum. Since World War II liberal mainline Protestant denominations have been more involved than evangelicals in denominational mergers and other ecumenical efforts. Mennonites show similar patterns. Those favoring ecumenism have more liberal attitudes on other issues. Those less favorable toward ecumenism scored higher on fundamentalism (r= -.27) and on general orthodoxy (r= -.13).

Summary

One purpose of this chapter was to locate Mennonites within the spectrum of Christian denominations, using a conservative-liberal continuum for locating fundamentalists, evangelicals, and liberal mainline Protestants. Some Mennonites and Brethren in Christ fall in the fundamentalist position. In regard to doctrinal orthodoxy, religious practices, moral codes, and separatism, Mennonites reflect evangelical emphasis. On peace and social issues, Mennonites find more congeniality with mainline Protestants.

A second purpose of this chapter was to present and analyze the differences among the five denominations participating in the 1989 survey. Although the differences were relatively small compared to differences between these and other Christian denominations, they were of sufficient concern and interest to merit our attention. The five groups cooperate and work together in many organizations, notably the Mennonite Central Committee, the Mennonite World Conference, many workshops and study conferences, Christian education projects, and many interdenominational councils, such as the Council of Mennonite Colleges. The success of these interdenominational activities attests to the prevailing similarities among the denominations.

In summarizing differences that do exist, we established rankings on the various dimensions of religiosity and social ethics that were included within the scope of the research. It is noteworthy that each of the five groups ranked highest on one or more measures.

The Evangelical Mennonites ranked highest on beliefs and Bible knowledge and on openness to the larger society. They were second highest on measures of religious practice and personal morality. On the basis of demographics, they were second most modernized.

The Brethren in Christ had the highest ranking on issues of personal morality. They tended toward middle ranking on most scales.

From the standpoint of demographics, the Mennonite Brethren were the most modernized. However, they rated highest on measures of religious practice and were the second highest on beliefs and Bible knowledge, Anabaptism, and in-group identity.

The General Conference Mennonites were the highest on dimensions of social ethics, indicating their strong concern for alleviating the problems of church and society. They were the highest also on the concomitants of modernization.

The conservatism of the Mennonite Church is evident in its highest ranking on Anabaptism and in-group identity, and lowest ranking on openness to the larger society. However, MC members were more liberal on aspects of social ethics, where they ranked second.

It is noteworthy that GC and MC members held adjacent rankings on four of the nine clusters of rankings, and were only two ranks apart on four others. The GCs and MBs held adjacent rankings on two of the clusters; MCs and MBs on six; MBs and EMCs on five; MBs and BICs on four; GCs and BICs on five; and GCs and EMCs on one.

The data explored in this chapter, together with supplementary analyses from previous chapters, led to the conclusion that the forces of modernization are having minor negative effects on Mennonites and Brethren in Christ. The negative effects would be greater if not offset by sacralizing forces and church-related higher education.

CHAPTER 11

Sorting the Indicators of Modernization

IN PREVIOUS CHAPTERS we presented data showing that the Mennonite mosaic contains considerable diversity with respect to religious beliefs, attitudes, and behavior. Although sufficient consensus exists to identify a Mennonite sacred canopy, underneath that canopy the church members reveal a wide spectrum of views on many issues. The spectrum would likely be even broader if we were to include in our survey members of Mennonite congregations on other continents.

The Increasing Pluralism of Mennonites

Sources of Increasing Pluralism

One source of increasing pluralism among Mennonites is the growing internationalization of Mennonites. According to the data assembled by Lichdi (1990) in the *Mennonite World Handbook*, in 1989 there were 856,600 members of Mennonite bodies in Africa, Asia, Australia, Europe, North America, and South America. These members speak some 78 different native languages. Very soon the number of Mennonites in Africa, Asia, and Latin America will outnumber those in the older communities in Europe and North America. Nowhere was this Mennonite pluralism more in evidence than in the 1990 Mennonite World Conference held in Winnipeg, Manitoba, where a variety of native languages, costumes, and music forms were displayed from the platform. Future research will need to portray more accurately the variety of beliefs, worship patterns, social customs, and moral and ethical standards of these worldwide followers of Menno. By comparison, the differences between the Canadian and American respondents in our survey were very small.

Race composition is also a factor in Mennonite pluralism. Yoder's (1985:313) 1982 census of the Mennonite Church in Canada and the United States indicated that 10,259 individuals (7% of the population) were members of minority groups—3,613 blacks, 672 American Indians, 1927 Asians, and 4,047 Hispanics. The racial composition of the other groups in our survey is not available. The variant characteristics of Mennonite minority groups await further research, since the number of minority members in the 1972 and 1989 samples was too small to make reliable comparisons between racial categories.

Denominational differences is another source of Mennonite pluralism. North American Mennonites and Brethren in Christ are organized into some 22 separate bodies, ranging from a few thousand members to over 100,000 in the case of the largest body (Horsch, 1990:207). The spread from the most conservative bodies to the more liberal groups in our surveys was noted in chapter 10, together with the detailed analysis of the differences between the five participating denominations. As Wuthnow (1988:72) points out, denominationalism and interfaith divisions continue to be one of the essential features of American religion. Roof and McKinney (1985:26) state that since the middle of the 20th century the United States has become much more pluralistic in its religious life. Mennonites have provided more than their share of this North American pluralism.

The form of pluralism that we present in this chapter is the variation in beliefs, attitudes, and behavior among the individuals that comprise the membership of the churches. Earlier chapters in this volume have documented the wide range of responses to questions regarding beliefs and behaviors.

Mennonites and Brethren in Christ show the least diversity with respect to theological beliefs. Data presented in chapter 3 indicate that less than 10 percent diverge from the most orthodox position on doctrinal items. More diversity is found in adherence to 16th-century Anabaptist principles.

With respect to issues of a moral or ethical nature, however, wide attitudinal differences appear. Why do such variations appear when we found fairly uniform religious traditions and practices? Are the variations a matter of age and gender differences, possibly reflecting a generation gap? Is this growing pluralism due to increasing educational, occupational, and income diversity, or the changes wrought by increasing urbanization? Can these factors explain the variations among the participants in our survey?

Sociologists believe that people vary in their beliefs and behavior according to their social environments. That is, people are rigid or flexible, conservative or liberal, religious or nonreligious, depending on the social conditions within which they live. If their life conditions change, their views will also change. Political or religious views will become more conservative as persons gain wealth, grow older, or join organizations of a different social rank (Niebuhr, 1929; Roof and McKinney, 1987:106-47).

The Indicators of Modernization

In this chapter we will explore differences among church members on the basis of several indicators of modernization that were identified in chapter 1: urbanization, educational achievement, occupational rank, income levels, and mobility. We will also explore variations among church members on the basis of age and gender. We do not expect that such factors will explain all variations observed. Even if we were to select a subsample of members of the same gender, age, residence, marital status, and socioeconomic status we would expect to find residual variations within that subsample. Such variations would be due in part to the freedom that individuals have to choose between social and religious options. Individual responsibility to God and associates assumes that people are rational beings, capable of making choices for good or bad, for gain or loss, in personal and corporate dimensions. Attitudes reflect rational choices at least in part, and are not wholly determined by social factors. As Rodney Stark (1990) put it, in defense of rational choice theory, "one could not do 'attitude research' on any basis other than the belief that cognitive factors are of primary importance."

In seeking to identify sources of doctrinal unity and diversity, Wuthnow (1983) summarized four popularly held arguments on the origin of an individual's Christian beliefs: (1) the programs of the church itself, (2) early religious socialization, (3) characteristics of a person's social biography, and (4) deeper concerns characteristic of the human condition. Using a "Salience of Faith Index" derived from data on Lutheran Church members, Wuthnow concluded that there is a strong relationship between faith and participation in church programs. He found little support for "the idea that religious commitment is largely a product of early religious training or the idea that it is mainly a function of one's social position." However, he observed some differences in "salience of faith" on the basis of church members' education, gender, age, and geographic region.

Modernization as Increasing Urbanization

We turn now to an examination of the differences in beliefs, attitudes, and behavior of Mennonites on the basis of Wuthnow's third argument, namely, the social or demographic characteristics of the respondents. How much difference between individuals can be explained by the shift of Mennonites from rural to urban residence?

Table 11-1. Demographic Variations by Residence

Variables	Residence			
	Rural farm	Rural nonfarm	Small city	Large city
Education				
Percent high school graduates	72	76	81	83
Percent college graduates	18	29	38	46
Socioeconomic status				
Percent professional occupation	14	25	31	40
Median household income	$28,333	29,672	30,279	36,111
Mobility				
Percent lived in community less than five years	6	12	16	16
Percent nonresident members	4	6	7	10
Percent ever a member of another denomination	20	25	31	28
Family characteristics				
Percent ever divorced or separated	3	4	4	7
Percent married women employed	54	58	52	61
Median number of children (persons 30 years and older)	3.2	2.8	2.9	2.4
Median number of persons living in household	3.6	2.9	2.8	2.8

Urbanization and Demographic Trends

We have assumed that urbanization is a major facet of modernization. Before examing the effects of urbanization on religious beliefs and attitudes, we will note the relationship of urbanization to other demographic trends among Mennonites.

In chapter 1 we demonstrated (see Table 1-5) that urban Mennonites have significantly more education, higher socioeconomic status, more liberal political leanings, and more favorable attitude toward expanded roles for women. Table 11-1 shows additional demographic comparisons, following residence categories outlined in chapter 1 and grouping variables according to indicators of modernization plus family characteristics.

Among rural Mennonites in 1989 slightly smaller proportions had completed a high school education, and substantially fewer persons had gained a college degree. The higher socioeconomic status of urban residents was evident in the substantially larger proportions entering professional occupations and in their somewhat higher household incomes. However, the urban incomes may not be sufficiently larger to offset the higher costs of living in cities.

Urban Mennonites had greater residential mobility, indicated by the slightly larger proportions who had moved within the last five years and currently were not residing near the congregations of which they were members. A slightly larger proportion of urban persons moved their church affiliation from another denomination to a Mennonite or Brethren in Christ church.

In regard to family characteristics, the number of children in families and the number of persons in households was about one-third larger on farms than in large cities. Rates of female employment and broken marriages moved upward with urbanization.

Urbanization and Changes in Religious Values

In regard to religious values, one would expect people living in rural areas, especially those residing on farms, to exhibit less modernized, more traditional religious beliefs and social attitudes. This assumption has been generally supported whenever research findings revealed statistically significant rural-urban variations.

The effects of urbanization vary considerably depending on what characteristic is examined. In a survey of the United Church of Christ, Campbell and Fukuyama (1970) found that rural members were less involved in church organizations, but rated higher on orthodoxy of beliefs and devotionalism. On the matter of church and public (government) policies, rural-urban differences were small and inconclusive.

Reviewing studies more recently, Hoge and Roozen (1979:47) concluded that "all research has found weak relationships, if any at all, between community size and church attendance and participation."

Recent polls in the United States by the Gallup organization (Gallup, 1982; 1985) revealed small rural-urban differences on a number of religious variables. Persons living on farms and in small towns were more likely to believe in God and in the divinity of Christ, attend church more regularly, read the Bible more frequently, and rate higher on evangelism than people in large cities. They were more conservative in religion and politics. No differences were found in frequency of prayer.

Reviewing the findings from the 1972 survey, Kauffman and Harder (1975:342) concluded that rural-urban differences with respect to faith and life variables were "real but relatively unimportant"—not unlike a conclusion arrived at long ago by Dewey (1960) who reviewed many earlier sociological studies of a more general nature. Are there still real differences between rural and urban? What changes in religious values occur as Mennonites move from rural areas to the cities?

Table 11-2 provides a summary of the relationships between religious variables and rural-urban residence categories. Instead of reporting the entire distribution for each variable, we report only the percentage of respondents who scored "high" on the scale, which is adequate for comparing the residence categories.[1] In order to highlight the residence category with the highest ranking, the highest percentage in each row has been underlined.

Only small variations between residence categories were observed on most scales. Indeed, on five of the scales the differences were not statistically significant. However, on a number of scales the residence variations were great enough to be important in our analysis.

Rural respondents scored higher on the scales measuring beliefs, moral attitudes and behavior, and in-group identity. Small-city residents were highest on church participation and evangelism. Large-city residents were strongest on ethical issues (pacifism, race relations, welfare programs for the poor, and expanded roles for women). They were also substantially higher on ecumenism and political participation.

Not surprisingly, these results indicate greater conservatism among rural church members and more liberal views among the more highly urbanized. A careful examination of the data in Table 11-2 reveals that the large-city residents in 1989 were more different from the other three categories than the latter were different from each other. In most cases the small-city residents were quite similar to the two rural categories. It was the large-city group that differed significantly from the others, being significantly lower on beliefs, church participation, and the moral scales, and significantly higher on the ethical issues, ecumenism, and political scales.

As measured by our concomitants of modernization, rural and urban respondents showed no significant differences. We conclude that the urbanization process among Mennonites leads to diminished orthodoxy of beliefs, diminished support for traditional moral standards, greater support for liberal ethical principles, and greater acceptance of ecumenical programs and participation in political affairs.

These findings were essentially the same as those in 1972. The urbanites scored highest on the same scales that they did in 1972, as did the rural respondents. Where significant differences between rural and urban residents are found, these differences seem to persist over time; at

Table 11-2. Variations in Religious Dimensions by Residence

"High" rating on:**	Percentage by residence			
	Rural farm	Rural nonfarm	Small city	Large city
Beliefs:				
General orthodoxy	79	80	73	65
Fundamentalist orthodoxy	27	28	23	18
Anabaptism	27	23	26	19
Religious practice:				
Church participation	30	31	32	23
*Devotionalism	21	22	20	18
Evangelism	13	19	22	20
Moral and ethical issues:				
Moral attitudes	37	34	30	16
Moral behavior	34	34	29	19
Pacifism	16	13	25	26
Race relations	23	23	35	42
Welfare attitudes	13	12	22	26
Role of women	20	25	36	43
In-group identity:				
Ethnicity	21	27	24	21
Communalism	24	24	21	19
*Separatism	16	17	20	15
Separation of church and state	29	34	26	19
Openness to the larger society:				
Ecumenism	21	23	30	37
*Memberships in organizations	18	14	16	18
Political participation	18	19	20	30
Political action	34	36	41	51
Concomitants of modernization:				
*Secularism	19	18	21	20
Individualism	19	16	15	18
*Materialism	18	19	15	17

*Percentage variations are not statistically significant.
**Highest percentages are underlined.

least they did so over the relatively short period of 17 years between our two surveys.

The amount of difference between rural and urban categories in the two surveys varied somewhat from scale to scale. For example, on the political action scale the difference between the percentage scoring "high" for rural farm and large-city categories was 12 percent in 1972 but 17 percent in 1989. By contrast the differences on the fundamentalism scale were 17 percent in 1972 and 9 percent in 1989. On most scales the differences were greater in 1989 than in 1972, leading to the conclusion that rural-urban differences may be slowly increasing.

One might suspect that the rural-urban differences are due to factors other than residence per se, such as age or education. Since in 1989 rural and urban Mennonites were similar in average age, variations in religiosity were not likely to be due to the age factor. Regarding education, there was a correlation of .23 with residence, indicating that increasing education followed increasing urbanization. Would rural-urban differences diminish or disappear if the relationship between residence and religious variables were examined when educational level is controlled in the analysis? A partial correlation analysis revealed that controlling for education reduced, but did not eliminate, the significant correlations between residence and a variety of religious scales. We conclude that rural-urban variations partially reflect differences in educational achievement, but residence itself is also a differentiating factor (albeit weak) with respect to religiosity.

Rural-urban differences among Mennonites are similar to such differences in other populations that have been studied. Bibby's 1985 survey of Canadians (1987:91-94) showed few significant rural-urban differences. However, his rural respondents scored slightly higher than urbanites on scales measuring orthodoxy of beliefs, as among Mennonites. Also like Mennonite respondents, the rural and urban Canadians in Bibby's study showed no significant differences in the frequency of devotional practices.

To summarize, rural-urban differences among Mennonites in 1989 were very small on about half of our scales. On other scales the large-city respondents were significantly different from small-city and rural groups, indicating that increasing urbanization is associated with lower scores on scales measuring orthodoxy of beliefs and attitudes on moral issues, and with higher scores on scales measuring ethical issues, ecumenism, and political participation.

Modernization as Increasing Social Status

What happens to Mennonites as they move up the social ladder to greater educational achievement, higher occupational ranks, and larger incomes? In this section we will discuss the difference between respondents on the basis of the components of socioeconomic status. Although the socioeconomic status scale is comprised of all three components—education, occupation, and income—we will first take a look at education separately because of the major effect that it has on variations in the religious beliefs and attitudes of Mennonites. It tends to have a greater effect on beliefs, attitudes, and behavior than do all other demographic factors.

Increasing Educational Achievement

Education is a significant factor in the liberalization of beliefs, attitudes, and behavior. The study of the "liberal arts" is designed to broaden the horizon of personal knowledge and understanding, increase awareness and tolerance of social and cultural differences, and increase the critical and rational skills needed to face the issues of life.

Education tends to emphasize experimentation, innovation, and other aspects of social change, which encourages examination of traditional views. The engine of modernization, with all its technological and industrial advances, has been fueled by higher education and the research programs associated with it. From the Reformation onward, education has been a major factor in evaluating, distilling, and changing traditional elements of religious faith and life. This process has had both positive and negative effects. Scholars have been vital forces in the translation of the Bible, development of the hymns of the church, the writing of Christian literature, the training of church leaders, and many other elements on which the vitality of the church depends.

In our study of the modernization of Mennonites and Brethren in Christ, we need to ask whether higher education has had a positive or negative impact on their faith and life. In chapter 6 we reviewed the impact of church schools on Mennonite and BIC beliefs and attitudes. In this chapter we look at education in general, in order to discover similarities and differences between people with different levels of education. At times and places in the past, rural Mennonites have distrusted the influence of higher education, but in recent times only the most conservative groups (Hutterites, Old Order Amish, Old Colony Mennonites) have shunned education beyond the elementary level, fearing that their faith and life might be compromised.

According to Roof and McKinney (1987:65), in many of the mainline Protestant churches in the 1950s only a small proportion of the members were college educated, but by the 1980s a third or more of their members had attended college. Commenting on the significance of this trend, they say:

For organized religion the consequences have been important. It has had to try to accommodate a more informed and less parochial constituency; adjust to new cultural orientations and values brought on by expanding scientific and technological constituencies; bridge growing gaps between the better educated and the lesser educated on a wide range of social, political, and moral issues; and confront continuing, and at times tense, divisions between those arguing for symbolic interpretation of the scriptures and those insisting upon a more literal approach. Perhaps no aspect of change in the social basis of American religion has produced greater strains in the past couple decades than the shifts in education and class.

Mennonites also have experienced these consequences of higher education, particularly as shown by the harsh criticism leveled at some college and seminary professors by church leaders with less formal education.[2]

Among Mennonites and Brethren in Christ, those who had achieved a college degree or done graduate study were 19 percent in 1972 and 31 percent in 1989. In 1989 only 14 percent of those aged 70 and over had earned a college degree, but 42 percent of those aged 30 to 49 had done so—further evidence of the major shift toward pursuing higher education.

A variety of studies have reported on the relationships between education and religiosity, but the findings have varied depending on the church populations studied and, more particularly, the measures of religiosity used. Several surveys have indicated higher church participation with increasing educational levels. In his Detroit sample Lenski (1963) found higher church attendance among persons who had attended college than among those with less education. The survey of Lutherans reported on by Johnson (1983:40) revealed only minor variations between educational categories. Educational differences were not reported in Hunter's (1983) survey of evangelicals and the Roof and McKinney report (1987) on mainline Protestants. In their sample of members of the United Church of Christ, Campbell and Fukuyama (1970) found higher "organizational involvement" and greater "religious knowledge" as educational level increased. However, scores on belief orientation and devotionalism declined with increasing education.

Among Canadians, Bibby (1987:98) found that more education was associated with modest decreases in belief in God and the divinity of Jesus, and in the practice of prayer. Respondents with more education had slightly higher rates of church attendance but were similar in "religious commitment" to those with less education. In Bibby's study education was less potent than age in effecting differences among the respondents, but we found the opposite to be true among Mennonites.

Gallup's poll (Gallup, 1982) of Americans revealed similar rates of church attendance for those with college and those with less education. Lower proportions of the college-educated reported being "born again" and believing in the divinity of Christ and a literal interpretation of Scripture. Also, the college-educated reported praying and reading the Bible less often than did those with less education.

Table 11-3 presents the findings for Mennonites. The percent of respondents arbitrarily rated "high" is given for each of four educational levels: elementary school only, high school but not beyond, college but not beyond, and graduate school, with or without a graduate degree.

Those with only elementary education scored highest on the scales measuring beliefs (including Anabaptism), personal morality, in-group identity, and the concomitants of modernization. Increasing education was associated with higher scores on the scales measuring religious practices, social ethics, and openness to the larger society.[3] Church attendance (not shown in the table) was highest for the college-educated. The substantial percentage differences between educational categories lead to the conclusion that among Mennonites education is more potent than any other demographic variable in its impact on religious beliefs, attitudes, and behavior.

Where comparable, most of these findings reflect the results of the surveys on other religious populations noted above, except that higher education among Mennonites was associated with increased, rather than decreased, devotionalism. We conclude that advancing education among Mennonites leads to a decline in religious orthodoxy and support of conservative moral standards, but leads to an increase in religious practices (church participation, devotionalism, and evangelism), much greater support for social-ethical issues, and much more openness to participation in the larger society. More education is associated with somewhat less materialism, individualism, and secularism as indicated by the measures developed in this study. This finding—not expected—suggests that education—particularly in church schools—may provide a rational, more reflective consideration of human values and may lead to personal decisions to pursue alternatives to these concepts that are often regarded as facets of modernization.

Increasing Socioeconomic Status

Individual socioeconomic status (SES) scores were obtained by adding the scores from eight educational levels, eight occupation ranks, and 11 income levels. It has been common practice to define SES in terms of these three variables, although some researchers have preferred to use only income and occupation.

Table 11-3. Variations in Religious Dimensions by Education

"High" rating on:**	Percent by education			
	Elemen-tary	High school	College	Graduate school
Beliefs				
General orthodoxy	<u>86</u>	77	74	63
Fundamentalist orthodoxy	<u>44</u>	30	18	9
Anabaptism	<u>33</u>	19	20	30
Religious practice				
Church participation	18	22	31	<u>43</u>
Devotionalism	23	17	18	<u>26</u>
Evangelism	25	13	16	<u>28</u>
Moral and ethical issues				
Moral attitudes	<u>55</u>	36	22	14
Moral behavior	<u>45</u>	33	24	19
Pacifism	15	11	21	<u>34</u>
Race relations	9	19	38	<u>53</u>
Welfare attitudes	11	11	20	<u>32</u>
Role of women	9	21	36	<u>56</u>
In-group identity				
Ethnicity	<u>46</u>	20	19	23
Communalism	<u>28</u>	19	18	<u>28</u>
*Separatism	17	17	16	<u>19</u>
Separation of church and state	<u>44</u>	31	24	16
Openness to the larger society				
Ecumenism	23	21	29	<u>40</u>
Memberships	5	10	18	<u>32</u>
Political participation	6	15	30	<u>33</u>
Political action	25	35	48	<u>50</u>
Concomitants of modernization				
Secularism	<u>32</u>	23	15	14
Individualism	<u>21</u>	18	17	13
Materialism	<u>20</u>	<u>20</u>	17	11

*Percentage variations are not statistically significant.
**Highest percentages are underlined.

Using only income and occupation to define SES, Campbell and Fukuyama (1970:88) found SES, like education, to be associated with greater church participation and religious knowledge, and lower scores on devotional and belief scales. Variations in church participation were greater for SES than for education. Among Mennonites in 1989 (see Table 11-4), higher SES was also associated with greater church participation and Bible knowledge (not shown in the table), and lower scores on orthodoxy of beliefs. However, devotionalism rated slightly higher, rather than lower, among respondents with higher SES.[4]

In Detroit (Lenski, 1963) white Protestants with higher SES scored higher on church attendance but lower on belief orthodoxy and devotionalism. Among Catholics, however, increasing status was associated with *increasing* devotionalism but unchanging orthodoxy. The Gallup survey (1982) reported variations by income alone; higher income was associated with greater political conservatism and less Bible reading, and lower proportions of high-income respondents believed in the divinity of Christ and a literal interpretation of Scripture.

A review of Table 11-4 reveals percentage distributions quite similar to those for education in Table 11-3, except that the range of percentages in most cases was not as great as it was for education. This indicates that income and occupation are less potent factors than education in their effect on religious dimensions.

We conclude that upward socioeconomic mobility leads to some erosion of orthodox beliefs and adherence to traditional moral standards. It leads to more liberal views on social-ethical issues, less in-group identity, and more openness to participation in the larger society.

Increasing SES was negatively rather than positively related to secularism, individualism, and materialism (the last not significantly). This unexpected finding calls for more discussion.

Since urbanization is an indicator of modernization, and is significantly related to education (r=.23) and SES (r=.24), how then can SES be negatively related to what we have called "concomitants of modernization"? Does not increasing SES imply increasing modernization? Or are secularism, individualism, and materialism (as we have attempted to measure them) not really concomitants of modernization as previous theory has suggested they are?[5]

Are these findings peculiar to Mennonites? We have not found other studies that attempted to quantify these rather complex concepts (secularism, individualism, and materialism) and treat them as dimensions of modernization. We hope that this might be done by scholars studying other populations so that further tests can be made of modernization theories. We must conclude from our data that increasing socioeconomic

Table 11-4. Variations in Religious Dimensions by Socioeconomic Status

"High" rating on:**	Percent by SES			
	Lower	Lower middle	Upper middle	Upper
Beliefs				
General orthodoxy	79	75	74	60
Fundamentalist orthodoxy	33	26	17	8
*Anabaptism	23	23	21	27
Religious practice				
Church participation	17	28	36	40
*Devotionalism	14	16	19	21
Evangelism	15	17	22	27
Moral and ethical issues				
Moral attitudes	40	30	20	10
Moral behavior	28	22	23	15
Pacifism	12	16	19	33
Race relations	16	24	33	54
Welfare attitudes	12	14	18	31
Role of women	19	28	38	56
In-group identity				
Ethnicity	28	22	22	21
Communalism	20	17	21	29
*Separatism	16	17	15	17
Separation of church and state	34	29	23	17
Openness to the larger society				
Ecumenism	26	22	33	41
Memberships	6	14	20	39
Political participation	13	21	28	38
Political action	35	40	46	49
Concomitants of modernization				
Secularism	29	19	16	15
Individualism	19	15	14	12
*Materialism	19	15	17	15

*Percentage variations are not statistically significant.
**Highest percentages are underlined.

status among Mennonites has not led to greater secularism, individualism and materialism.

Other Variables in Mennonite Pluralism

Although not a part of our model of modernization, age and gender are important variables in any analysis of the factors that affect religious beliefs, attitudes, and behavior. Age and gender are also contributors to Mennonite pluralism.

Age Differentials

Past research has shown that on most variables there are significant variations according to age. In reviewing studies done in England and the United States several decades ago, Argyle (1959) concluded that a decline in religious interest and activity takes place between age 16 and approximately age 30, although the low point for some people comes earlier than age 30. He noted a gradual increase in religious activity and interest after age 30 and through the remainder of life.

Schroeder (quoted in Roof and McKinney, 1987:58) noted:

> The typical American Protestant reduces his church participation markedly in late adolescence and early adulthood. During this period of his life, a person is leaving his family of origin and is making the transition to the adult world. . . .

> After people form families of their own, they are likely to increase their involvement in church life. As did their parents before them, people in their late twenties or early thirties are likely to desire a religious instruction for their children. Consequently they are apt to reaffiliate as their children reach Sunday School age, for they feel some increased responsibility to participate in the institution to which they are sending their children for religious instruction.

Reviewing many surveys more recently, Hoge and Roozen (1979:46) were less certain about the effect of age on religious activity. In their opinion most studies show that the process of aging is not a reliable explanation of religious participation. They suspect that age differences depend in part on the historical period in which studies are made (e.g., the 1950s vs. the 1970s) and on the "cohort effect" resulting from comparing similar age-groups socialized in different decades. For example, the differences between youth and older persons might have been greater in the 1960s than they were in the 1980s.

Hoge and Roozen concluded that aging, in itself, has a small effect on church participation, although many studies indicate a decline between 18 and 30 that "may be well-nigh universal over recent decades. Beyond that no general statements can be made." We must note, however, that these scholars were focusing primarily on church participation rather than beliefs and attitudes on social issues.

To study the effects of aging on beliefs and behavior would require a longitudinal study of a particular group of teenagers, followed up with surveys every ten years until the sample members had all died. To our knowledge this has never been done, as it would require a lifetime of research. Most studies are limited to comparing all age-groups at a single moment of time, which ignores the impact of time periods and cohort effects. In our study of Mennonites at two different time periods we were able to make cohort comparisons, although the sample members were not the same persons in 1989 as in 1972.

Recent national surveys have expanded the data base on religious beliefs and behavior and provide a more comprehensive analysis of the effects of demographic factors on religion.[6] The Gallup poll (Gallup, 1982) investigated age variations among a national sample in the United States. Compared with younger groups, persons aged 50 years and older attended church more regularly, read the Bible more frequently, and prayed more often. Slightly higher proportions of the older group reported being born again, witnessing for Christ, and believing in a literal interpretation of the Bible. They viewed themselves as more to the right on "religious position" and on political views.

Table 11-5 shows the proportions of our 1989 respondents who scored "high" on the principal scales for each of five age categories. For some scales, there is a gradual increase or decrease from younger to older groups. On other scales the variation is curvilinear, that is, the youngest and oldest groups were similar with the middle groups being higher or lower, as in the case of church participation.

The variations between age categories were considerably greater than between residence categories, indicating that age is an important factor in explaining variations in religiosity, although not as powerful a factor as education. As expected, older persons, on the average, exhibited more strongly conservative positions on religious beliefs, attitudes, and behavior. Within each age category, however, there was a wide range of scale scores (not shown in the table), indicating that many older people have nontraditional views and many young people hold to conservative views.

The highest scores were found among the oldest age-groups for the following measures: all of the scales measuring beliefs, devotionalism, evangelism, moral attitudes and behavior, and in-group identity. The middle-aged group (30-49) scored highest on the scales measuring church participation, role of women, and political participation. The young adults (20-29) scored highest on two ethical scales (pacifism and race relations) and the ecumenism scale. For the latter, however, differences were not statistically significant.

Table 11-5. Variations in Religious Dimensions by Age

"High" rating on:**	Percent by age categories				
	13-19	20-29	30-49	50-69	70+
Beliefs					
General orthodoxy	57	72	71	80	<u>82</u>
Fundamentalist orthodoxy	11	16	20	30	<u>36</u>
Anabaptism	16	19	20	<u>28</u>	<u>28</u>
Religious practice					
Church participation	11	22	<u>36</u>	29	17
Devotionalism	7	12	16	27	<u>31</u>
Evangelism	8	9	16	24	<u>27</u>
Moral and ethical issues					
Moral attitudes	20	17	21	38	<u>54</u>
Moral behavior	35	15	17	41	<u>53</u>
Pacifism	16	<u>24</u>	20	19	14
Race relations	42	<u>47</u>	37	20	10
Welfare attitudes	<u>24</u>	21	18	17	14
Role of women	26	33	<u>36</u>	29	17
In-group identity					
Ethnicity	16	11	16	33	<u>43</u>
Communalism	17	15	18	27	<u>32</u>
Separatism	11	16	17	<u>18</u>	<u>18</u>
Separation of church and state	17	19	21	32	<u>51</u>
Openness to the larger society					
*Ecumenism	29	<u>31</u>	26	28	29
Memberships	<u>23</u>	16	22	12	8
Political participation	4	24	<u>27</u>	21	13
Political action	<u>48</u>	<u>48</u>	46	33	31
Concomitants of modernization					
Secularism	<u>38</u>	22	15	18	31
Individualism	<u>28</u>	17	15	14	25
Materialism	<u>36</u>	22	14	15	24

*Percentage variations are not statistically significant.
**Highest percentages are underlined.

The teenagers rated highest on the concomitants of modernization. Is this a characteristic of the age we live in, or will the teenagers of any time period have less secular, materialistic, and individualistic attitudes when they grow older? The teenagers scored highest on welfare attitudes and political action. The fact that they are involved in many youth organizations placed them highest on the memberships scale.

The church participation scale illustrates the curvilinear relationship between age and some measures of religiosity. Middle-aged persons rated highest—probably because they were most active in leadership positions—as compared with younger and older persons who carried fewer leadership responsibilities. Church attendance rates (not shown in the table, but a part of the church participation scale) were lowest in the 20-29 age-group and were somewhat higher and similar for teenagers and groups over age 30. This is in line with the findings on other church populations reported earlier in this section. Interestingly, attendance of the 70 and over group slacked off a bit, probably due to increasing health problems.[7]

We conclude that for our Mennonite and Brethren in Christ populations age is a significant factor in explaining variations in religiosity. The failure of some studies to show an important relationship between age and church participation (as indicated by Roof and McKinney) may reflect an assumption of linear rather than curvilinear relationships between age and church attendance and leadership. Our data suggest that church participation is higher among middle-aged persons than among either youth or older persons.

Gender Differentials
Differences between males and females are a matter of considerable interest, much speculation, and some scientific data. When we consider activities and behavioral roles, males and females differ considerably (though less as time goes on), whether because of biological factors or cultural conditioning. When it comes to beliefs and attitudes, however, there is much greater similarity. Undoubtedly one reason is that men and women interact so much with each other. As one sage said, the battle of the sexes will never be won—there is too much fraternizing with the enemy!

Argyle (1959) summarized findings on sex differences in religion from studies done in Britain and America. He concluded that women were more religious than men on all criteria. Women were more conservative in beliefs, but the differences were small. While the Episcopalian women in one study attended church more regularly than did the men (Glock, et al., 1967), Campolo (1971) found that among the American

Baptists the men attended more regularly than the women. Our data for Mennonites, both in 1972 and in 1989, gave men the slight edge in attendance.

Campbell and Fukuyama (1970) surveyed members of the United Church of Christ and found that women scored higher than men on all religious variables except "organizational involvement"; that is, men tended in larger proportions to get into organizational leadership. Likewise Mennonite men in both surveys scored a bit higher on the church participation scale, likely on account of their holding leadership positions in larger proportions.

Bibby's (1987:100) 1985 survey in Canada confirmed the earlier studies. Women joined and attended church at slightly higher rates, and scored higher on measures of orthodox beliefs and religious practices. In a survey of eight samples of high school and university students in Canada and Australia (Fullerton and Hunsberger, 1982) females scored consistently higher than males on a scale measuring Christian orthodoxy.

The Gallup organization's poll in 1988 (Gallup and Jones, 1989) yielded similar results. Women scored higher than men on several orthodoxy items (belief in God, Jesus, and miracles) and had more frequent church attendance and private prayer.

As in 1972, Mennonite males and females in 1989 were very similar on the religious variables. There were no statistically significant differences on Bible knowledge and devotionalism. Likewise there were no differences on the four social issues—pacifism, race relations, welfare attitudes, and women's roles. Men and women were very similar on the secularism and materialism scales, but women were slightly higher on the individualism scale. Women were slightly higher on beliefs and on moral attitudes and behavior. Men rated a bit higher on Anabaptism, ecumenism, communalism, and evangelism. They were slightly higher than women on the scale measuring attitudes that favor expanded roles for women (as in 1972), and they held more memberships in community organizations.

These findings seem to indicate that gender differences among Mennonites are slight—even slighter than the differences found in other church populations. Although Mennonite women were more orthodox on beliefs and moral behavior, the men scored a bit higher on a few of the other religious measures. The number of scales on which one sex scored higher than the other were about evenly divided between males and females. On about half of the scales in this study there were no differences at all.

Summary

In this chapter we observed and attempted to explain differences between church members on the basis of increasing urbanization, educational achievement, and socioeconomic status.

In comparing rural and urban church members we found significant differences on some scales but not on others. Rural members were more conservative in orthodoxy of beliefs, moral attitudes, in-group loyalties, and political preferences. Urban members expressed more liberal attitudes on social issues and were more open to participation in society beyond Mennonite boundaries. Rural and urban members' scores did not differ on scales measuring secularism, individualism, and materialism.

There were some significant variations between age-groups. As expected, older persons were more conservative on beliefs, moral attitudes, in-group identity, and political stance. Middle-aged respondents—joiners and activists—scored highest on church participation, political participation, and the number of memberships in community organizations. Young adults (aged 20-29) scored lowest on church attendance but highest on pacifism and race relations. Teenagers were highest on secularism, individualism, and materialism.

Females and males were similar in social and religious beliefs and attitudes, but females showed slightly more conservative responses on some scales. Males joined more groups, exercised more leadership in church and community, and they were less conforming to social mores.

Of all the demographic variables, education had the greatest effect, among Mennonites, on religiosity and social values. Higher education was strongly related to church participation, political participation, and other measures of openness to the larger society. Higher education was strongly related to social issues—to favorableness toward pacifism, other races, welfare for the poor, and especially, expanded roles for women. Higher education was related to lower scores on orthodoxy of beliefs, especially fundamentalism. Education was negatively related to the concomitants of modernization. The relationship of socioeconomic status to the measures of religiosity and social issues discussed in this chapter was very similar to the findings on education.

Demographic variables explained some of the variations among church members, but many differences remain unexplained. Individuals often deviate from expected patterns for complicated and unknown reasons. Moreover, the mystery of divine influence and the multitude of uncontrolled social forces making an impact on a person's beliefs and behavior defy explanation within the limited scope of this type of research. Nevertheless, the possibilities for greater understanding drive us toward greater precision in explaining personal beliefs and behavior.

CHAPTER 12

Emerging New Identities

MODERNIZATION (including urbanization, greater mobility, and higher levels of education, occupations, and income) and Mennonite identity (involving religiosity, community, family, institutions, and ethnicity) are polar in nature and are continuously involved in dialectical processes of change (secularization vs. sacralization, individualism vs. communalism, and materialism vs. peoplehood).

After comparing the five denominations participating in the 1972 and 1989 surveys, we conclude that Mennonite canopies are still firmly held in place by strong theological, community, family, and institutional stakes, so that Mennonite peoplehood and consciousness of kind persist, while adaptations and adjustments to the larger society occur. Mennonites are also reaching out in evangelism and church planting, especially in cities; and the personnel and resources assigned to missions and service extend into more than 50 countries. Modern Anabaptists are seeking to hold together in-group solidarity and outreach—a sense of peoplehood blended with concern for others. Changing leadership patterns—based on the priesthood of all believers—are at work, increasingly involving women (Fast, 1980:108-10; Harder, 1990:199-200). The mass media and ever more sophisticated technological means of communication are part of the changing modern scene. Some things have not changed since 1972, a generation ago; on the other hand a comparison of older and younger Mennonites shows that the youth are shifting their interests and loyalties to foci quite different from those their elders emphasize. As David Brinkley (1990) recently commented, "We live at the end of an era almost every twenty-four hours." What will the next Mennonite era bring?

The Struggle for Change

The early Christians followed Christ as the new way toward a fuller truth and more meaningful life. Our Anabaptist forebears sought to find that new way for their time. Mennonites in modern, urban North America are also in a quest for renewal. In chapter 1 our model presented the dialectic between modernization and identity, but it has become clear that Mennonites face a variety of struggles—between Mennonites and the larger society; between Mennonite denominations within those denominations; between Anabaptist and fundamentalist theologies; between faith and life, communal needs and service outreach, leaders and laity, men and women, and young and old. How do we summarize such complex dynamics?

Identity Versus Modernization

As the model in figure 1-4 suggests, the modern influences of urbanization and increased education are pulling in the direction of secularization, but are counteracted by the sacralizing forces of religiosity and community that seek to maintain a dynamic Mennonite identity. In chapters 3 and 4 we observed that commitment to religious beliefs, religious experiences, devotional practices, and service remained strong between 1972 and 1989. In the struggle between secularization and sacralization, the sacred seemed to be holding its own.

As Mennonites rise in socioeconomic status in the capitalist societies of Canada and the United States, they are also increasingly drawn toward individualism, but this trend is counteracted by the communalism of the Mennonite community and the Mennonite family. The findings reported in chapters 5 and 6 suggest that while families and communities change, Anabaptist theology and communal networks in the city do hold individualism in check.

Nor are those with more income and greater mobility necessarily more prone to materialism, especially when counteracted by the support of family, institutions, and ethnicity, which enhance a sense of peoplehood. In the dialectic between materialism and peoplehood, many Mennonites are able to develop a sense of belonging and commitment to a Mennonite identity rather than focusing on material things.

Throughout this volume we have shown the struggle between modernization and Mennonite identity, and we do not want to become repetitious. In particular, chapters 10 and 11 summarized some of the details of our findings. However, some points require highlighting, and some dialectics have not yet been covered.

Tensions Between Anabaptism and Fundamentalism

In two recent volumes, Robert Wuthnow (1988, 1989) describes the struggle in America between evangelicals and liberals, who, he thinks, have increasingly become two theological solitudes in conflict with each other. He makes a strong plea for reconciliation between mainline Protestants and evangelical groups. Our study shows that there are few Mennonite liberals, so the tensions among Mennonites are more between two theologies—the original Anabaptist heritage and recent fundamentalism. Thus we found an internal dialectic between Anabaptism and fundamentalism, two theologies that are contrasting, if not polar.

The Anabaptist movement was part of a larger quest for religious renewal in the 16th century. According to Walter Klaassen (1990:13-26), 1975 was the modern watershed between two very important and distinct historical theological interpretations of the Anabaptist vision or visions (Driedger and Harder, 1990:2).

The move from a monogenetic view of Anabaptist beginnings to a polygenetic view was best expressed in 1975 by Stayer, Packull, and Deppermann (1975). "That essay marked a turning-point in the understanding of 16th-century Anabaptism. It was a revision of the view normally associated with Harold S. Bender" (Klaassen, 1990:12). Bender's understanding was that within the movement there was a common, solid core of beliefs, with softer expressions of its main affirmations further away from the center. Since 1975 the revisionist model has claimed that Anabaptism started in at least three or more places—including Switzerland, South Germany, and the Netherlands—and that the Anabaptist groups in the various areas exhibited distinct characteristics (Klaassen, 1990:14). So the revised model is more pluralistic.

Figure 12-1 shows some of the correlations of Anabaptism and fundamentalism with the major variables that have emerged in this study. The two theological positions are portrayed in the top corners of the figure. For the factors that related most positively to Anabaptism, but less strongly with fundamentalism, see the top left corner; for the reverse, the top right corner. Similarities between these two positions are shown at the bottom.

What makes Anabaptist Mennonites unique—especially in contrast to fundamentalist Mennonites—are peacemaking, in-group identity, communalism, service to others, and less evidence of individualism. Peacemaking related positively to Anabaptism (r=.48) but negatively to fundamentalism (r= -.30). Anabaptist Mennonites exhibited strong in-group identity (r=.37), while fundamentalist Mennonites exhibited much less (r=.08). The contrasts were similar for communalism (r=.36 vs .02) and service to others (r=.29 vs .07). Anabaptist Mennonites also related negatively to individualism, much more strongly than did fundamentalist Mennonites (r= -.42 vs -.14). Figure 12-1 shows that Anabaptist Mennonites are unique in that they are strong on peacemaking, in-group identity, communalism, and service to others, and are wary of excessive individualism.

In contrast, fundamentalist Mennonites represent a unique counter set of relationships. As shown in Figure 12-1, general orthodox beliefs (r=.71) are their doctrinal flagship. While Anabaptist Mennonites also adhere to orthodox theology (r=.23), the correlation was not nearly as strong. Traditional female roles, in which the female adopts a submissive role in both the home and church, also distinguished the fundamentalists from the Anabaptists (r=.49 vs .10). Three of the five correlations were negative for fundamentalism with welfare aid (r= -.29 vs .14 for Anabaptists), race relations (r= -.31 vs .07) and education (r= -.35 vs -.02). Fundamentalist Mennonites are less educated, less open to people of other races, and less willing to help others in the form of welfare than are Anabaptist Mennonites. Fundamentalism is a theological option which is much more conservative in doctrine, less accepting of equality between males and females, and less openness to other groups.

While Anabaptists and fundamentalists contrast greatly, they also have some similarities, as noted in Figure 12-1. Both had high scores on moral issues (rs=.41 and .51, respectively), devotionalism (rs=.42 and .40), quality of religious life (rs=.41 and .36), evangelism (rs=.26 and .24), and opposition to secularism (rs= -.35 and -.34). Anabaptism and fundamentalism are two major tiles in the Mennonite mosaic—two quite different tiles but with some common characteristics.

Anabaptism clearly appeals more to urban, educated, professional Mennonites of higher socioeconomic status, while fundamentalism appeals more to rural, less educated Mennonites of lower socioeconomic status, employed in blue collar occupations. Since urbanization and social status continue to increase among Mennonites, Anabaptism may in the future receive even greater support. However, Anabaptism is a more demanding theology, which comfortable, urban, higher-status Mennonites may find too costly.

At the same time, a multitude of other forces are at work, especially in the city. James Reimer (1988:147-59) has identified 13 contemporary theological trends among Mennonites: evolutionary, shalom, liberation, narrative, feminist, political, historical, existential, eschatological, evangelical, Anabaptist, therapeutic, and ethno-cultural. Paul Toews (1990:55), in a review of Mennonite periodicals, found that Mennonite theology was becoming more pluralistic. Norman Kraus (1990:32-49) has also wrestled with the complexity of both the conservative and more

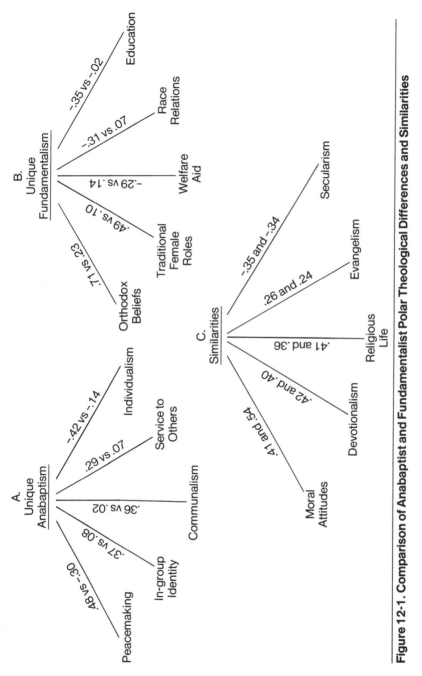

Figure 12-1. Comparison of Anabaptist and Fundamentalist Polar Theological Differences and Similarities

A. First coefficient represents Anabaptists vs. second, Fundamentalists.
B. First coefficient represents Fundamentalists vs. second, Anabaptists.
C. First coefficient represents Anabaptists and second, Fundamentalists.

liberal theological wings of the Mennonites in North America. As Mennonites are increasingly exposed to the larger, urban society, and as they drink more and more at a variety of theological wells, diversity is sure to increase. The trend toward theological pluralism is clear. Only the future can tell what new foci will emerge and how Anabaptism will ultimately fare.

Blending Faith and Life

Our study of the Mennonite faith, community, family, and institutions points to a complex, internal Anabaptist-Mennonite dialectic emerging from a crucible of change. It has always been difficult to sort out the essentials that have bogged Mennonites down in cultural differentiation and religious extremism in their quest for an ideal sacred canopy. Figure 12-2 presents five essential elements of Anabaptist-Mennonite faith and life, sometimes in conflict with each other: in-group identity, Anabaptism, communalism, welfare aid for the poor, and peacemaking. Such a complex sacred canopy will require costly discipleship.

In chapter 3 we examined in more detail the various components of "the sacred" and observed that, of the three sets of beliefs (orthodoxy, fundamentalism, Anabaptism) Anabaptism was most strongly associated with three elements of religiosity—Bible knowledge, church participation, and religious experience.

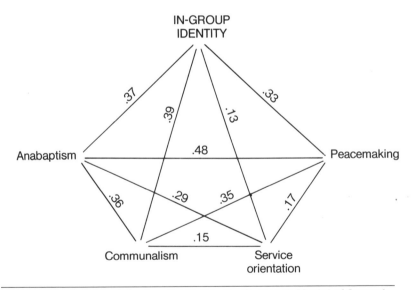

Figure 12-2. A Modern Anabaptist Solidarity-Outreach Model of Sacred Identity

We also observed a much stronger association between Anabaptism and various forms of outreach—service to others, support of MCC, and peacemaking—than we did for orthodoxy and fundamentalism. While the three belief systems were equally associated with evangelism, Anabaptism was more strongly associated with service to others. With peacemaking, one of the major tenets of the original movement, Anabaptism correlated highly and positively (r=.48), while both orthodoxy and fundamentalism correlated negatively (-.17 and -.30 respectively). Anabaptist Mennonites clearly demonstrated the capacity for strong outreach, through both evangelism and peacemaking activities, while Mennonites of the other two belief orientations were negative toward a broader outreach, especially peacemaking.

Anabaptism was the most negatively associated with individualism (-.42) and materialism (-.23), and as negatively correlated as orthodoxy and fundamentalism were with secularism. Anabaptist Mennonites were especially negative toward materialism (-.35), more so than the other two (-.04 and -.06).

Because of the more positive association of Anabaptism with several aspects of religiosity and with service to others; because of the more negative association of Anabaptism with individualist and materialist trends; and because of the greater capacity of Anabaptist Mennonites to integrate their faith under the influences of modernization, Anabaptism appears to be the most viable engine for fueling the reconstruction of the Mennonite canopy, in a holistic way, amidst modern complexities (Driedger, et al., 1983).

Figure 12-2 shows a strong association (r=.37) between Anabaptism and in-group identity, which demonstrates the integral part that Anabaptist beliefs have had in the larger, complex modern world that Mennonites find themselves "in but not of." Religion has always been central to this movement in the past; and Anabaptism is central in the future survival of a distinctive Mennonite witness (Ainlay, 1990; Driedger, 1990; Hamm, 1990; Redekop, 1990; Sawatsky, 1990; Toews, 1990).

Balancing Communal and Service Networks

In part two we discussed the extent to which community networks have changed as Mennonites have moved from rural to urban areas under the increased influence of modernization. The strength of communalism—measured by the participation of the respondents' families in the past, the length of participation, how well the respondents fit into congregational life, their satisfaction with being Mennonite, and whether they planned to stay part of the Mennonite community—remained about the same from 1972 to 1989.

Figure 12-2 shows a strong association between in-group identity and communalism (r=.39), suggesting that identification with Mennonite peers and structures (organizations, schools, family, language, and friends) is strongly correlated with developing satisfying communal networks (satisfaction, durability and strength of loyalties). As Mennonites increasingly move from rural areas to less boundaried, urban areas, they seem to be merging an earlier identity based on structures with a newer identity based on social networks.

While Mennonites favored in-group identity, Figure 12-2 shows they were also concerned with serving others. A majority visited the sick, did community volunteer work, used resources for the good of others, and wanted to be at peace with others and treat them well. This service orientation correlated positively with in-group identity (.13), Anabaptist beliefs (.29), communalism (.15), and peacemaking (.17). While these correlations were smaller than some of the others, they indicate that a majority of the respondents wanted to combine communalism with service networks.

Casting Nets for Peacemaking

One of the most distinctive components of Anabaptist-Mennonite faith and life has been the principle of nonresistance/pacifism/nonviolence/peacemaking. This issue separated the early Anabaptists (Menno Simons and Thomas Muentzer), and it is a controversial issue even today. Nonresistance has also been one of the most costly elements of discipleship; many of our ancestors lost their lives because of their understanding that the gospel is a gospel of peace.

Peacemaking in the 1989 survey was moderately associated with in-group identity (r=.33), as shown in Figure 12-2. This "in-but-not-of-the-world" model is held together by a strong sense of peoplehood. The four factors (Anabaptism, communalism, service orientation, and peacemaking) correlated highly with in-group identity; they make up a complex, integrated sacred network that Mennonites in the past have found hard to keep in balance. Many internal schisms have resulted because some elements were emphasized more than others, and external pressures have often resulted in persecution, migration, and conflict. The Anabaptist faith and life dialectic has been difficult to integrate and will likely remain that way in the future.

Changing Leadership and Communication Patterns

Leadership plays a crucial role in the process of modernization and change. Leaders perform crucial roles as symbols of trust, preservers of a past heritage, or strategic planners of new futures.

Although leadership has often been played down in the Anabaptist tradition, because all believers are considered "priests," it has nevertheless shaped Mennonite history in important ways. Menno Simons gathered together the early Anabaptists, who were scattered under persecution and in desperate need of encouragement and shepherding. More recently, Orie Miller and P. C. Hiebert guided the fledgling relief work in Russia into the Mennonite Central Committee, which has transformed our capacity for worldwide service. Harold S. Bender had the courage to present "the Anabaptist Vision," tailoring it to a constituency that was drinking theology at many different wells. David Toews brought refugees from Russia and signed promises to pay for their travel when the organizational coffers were empty. Mennonites have had leaders whose roles were crucial. We need to examine Mennonite leadership in greater detail.

Leader and Laity Differentials

Max Weber (1978) has suggested that there are at least three types of leaders—traditional, rational, and charismatic—who perform quite different functions, depending on the situation. Mennonites have long been under traditional, rural leadership, with the characteristics noted by Weber: authority, preservation of the past, respect for tradition, reluctance to change, and emphasis on traditional morals and a traditional social order. The reluctance to affirm leadership roles for women, to participate in politics, and the like was still strongly evident in the 1972 and 1989 surveys. Traditional leaders play a useful role in the resistance to change that is too rapid. But, traditional leadership has been dysfunctional when leaders of this type did not appropriately discern between the preservation of essentials and the preservation of nonessentials (Lindley, 1980:67-70; Miller and Rupp, 1980:111-12; Nyce, 1980:100-101; Wiebe, 1979). Traditional leaders create an antithesis to modernization, secularization, individualism, and materialism, and stimulate the essential dialectic between traditional and modern opposites.

Rational leaders, according to Weber (1978), are usually located in urban settings, where—in larger bureaucracies—there is a need for good administrators, organizational efficiency, and competence in specialties. These leaders are bureaucrats or technocrats, often working for business or government. Now that one-fourth of North American Mennonites are in the professions, one-tenth are in business, and one-half are urban, they are increasingly working in administration, economic enterprise, and services which need steady, trustworthy, competent specialists.

Charismatic leaders are able to link the traditions of the past with the trends of the present, and mold them into a relevant vision for the future.

Charismatic leaders must be sufficiently successful in taking their followers with them until traditions change, new adaptations are made, and all adopt the new vision that joins both valued traditional ideals and modern needs—as Harold S. Bender, J. J. Thiessen, and J. B. Toews demonstrated. Of crucial importance for a vision of the future, is whether such leaders will continue to emerge, whether they will be willing to commit themselves to leading the followers of the distinctive Anabaptist vision, and whether there will be enough followers willing to make the sacrifices required by Anabaptist visions.

Most surveys of other religious populations have not reported clergy-laity differences. However, the survey of Lutherans reported by Johnson (1983) compared over 500 pastors with some 1,500 laypersons. Some of the items used in this survey were similar to ours.

Lutheran pastors held more liberal views on social issues; in particular, they were more favorable than laypersons toward the ordination of women, discussing political issues from the pulpit, and spending more government money for welfare. They were more opposed to the death penalty. On moral issues, pastors were more liberal; smaller proportions of pastors responded "always wrong" on smoking marijuana, premarital intercourse, homosexual relations, and abortion. Slightly smaller proportions of pastors expressed no doubt about the existence of God and fewer would interpret the Bible literally.

The priesthood of every believer was a central part of Anabaptist theology. Both the 1972 and 1989 surveys probed the extent to which such broadly shared leadership was a part of Mennonite beliefs at the time. Over one-half (58%) of the respondents in 1972 and two-thirds (66%) in 1989 agreed that "a proper view of congregational leadership is that all members should share, as they are able, in the ministerial functions of the congregation."

Over one-half (59%) in 1972 agreed that "a church congregation cannot be complete unless there is an ordained minister to lead the congregation and perform the ministerial functions," while just under half (48%) in 1989 agreed (41% disagreed). Better educated lay members who work in professional and business occupations in the city tend to feel more at ease in sharing ministerial functions.

While the trend in 1989 was for all members to be more involved in leadership, there were some striking differences between clergy and laity. Table 12-1 compares three categories of leadership—ordained persons, lay leaders, and non-leaders—on seven categories of faith and action. The data show that three-fourths of all Mennonites were holding to the orthodox doctrines; however, one-fourth of the laity scored high on fundamentalism, whereas very few (13%) of the ordained leaders did so.

Table 12-1. Relationship of Faith and Action Variables to Leadership
Categories

Faith and life variables	Leadership categories			Total
	Non-leaders	Lay leaders	Ordained leaders	
	(Percent scoring "high")			
Beliefs				
General orthodoxy	70	77	72	74
Fundamentalism	26	24	13	24
Anabaptism	18	22	49	23
Religious practice				
Church participation	0	41	73	29
Stewardship	22	29	44	28
Devotionalism	14	20	45	20
Outreach and service				
MCC support	14	23	31	20
Peacemaking	16	17	40	19
Evangelism	11	16	59	18
Welfare attitudes	15	17	36	18
Mennonite identity				
Support of church schools	50	55	73	55
In-group identity	25	20	34	23
Communalism	17	22	42	22
Separatism	15	17	29	17
Moral and ethical issues				
Women in leadership	29	35	52	34
Race relations	22	32	57	31
Moral attitudes	31	28	27	29
Moral behavior	32	27	28	29
Involvement in society				
*Political action	38	43	37	41
Ecumenism	25	26	48	28
Political participation	18	25	22	22
Memberships	12	20	16	16
*Use of mass media	12	15	9	14
Concomitants of modernization				
Personal independence	30	21	13	24
Secularism	33	13	5	20
Individualism	28	11	1	17
Materialism	22	16	7	17

*Not statistically significant at the .01 level.

One-fourth (23%) of the laity scored high on Anabaptism, with twice as many of the ordained ministers (49%) doing so. Earlier we saw that higher education (Mennonite schools, theological training) and professional occupations correlated highly with Anabaptist beliefs, while less education and rural residence correlated highly with fundamentalist beliefs.

One-half or more of the ordained leaders rated high on the general orthodoxy and Anabaptism scales; they were substantially higher than others on Anabaptism. They rated much higher than the laity on the religious practice variables. As expected, because of their leadership responsibilities in the congregation, their rating on church participation was very high compared to the laity. Few lay members scored high on any of the four indicators of religious practice.

Average Mennonite identity scores tended to follow the same pattern as religious practice, except that support for church schools (55%) was very high, with clergy scoring higher than laity. In regard to Mennonite identity, the differences between the laity and ordained leaders were moderate, but they were significant in each case.

Compared to the laity, roughly twice as many ordained ministers scored high on ethical issues, such as race relations and women in leadership. On moral attitudes and behavior, the differences between ordained leaders and the laity were too small to generalize. Personal morality tends to increase with fundamentalism and decline with modernization, while social concerns increase with adherence to Anabaptist principles and with higher socioeconomic status and urbanization.

About one in five in the sample was highly involved in outreach and service, and again ordained leaders were more highly involved. While two and three times as many of the ordained strongly supported MCC, peacemaking, and welfare programs, they were five times more involved in evangelism (11 vs. 59%) than were the laity. On most of these matters, lay leaders were closer to the non-leaders than to the ordained leaders. With more education, higher socioeconomic status, and greater urbanization, the clergy seemed to be better prepared for and more involved in outreach than were the laity.

The differences in involvement in society were not great. While ordained leaders scored twice as high on ecumenism, the differences in attitudes toward political action and participation were minimal. Lay leaders scored higher than the others on both political action and membership in community organizations, perhaps because of wider contacts with people in their places of work.

Finally, Table 12-1 showed that non-leaders scored much higher than lay leaders, and lay leaders than the ordained leaders, on the concomitants of modernization—personal independence (30 and 13%), secularism (33 and 5%), individualism (28 and 1%), and materialism (22 and 7%). Lay members reflect the dominant spirit of the modern world more fully than do the clergy. In summary, Mennonite leaders tend to spearhead efforts to foster Anabaptist identity and outreach, and serve as a brake on excessive secularization, individualism, and materialism.

Male and Female Variations

Table 12-1 showed that one-third (34%) of the respondents scored high on participation of women in church leadership, with one-half (52%) of the ordained leaders doing so. Support for women in church leadership was also greater among the better educated (r=.40), those of higher socioeconomic status (r=.36), and the more urban (r=.20). For example, twice as many large-city residents (45%) supported greater leadership roles for women as did rural-farm respondents (26%).

The level of education differentiated most strongly the concern for women's participation in leadership. Table 12-2 ranks the levels at which the respondents accepted women's leadership in the church, with three out of four (76%) supporting the role of deaconess. However, only one in three (37%) felt it appropriate to have women conduct ordinations. Two-thirds to three-fourths (62-76%) were willing to have women fill church positions with lower status and power, such as deaconess, worship leader, minister of Christian education, reading Scripture in the worship service, youth minister, and chairperson of the church council.

Table 12-2. Responsibilities Appropriate for Qualified Women to Fill in Congregational Leadership by Gender and Education, 1989

Leadership positions	Gender		Education				Total
	Male	Female	Elementary	High school	College	Graduate school	
Deaconess/deacon	76	76	53	65	87	93	76
Worship leader	73	70	44	64	81	88	71
Minister of Christian education	72	67	35	60	82	88	69
Read Scripture in worship service	71	66	46	58	79	85	68
Youth minister	65	59	29	54	72	80	62
Chairperson, church council	63	62	36	56	70	77	62
Chairperson, board of elders	52	46	23	40	56	70	49
Preaching	50	41	17	32	56	69	45
Conduct communion service	48	38	15	30	54	67	43
Conduct funerals	46	37	13	28	51	66	41
Ordained minister	45	37	15	28	50	63	40
Conduct weddings	46	35	13	27	50	64	40
Conduct baptisms	45	36	14	28	50	65	40
Conduct ordinations	41	33	14	25	46	59	37

Less than one-half of the respondents, however, were willing to support women in higher-profile positions and activities, such as chairing the board of elders (49%); preaching (45%); conducting communion services (43%), funerals (41%), weddings (40%), baptisms (40%), and ordinations (37%). Ordination seems to be the crux of church power and influence—a door to what might be considered most-needed "status" services, which Bibby (1987) calls rites of passage. Interestingly, in 1989 40 percent of the respondents were willing to support women in the entire range of leadership roles—a considerable increase judging from data reported elsewhere (Ropp, 1980:11-14; Turner and Emery, 1983; Woudstra-Gorter, 1980:102-07).

The willingness to support qualified women in leadership roles was highly correlated with education; two to four times as many respondents with graduate education as with elementary education alone were willing to let women serve in leadership positions. In fact, respondents with a graduate education ranged from 59 percent accepting the role of conducting ordinations to 93 percent accepting the role of deaconess. The concept of the priesthood of all believers is increasingly being extended to the other half of the Mennonite membership, a concept which the early Anabaptists pioneered 475 years ago, judging from the accounts of female martyrs in the *Martyrs Mirror* (van Braght, 1964).

While three-fourths of both male and female respondents agreed that it was appropriate for women to serve as deaconesses in the church, significantly more males than females thought it appropriate for women to serve in other positions in the church. The gap between male and female support widened with higher status positions. For example, while 41 percent of males consented to women conducting ordinations, only 33 percent of women agreed. The fact that education is such an influential factor in support of female involvement, and women have somewhat less education than men, may account for most of the difference. Those who wish to increase involvement of women in the leadership of the church will need to work at least as much with women as with men. Younger Mennonites and those subscribing to Anabaptist beliefs favor leadership for women in the church more than do older respondents and fundamentalist Mennonites.

Recently, Ruth Vogt (1990:30) was angry that women were not given sufficient opportunity to participate in the program of the 1990 Mennonite World Conference, held in Winnipeg. Our data suggest that in North America there is still much to be done in this area. However, there is hope, as education and urbanization increase, that the younger generation and those who commit themselves to the Anabaptist way, will increasingly include women in the leadership of the church.

Secular and Sacred Communications

While leadership plays an important part in the search for a new identity, the use of the media is also important. The early Anabaptists made good use of the products of printing with movable type, newly invented by Gutenberg when he published the Gutenberg Bible in 1456. Luther translated the Bible from Latin into the vernacular German, and the Bible became a cornerstone of Anabaptist beliefs and discipleship, and made practical and possible "the priesthood of every believer." The laity were no longer dependent on learned priests who knew Latin to interpret the Scriptures for them; they were able to read and interpret the Scriptures for themselves.

Mennonites have always stressed at least minimal literacy because of the importance of reading the Bible for an active life of faith. More recently, however, with greater urbanization and more education, Mennonites have increasingly been exposed to the printed and electronic media. Table 12-3 shows to what extent Mennonites in both 1972 and 1989 were reading newspapers and books, listening to radio and recorded music, and watching television; the 1989 questionnaire added video cassettes.

Table 12-3. Percentage of Respondents Using the Media, 1972 and 1989

| | 1972 | | | | | 1989 | | | | |
| | Hours per day | | | | | Hours per day | | | | |
	None	Under 1 hour	1-2.9 hours	3-4.9 hours	5+ hours	None	Under 1 hour	1-2.9 hours	3-4.9 hours	5+ hours
Reading newspapers/ magazines	3	63	29	3	2	4	64	26	4	2
Reading books	14	51	25	6	5	13	52	25	6	4
Listening to radio	5	44	30	12	10	6	44	26	12	12
Watching TV	15	31	38	12	5	7	29	42	16	6
Listening to recorded music	19	53	19	5	3	23	55	16	4	2
Watching video cassettes*						62	33	4	1	0

*Not included in the 1972 survey.

In 1972 most respondents (all except 3%) were reading newspapers, although two-thirds (63%) spent less than an hour per day doing so. Two-thirds either did not read books at all (14%) or spent less than an hour per day reading books (51%). Most Mennonites still used the printed page, although relatively few did so extensively, with only 5 percent reading books for five hours a day or more. The extent of reading remained unchanged a generation later. Most Mennonites in 1989 were reading a little, but very few were reading extensively—a fact that writers and editors should bear in mind.

In both surveys most respondents listened to the radio (only 5-6% did not); one-fourth (22% in 1972 and 24% in 1989) listened three or more hours per day. This habit also had not changed during the previous two decades. These three ways of acquiring information (reading newspapers, reading books, and listening to the radio) seem to have stabilized into a pattern of moderate use.

In 1972 Mennonites were in the closing stages of a controversy over whether they should use television; many families were still reluctant to do so. One in seven respondents (15%) in 1972 did not watch television; the figure had dropped to 7 percent by 1989. Mennonites in 1989 had accepted television as a source of information, and their pattern of use was similar to that for the other three forms of media, except that almost half (42%) watched television somewhat more (one to three hours daily). Listening to recorded music actually showed a decline in the 1989 survey, presumably because one-third of the respondents shifted over to watching videocassettes, a more modern form of electronic communication.

To what extent were Mennonites in 1989 reading their own literature? Three-fourths (77%) of the respondents received one of their principal denominational magazines, such as *The Mennonite, The Mennonite Reporter, Gospel Herald, Evangelical Visitor, EMC Today, Christian Leader,* and *Mennonite Brethren Herald.* More than one-half (59%) of those who received such periodicals said they read most or all of the issues at least in part—one-fourth (23%) read none or only a few of the issues. Those who did not receive one denominational periodical stated a variety of reasons: one-third did not have time to read; one-fourth were uninterested; and 13 percent felt that such periodicals did not meet their needs.

One-fourth (27%) listened most to news, public affairs, and talk shows on the radio, and about as many (26%) listened to religious and inspirational programs. The other half depended on the radio for a variety of music, including popular or rock (13%), easy listening (12%), classical (9%), and country (9%). Only one percent mostly depended on the radio for sports events. The radio, being more mobile, seems to fill information and entertainment needs in cars, offices, travel, and other places where television is less practical.

Table 12-3 shows that the respondents in 1989 used television more than radio. Practically all respondents (94%) now had television sets, and half of these owned two or more sets. Almost one-half (46%) also had VCRs (videocassette recorders), one-third (37%) subscribed to basic cable TV service, and one-fifth (21%) owned personal computers. Mennonites are strongly committed to the use of electronic media. However, three-fourths (75%) felt that television has a more negative than positive impact, while only 8 percent perceived TV as a positive influence. There was a time when Mennonites combated the negative influences by not owning such devices, but now, presumably, selectivity is the procedure for minimizing the negative impact. Seventy percent of the respondents said they never contribute money to religious TV programs—only 4 percent did so several times a year.

Relatively few (10%) of those who scored high on the use of the media lived on the farms, and almost twice as many who used the media extensively (17%) lived in large cities. There was a gradual increase in use as place of residence shifted from rural farm (10%) to rural nonfarm (12%), to small city (15%), to large city (17%). As urbanization increases, there is also more use of modern media, which will likely increase still more in the future.

Education had the same effect except that the range was greater. Only 5 percent of the Mennonites with only elementary education scored high on use of the media, and the percentages increased with higher levels of education: high school (13%), college (16%), and graduate school (16%).

The range of differentiation was greatest when controlling for socioeconomic status. Only 5 percent of those of lower SES used the media extensively; the percentages increased with increases in socioeconomic level (5, 11, 19 and 21%)—to the point that the highest level used the media four times as much as did the lowest level.

In summary, the correlations were all significant between high media use and greater education (r=.15), urbanization (r=.18), and higher socioeconomic status (r=.28). Use of the media also varied slightly among denominations; the percentage that scored "high" on the media use scale were: Mennonite Church, 13 percent; Mennonite Brethren, 13 percent; General Conference Mennonite, 14 percent; Brethren in Christ, 15 percent; and Evangelical Mennonites, 18 percent.

Predicting Future Trends

Throughout this volume we have examined changes over a generation—the effects of modernization on Mennonite identity between 1972 and 1989. As noted earlier, age is a factor that provides an important clue to future trends. What about those who have left the Mennonite and Brethren in Christ churches? Little can be said about those who have left—more research needs to be done.

The Generation Gap

In chapter 11 we observed that younger respondents scored significantly lower on religious beliefs and practice, moral issues, and in-group identity. These findings suggest that younger Mennonites do not commit themselves to the same issues and concerns as do the older generations. What do these findings suggest for the future?

Table 12-4 lists 29 variables used in this research on Mennonite life and thought, ranked according to their correlation with the age variable. The proportion of respondents who scored high on these dimensions is given for each of five age categories; this shows which issues older Men-

Table 12-4. Faith and Life Variables, Ranked by Correlation with Age

Variables	Age of the respondents					Pearson's r
	13-19	20-29	30-49	50-69	70+	
	(Percent scoring "high")					
Older persons' values						
In-group identity	16	11	16	33	43	.31
Moral behavior	35	15	17	41	53	.31
Church participation	11	22	36	29	17	.31
Devotionalism	7	12	16	27	31	.29
Moral attitudes	20	17	21	38	54	.28
Evangelism	8	9	16	24	27	.26
Separation of church and state	17	19	21	32	51	.23
Serving others	6	19	29	37	37	.22
Stewardship	14	38	38	29	20	.18
Communalism	17	15	18	27	32	.16
Anabaptism	16	19	20	28	28	.16
Fundamentalism	11	16	20	30	36	.12
Common values						
General orthodoxy	57	72	71	80	82	.09
Separatism	11	16	17	18	18	.07
MCC support	13	19	22	19	25	.06
Bible knowledge	17	32	38	41	32	.03
Secularism	38	22	15	18	31	.03
Individualism	28	17	15	14	25	.02
Political participation	4	24	27	21	13	.01
Peacemaking	16	24	20	19	14	.01
Materialism	36	22	14	15	24	.01
Welfare attitudes	24	21	18	17	14	-.03
Ecumenism	29	31	26	28	29	-.04
Younger persons' values						
Greater roles for women	26	33	36	29	17	-.08
Political action	48	48	46	33	31	-.18
Use of mass media	22	14	19	9	2	-.18
Memberships	23	16	22	12	8	-.19
Women in leadership	34	44	42	29	11	-.23
Race relations	42	47	37	20	19	-.36

nonites value most, and which issues younger Mennonites are most concerned with. At the top of the list is in-group identity (r=.31) on which
four times as many respondents aged 70 or over (43%) scored high as
did those in the twenties (11%). More older respondents clearly valued
their ethnic heritage and were more concerned with moral attitudes and
behavior; they felt a greater need for social and ethical boundaries than
did the younger respondents.

Four to six times as many older Mennonites were stronger on
devotionalism, evangelism, and serving others. Many more older people
than teenagers favored separation of church and state; they participated
much more in Sunday school, adhered more to fundamentalist and orthodox beliefs, showed more evidence of communalism, and read the Bible more frequently. Older respondents showed more support for the
religious stake in the sacred canopy that some of these indicators represent.

Scores on the service and outreach variables did not differ greatly by
age. Very few scored strongly on separatism, while the differences in
support for MCC, stewardship, and peacemaking were not great.

Perhaps surprisingly, the least age differences appeared in the concomitants of modernization. The myth that youth are more materialistic,
individualistic, and secular are not supported by our data. However, we
must also note that as many as a fifth to a third (ranging from 14 to 38%)
did score high on these concomitants of modernization; this substantial
block of respondents represented about one-fourth of the Mennonites
and Brethren in Christ. This finding must be of considerable concern. Interestingly, those in the middle age range exhibited the least secularism,
materialism, and individualism. Does raising children nudge parents
more toward familial, communal, and religious interests?

Youth are more action-oriented than older people. Mennonite
youth in 1989 favored a more active role for women in the church and
political action to a greater extent than did the older people; they used
the mass media much more and were much more involved in various
community organizations. Their concern for social action was most evident in the area of social justice. Five times as many younger Mennonites
favored equal treatment for other races, and four times as many youth favored more church leadership for women. The age differences were
greatest on these two issues (r=.30 and .34). Mennonite youth felt as
strongly about equality for women and other races as older Mennonites
felt about ethnicity and moral issues. These age-groups were clearly po-
larized on social justice and preservation of boundaries.

Table 12-4 clearly shows great differences between youth and older
people on very important issues. What implications are there for the

future—for Mennonites in 2010—in the fact that the youth, two generations younger than their grandparents, scored much lower on ethnicity
and morality? Furthermore, will the youth's greater openness to other
races and leadership for women create a more just and equal society and
church? What implications does this trend have for theology?

The Future: Growth or Decline?

The 1972 and 1989 surveys have provided readings on the core of
Mennonites who have remained in the church and who took the time to
respond to the questionnaire. What about those who have left? It is common knowledge that many leave to join other churches and that increasingly many do not relate meaningfully to any Christian fellowship. We
have not surveyed the extent to which members are leaving. Future research should focus on the extent of membership loss and the reasons
why some are leaving for other churches and why some are not attending church at all.

In the past, Mennonites were mostly rural, located in boundaried,
solidly Mennonite enclaves. Some were more segregated and more exclusively Mennonite than others, but individuals and families were usually aware of the needs of other members. It was easier then to think of a
Mennonite church as a community, when it was circumscribed by space
and a sense of peoplehood was nurtured therein. These religious, ethnic,
and communal enclaves were replenished mostly by new births, occasionally by immigrants of kindred and kind, rarely through recruitment
of members from other backgrounds. The emphasis was more on preservation of kind, and growth occurred through having large families. Loss
of members from the relatively closed communities was a traumatic experience, like having a limb severed from one's body.

Birthrates in North America are declining among Mennonites as
well as in the general population. Church growth will be difficult to
maintain even if all descendants remain Mennonite—which is not the
case. The urban environment offers new opportunities for recruitment,
but it is far from clear whether new recruits will be sufficient to replace
losses. We need research on the extent to which urban witness results in
new recruits, the extent to which losses are occuring, and the extent to
which new members of non-Mennonite background revitalize or blunt
the Anabaptist vision. Our data show a modern dispersion of Mennonites. On the basis of annual membership statistics, comparing Lichdi's
1989 data and Kauffman and Harder's data for 1972, we find that the
membership of the Brethren in Christ Church increased most—by 78
percent—followed by the Mennonite Brethren Church (28%), Evangelical Mennonite Church (22%), General Conference Mennonite Church

(13%), and the Mennonite Church, (4%). More research is needed to determine what part birthrates, recruitment, and immigration have each played in these growth patterns.

Summary

Our general conclusion is that while modernization tends to seduce people toward secularization, individualism, and materialism, this tendency is, for the most part, counteracted by strong religious, family, community, and institutional identity that provides a sense of peoplehood.

In 1989 Mennonites exhibited the influence of both Anabaptism and fundamentalism, each having its strong adherents. The Anabaptist Mennonites were strong on peacemaking, in-group identity, communalism, helping others and avoiding excessive individualism. The fundamentalist Mennonites, on the other hand—having lower educational achievement—were strong on orthodox beliefs and traditional gender roles, and were less accepting of welfare aid to the poor and racial equality. We expected these theologies to be different—if not polar opposites—in many ways, although they share strong moral attitudes, devotionalism, religious life, and evangelism, and both were negative on secularism. These contrasting types represent a range of theologies among Mennonites. The Anabaptist Mennonites are, on the average, more urban, better educated, and they occupy higher status, while fundamentalist Mennonites are more rural, less educated, and occupy lower status. Theological pluralism is very much a part of the Mennonite mosaic.

In our examination of leadership we found considerable differences between the laity and leaders. Compared to lay members, ordained leaders were more strongly Anabaptist and were more involved in religious practices, such as stewardship, devotionalism, and church participation. Leaders—compared to non-leaders—more strongly favored outreach through peacemaking, evangelism, MCC work, and service to the poor. Their Mennonite identity was stronger. They more heavily supported women in leadership and racial equality. There were few differences between clergy and laity on personal morality, however. The laity tended to be more independent, secular, individualistic, and materialistic.

In 1989 Mennonites continued to use all forms of media; the pattern of use had not changed much since 1972. While most subscribed to Mennonite periodicals, they spent very little time reading. Use of radio and television was modest. Some Mennonites also used VCRs and personal computers. Use of the media was highest among the better educated, the more urban, and those of higher socioeconomic status. Most Mennonites had access to all forms of communication, but overall they seemed to use the media only to a modest degree. Neither did they depend heavily on the media for their religious and spiritual guidance.

Can we predict the future by examining age differences? While older Mennonites in North America were somewhat stronger on religious beliefs, in-group identity, and moral issues, younger Mennonites were more concerned about social equality and justice. There is evidence of loss of members, but this study did not cover members who have left. Movement from the farm to the city has its opportunities for recruitment as well as the risk of losses. This is an important subject for future research.

We believe that effective leadership and skills in communication are essential for the creation of new identities in modern society and for blending Mennonite solidarity with outreach. The model prepared for such a task includes five intercorrelated variables (in-group identity, Anabaptism, communal networking, serving others, and peacemaking) and appeals more strongly to urban, educated, and higher-status Mennonites. Strong in-group identity energized by Anabaptist theology appears effective in weaving together communal networks, identification with the poor, and peacemaking—which our modern society desperately needs. Some might call it love in action.

Methods Used in the Survey

IMPETUS FOR A NEW SURVEY of Mennonite church members in the United States and Canada developed from an awareness that the data gathered in 1972 had become outdated. Indeed, the Mennonite Brethren Church had conducted its own follow-up survey in 1982 (published in *Direction* 14:2 [1985]) in order to validate the 1972 findings and identify trends in the 10-year interim.

Steps toward a new five-denomination survey were begun in 1985 with an assessment of interest among the leaders of the General Conference Mennonite Church and the Mennonite Church. Eventually all five groups agreed to participate, and the Administrative Committee was formed and met for the first time in June 1987. The Institute of Mennonite Studies, the research arm of the Associated Mennonite Biblical Seminaries, Elkhart, Indiana, agreed to sponsor the study and provide several administrative functions, including handling the project's finances.

In order to achieve maximum comparability, the planners agreed that Church Member Profile II should conform to the methods of the 1972 survey as closely as possible. This meant (1) gathering data by questionnaires administered in group settings, (2) repeating about two-thirds of the original questionnaire, with the same question and response wordings, (3) using the same methods of sample selection, and (4) using the same procedures in conducting the fieldwork.

Neither the original nor the present survey is a census of the Mennonite population. Only church members who had reached the age of 13 were included. Since the median age at baptism is 15, most children were excluded from the sample. Also excluded were persons attending a Mennonite or Brethren in Christ congregation but not having formal membership.

Objectives and Questionnaire Development

As in 1972, the objectives of the 1989 survey were to obtain a profile of the religious beliefs, attitudes, and practices of members of the participating denominations. A new objective was to identify trends in these areas that would provide clues regarding the impact of modernization on Mennonite life and thought. As noted in chapter 1, modernization was operationalized in demographic terms, that is, urbanization, higher socioeconomic status, and geographic mobility. There was also interest in determining whether modernization involved increases in secularism, individualism, and materialism.

Items repeated from the 1972 questionnaire probed the following dimensions: doctrinal orthodoxy; Bible knowledge; church participation and other religious practices; adherence to 16th-century Anabaptist principles; identity with congregation and denomination; membership in community organizations; attitudes regarding moral, ethical, and political issues; selected family characteristics; loyalty to and financial support of church institutions; attitudes toward ecumenism; and demographic characteristics of the respondents.

Dimensions added in the new questionnaire included measures of in-group identity, secularism, individualism, materialism, attitudes regarding male and female roles within and beyond the family, conforming and deviant personal behaviors, identity with the charismatic movement, and selected characteristics of the respondents' congregations. In a pretest, all new questionnaire items were administered to some 50 persons not included in the survey. The pretest provided a basis for determining appropriate scale items and eliminating those items that did not meet the tests of factor analysis and item-to-scale correlations.

Sample Selection

Since the method of sample selection was identical to that of the 1972 survey, we refer the reader to the appendix in Kauffman and Harder (1975) for details. Here we report only the results of the 1989 sample selection process.

The sample was selected in two phases: (1) selection of sample congregations, and (2) selection of members within each sample congregation. In the first phase all congregations that were affiliated with a conference and had at least 25 members were listed alphabetically within each district conference. (Omitting congregations with fewer than 25 members removed only 2 percent of the total membership from the sampling frame.) The number of members in each congregation was listed, and a procedure known as "probability of selection proportionate to size" yielded 186 sample congregations. Five of these were found to be ineligible, either because they were disbanding or had recently disaffiliated from a conference. Of the 181 eligible congregations, 153 (85%) agreed to participate.

In the second phase, the pastor of each participating congregation submitted a membership list, from which we drew a random sample of members: 26 for each MC congregation; 28, GC; 31, MB; 40, BIC; and 50, EMC. Each pastor was sent the sample list for verification that the individual was still a member of the congregation, was at least 13 years of age, could read English, was resident in the community, and would be otherwise able to complete a questionnaire. All persons meeting these qualifications were sent a letter explaining the survey and inviting them to the church on a given evening to complete the questionnaire under the supervision of a research visitor.

Follow-up arrangements were made for all persons not present on the appointed evening. Absentees were provided later with a copy of the questionnaire to be completed at home and mailed to the research office in the envelope provided. An address was obtained for each sample member who did not reside in the community of his/her congregation, and a questionnaire with return envelope was mailed to all such persons.

Field Procedures

Forty "research visitors" assisted in the survey, each of them traveling to from one to six congregations to administer the questionnaires. The project director met with these persons at various locations from eastern Pennsylvania to British Columbia, providing a research manual and reviewing the procedures to be used in carrying out the fieldwork and returning the questionnaires to the research office in Goshen, Indiana.

The fieldwork began in early March 1989 and was completed by the end of July. Depending on the respondent's speed, from one to three hours were required to fill out the 25-page questionnaire. The research visitors completed a report form for each congregation visited, indicating the persons present and persons absent (for follow-up), and giving addresses for all nonresident members. A total of 3,130 questionnaires were returned, of which 3,083 were usable, representing approximately 70 percent of all sample members eligible and able to complete a questionnaire.

Since the five denominations varied greatly in size, a different proportion of the total membership was obtained in the sample of each denomination. These proportions varied from less than 2 percent of the 102,150 members of the Mennonite Church in 1988 to approximately 12 percent of the 3,841 members of the Evangelical Mennonite Church. An adjustment needed to be made when the data for all five denominations were combined, so that each denomination would be represented in the combined data in proper proportion to that denomination's share in the total membership of the combined denominations. This adjustment is called weighting. Table A-1 reports—for each denomination—the total membership, the number of eligible sample congregations, the number of participating congregations, the number of usable responses, and the denominational weights.

Table A-1. Analysis of Sampling Results

Denomination	Members in 1988	Eligible sample congs.	Congs. partici- pating	Usable responses	Denomi- national weights
Mennonite Church	102,150	58	50	888	1.57
General Conference	64,460	47	41	713	1.16
Mennonite Brethren	41,956	37	35	727	.77
Brethren in Christ	18,898	27	18	455	.56
Evangelical Mennonite	3,841	12	9	300	.17
Totals	201,840	181	153	3083	

Data Analysis

All responses were coded and entered into the data bank for analysis at the Goshen College computer center, utilizing the Statistical Package for the Social Sciences. This volume reports on the development of some 40 scales, each constructed from two or more questionnaire items. The items were incorporated into scales if they met the tests of factor analysis and item-to-scale correlations. Pearsonian correlation coefficients (r) were utilized as an efficient device for describing the relationships between scales. An alpha level of .01 was required for determining the statistical significance of relationships between variables when scales were correlated and when chi-square was used as a test of significance in tables showing percentage distributions.

Following is a list of scales utilized in the study, grouped according to the results of factor analysis. These are the unidimensional scales (for which the analysis extracted only one factor, a preferred outcome):

Bible knowledge
church participation
ecumenism
evangelism
female equality

personal independence
political action
political participation
race relations
role of women

fundamentalism

general orthodoxy

individualism

marital role identity

materialism

moral behavior

moral values

pacifism

secularism

separation of church and state

spousal relationships

support of church colleges

stewardship

welfare attitudes

women's career development

Factor analysis extracted two factors for the following scales:

devotionalism

marriage agreements

serving others

separatism

Three factors were extracted for the following scales:

Anabaptism

communalism

in-group identity

mass media

moral attitudes

religious experience

As indicated above, further details on the methods used in the two surveys can be found in the appendix to Kauffman and Harder (1975). The authors will be happy to provide additional information to anyone desiring it.

Notes

Chapter 1: The Challenge of Modernization

1. Data for Church Member Profile II were collected in 1989 by Howard Kauffman and Leland Harder from 153 participating congregations in the same five denominations in the United States and Canada. These denominations—Mennonite Church, General Conference Mennonite, Mennonite Brethren, Brethren in Christ, and Evangelical Mennonite—represent about 60 percent of the members of some 20 Mennonite and Brethren in Christ denominations in North America. The 1989 survey collected 3,083 usable questionnaires—a return rate of about 70 percent. For more details, see the appendix.

2. The correlation coefficients are Pearson r, which has a range from -1.00 to 1.00. The relationship between education and occupation (.56) is strong. Urbanization is moderately related to education (.23), occupational rank (.22), mobility (.20), and income (.10). Occupational rank is moderately related to urbanism (.22), income (.23), and mobility (.08). Income is related to education (.27), occupation (.23), and urbanism (.10), but not to mobility (.01).

3. The first survey, made in 1972 and called "Mennonite Church Member Profile," was extensively reported in J. Howard Kauffman and Leland Harder, *Anabaptists Four Centuries Later*, published in 1975. This original North American survey included the same five denominations studied in 1989, with the number of respondents as follows: Mennonite Church, 1,202; General Conference Mennonite Church, 614; Mennonite Brethren Church, 712; Evangelical Mennonite Church, 444; Brethren in Christ Church, 619. There was a total of 3,591 respondents, representing a 71 percent return.

4. The two samples taken of the five denominations in 1972 and 1989 will be compared from time to time to show changes and trends over the span of seventeen years. Approximately two-thirds of the questions asked in 1989 were the same as those asked in 1972, so they are directly comparable. The 1989 survey devoted one-third of its questions to new concerns and issues. For more details regarding the 1989 sample, see the appendix.

5. To clarify, most of the men on farms are married to women who classify themselves as housewives. Many of these women do not work on the farm as much as did their mothers and grandmothers.

6. The decline in the proportion of respondents who were students, from 14 percent in 1972 to 6 percent in 1989 is not due to a lower proportion of youth attending school. It results from the decline in the proportions of our samples in the 13-19 age-group, from 13 percent in 1972 to 5 percent in 1989. This reflects a major decline in birthrates from the 1950s to the 1970s and an increase in the age at which Mennonite youth become church members through baptism.

7. Income reported in this study is not individual but household income, often in-

cluding two individual incomes—as women increasingly entered the labor force—and occasionally more than two. The respondent was asked to report the "combined 1988 net income (before income taxes) of all members of your household living at home."

8. The range in farm income is partially due to fewer farm women earning second incomes in the labor force.

Chapter 2: Sketching the Regional Settings

1. Hereafter, *South European* will designate Mennonites who lived in the southern Germanic cultural region—Switzerland, South Germany, and Austria. North European Mennonites are those who emerged in the Netherlands and northern Germany and then moved to Prussia, Poland, and Russia.

2. The very earliest Mennonite settlers in the American colonies were partly, perhaps largely, of Dutch origin and may have been somewhat more pro-urban than many Lancaster Mennonites. However, their descendants represent a very small portion of the eastern Mennonite population today.

3. The 1972 survey did not include a question about origins. In 1989 we asked the following question of all those respondents whose race was white (but not Hispanic): "What national background were your ancestors largely from before coming to Canada or the United States?" Respondents checked one of four answers: (l) Swiss/South German/Alsatian, (2) Dutch/North German/Prussian/Russian, (3) British, (4) other.

4. Table 2-4 reports the responses regarding origin: Swiss, Dutch, and other. Although the response categories were quite clear, we suspect that some of the Swiss Mennonite respondents, thinking of themselves as "Pennsylvania Dutch," checked the category "Dutch." Thus the category "Dutch," especially for the eastern United States, is likely somewhat contaminated. Later, when we compare the respondents of Swiss and Dutch origins, we do not include those who checked "Dutch" in the American East and Midwest, to make sure that the suspected contamination factor is eliminated from those regions. Any contamination in other regions should be very minimal.

5. Despite our sample of nearly 3,100, considered large by most social science standards, we were not able to get a sufficient number of respondents from among native Indians, blacks, Asians, Hispanics, and other visible minorities. The random selection of congregations yielded one church with primarily black members, two congregations of Hispanics, and a Chinese Mennonite congregation. The black congregation and one of the Hispanic churches participated; one Hispanic congregation was found to be disbanding, and the Chinese congregation did not wish to participate. The questionnaire item on race asked the respondent to check one of six answers: (1) Hispanic, (2) black, (3) white (not Hispanic), (4) American or Canadian Indian, (5) Asian, and (6) other. There were 75 respondents who checked "American or Canadian Indian." We believe these are virtually all in error, the respondents apparently thinking they were checking "American," rather than "American Indian" as was intended. Another problem was the inability or unwillingness of minority members whose mother tongue was not English to complete a long English questionnaire, as was the case with the Hispanic congregation. The Administrative Committee for the 1989 survey debated this problem at length and decided that it was impossible to enlarge the sample to include adequate numbers of visible minorities. It was decided to encourage other researchers to make a study of Mennonite minorities in the near future. Michael Yoder included other racial minorities in his census of the Mennonite Church (1985:307-47), and the results were most interesting.

Chapter 3: The Sacred and Secularization

1. Four of the scale items used in 1989 are identical to the items used in 1972. In 1989 the 1972 item on belief in "a flood in Noah's day" was replaced with the item on excluding from membership those persons who do not accept the fundamentals.

2. The items in the Anabaptism scale are based on the content of the Anabaptist vision as set forth by Bender in the 1940s. More recent emphases on the polygenesis of Anabaptism faced us with a dilemma—should we revise the scale in line with new thinking or use it again for the sake of comparability and determination of changes in beliefs since

1972? We opted for the latter. Elsewhere, recent pluralism in Mennonite beliefs was explored with the addition of questionnaire items not used in 1972.

3. A positive correlation has values from .00 (no correlation) to 1.00 (perfect positive correlation), indicating that scores on one variable increase when scores on the other variable also increase. A negative correlation (-.01 to -.1.00) indicates that increases on one variable are associated with decreases on the other variable.

4. Responses were coded from one to five, with "five" representing the most secular response. Total scores for the nine items ranged from 9 to 41 within a possible range of 9 to 45; the mean score was 18. A factor analysis resulted in all nine items loading on a single factor; thus we can claim unidimensionality for the scale.

Chapter 4: Community and Individualism

1. The movement sponsored the publication of the *Mennonite Community* magazine from 1946 through 1953 and undergirded the Conferences on Mennonite Educational and Cultural Problems, first held annually, later biennially, from 1942 to 1967.

2. We hope we are not amiss in implying that what Bellah and his associates write about American society may apply also to Canadian society. In subsequent references to the work, for the sake of simplicity, we will use Bellah's name in place of "Bellah and his associates."

3. We acknowledge helpful suggestions from Stephen Ainlay and Leland Harder. Using the Bellah volume (1985) and other sources, Harder drafted over 100 statements related to modernization, secularism, individualism, and materialism to which Likert-type, agree-disagree responses could be assigned. Sixty-four of these items were pretested with a group of 50 persons. On the basis of factor analysis and item-to-scale correlations, 22 were finally incorporated into the survey instrument. These items are the basis for the scales measuring secularism, individualism, and separatism.

4. The responses provided were "very important," "important," "somewhat important," "not very important," and "of no importance."

5. All three scales (individualism, personal independence, and materialism) factored as unidimensional in their final form—leading us to believe that they are valid measures of the aspects of individualism presented above.

6. Assuming that the inclusion of seminary-trained clergy in the sample may have affected the negative correlation between education and the concomitants of modernization, we tested the difference it would make if clergy (ordained persons) were omitted from the analysis. When the clergy were omitted, the negative correlations persisted although slightly diminished. For example, the correlation between education and secularism was -.17 with clergy omitted, -.20 with clergy included. The correlation between education and individualism was -.11 with clergy omitted, -.21 when included. The negative correlations persisted when the variables of age, residence, socioeconomic status, and mobility were controlled by partial correlation analysis.

Chapter 5: Changing Family Patterns

1. For a statement on family values from a biblical viewpoint by a Mennonite author, see Ross T. Bender, *Christians in Families* (1982).

2. The CMP II data for intermarriages are for *all* age-groups, not just for the younger, currently marrying couples as reported by the Canadian census.

3. Yoder's 1982 MC census indicated that 4.4 percent of the comparable adult "non-Hispanic white" population had experienced divorce or separation. The 1989 rate for ever-divorced or -separated MC members was 4.5 percent. Both sets of data are based on members 20 years of age and older.

4. Applying the U.S. Consumer Price Index to incomes of Mennonites of both Canada and the United States incurs some imprecision. Because of differences in the economies, inflation rates, and index computations it is difficult to make international comparisons. There are probably only small differences between the two countries in their inflation-adjusted income trends.

5. The responses to each item were coded from one to five, with the most equalitarian

response arbitrarily assigned the highest score. Respondent scores ranged from 3 to 15, the possible limits. Factor analysis resulted in all items loading on one factor—true also for the married women's career scale.

6. The 1956 and 1989 data are for the Mennonite Church only. Since the item was not used in the 1972 survey, it was not possible to compare the 1972 and 1989 respondents in this regard.

7. The differences in response distributions between the five denominations on these three items were slight and not statistically significant.

Chapter 6: Emerging Institutions

1. The 12 percent represents those who had one or more years in a Mennonite elementary school; it does not mean that 12 percent spent *all* their elementary years in a Mennonite school, nor does it mean that at any one time 12 percent of Mennonite elementary school children are attending a Mennonite school.

2. Category 1 includes those who attended non-Mennonite church-related colleges and/or public colleges and universities. Some respondents appear in both categories 2 and 3, having attended a Mennonite or BIC school at both high school and college levels.

3. The scale measuring support of church colleges was formed from responses to these two items: (1) "Do you think the benefits derived from our present church colleges justify the costs of maintaining them?" (2) "In general, every Mennonite young person who goes to school beyond high school should take at least one year of study in a Mennonite college or Bible institute" (responses: agree, undecided, disagree).

4. In a telephone survey, Rothenberg and Newport used a national population probability sample, but gathered data only from those who identified themselves as evangelicals. They did not first identify evangelical denominations and then take a sample of their members. The fact that 45 percent lived in southern states and 10 percent were black may have biased their sample in the Democratic direction.

5. See Kauffman and Harder (1975:237-39) for details on the 1972 pattern of giving.

Chapter 7: Changing Consciousness of Peoplehood

1. Factor analysis is the statistical technique of combining related variables into larger clusters independent from other clusters, called factors. Using this technique, we found that four of the questions, related to language and newspapers, clustered under "communications"; four more, related to dating and friendships, clustered under "social relations"; and two questions clustered under "Mennonite organizations."

2. We combined the responses to 10 questions, two for each of the five variables presented in Table 7-2, to form an in-group identity scale. Figures 7-1 to 7-3 give composite scores, indicating degrees of in-group identity.

3. As discussed in chapter 1, urbanization, socioeconomic status (composed of education, occupation, and income) and mobility constitute our model of modernization.

Chapter 8: Finding Networks of Service

1. The evangelism scale was constructed from the responses to three items: (1) How frequently do you take the opportunity to witness orally about the Christian faith to persons at work, in the neighborhood, or elsewhere? (2) How frequently have you invited non-Christians to attend your church and/or Sunday school services? (3) Have you personally ever tried to lead someone to faith in Christ?

2. In this volume the terms peacemaking and pacifism are used interchangeably. A pacifism scale was constructed using six items: not taking part in war, promoting the peace position, choosing nonparticipation in the military if drafted, viewing ownership of stock in companies producing war goods as wrong, opposing payment of the proportion of income taxes that go to the military, and disfavoring Israel's warlike treatment of the Arabs.

3. Respondents were asked to check numerous categories of service under MCC and other agencies (summer voluntary service, long-term voluntary service, alternative service during wartime, etc.). A few respondents had served in two or more of these programs; these individuals will slightly inflate the numbers listed under MCC service.

Chapter 9: Probing Moral and Ethical Issues

1. Table 9-1 omits the following moral issues already reported on in chapter 5: divorce and remarriage of divorced persons.

2. The question refers to public policy as established by legislatures rather than to what the individual would do if faced with the decision of whether to have an abortion herself.

3. The three items in this scale were the only behavior items included in the 1972 questionnaire. They do not constitute a strong measure of personal moral behavior, but were used in the 1989 data analysis only for the sake of comparability. For more detail on the rationale and construction of the moral attitudes and moral behavior scales, see Kauffman and Harder, pp. 126-27. The content of the scales was the same in both surveys.

4. Precise comparisons with the 1972 results is not possible since in 1989 the phrase "if otherwise compatible" was added to the 1972 statement. In 1972, 19 percent responded "never wrong"; in 1989, 42 percent. Some of this shift may be due to the rewording of the item.

5. The 1972 item had a somewhat different wording: "Capital punishment (the death penalty for a major crime) is a necessary deterrent to crime and should not be abandoned by our national, provincial, or state governments." The responses were: agree, 30 percent; disagree, 41 percent; and uncertain, 29 percent. These responses are very similar to those in 1989, but the rewording precludes a precise comparison.

Chapter 10: Comparing Mennonite Denominations

1. If the reader wishes more information on the origin, history, and characteristics of the five denominations than we have provided in this volume, chapter 2 in Kauffman and Harder, *Anabaptists Four Centuries Later*, will provide a review. More detail can be found in Dyck (1967) and Schlabach (1988).

2. The percentage was computed for each respondent by dividing the reported household amount given to church and charities in 1988 by the reported net household income in 1988. Class mid-values were used in the computations.

3. Additional behaviors were probed in the 1989 questionnaire, but for the sake of comparability only these three were used again in the 1989 scale for moral behavior. A high score on this scale represents avoidance of the behaviors.

4. One purpose of this scale was to examine how persons who are very traditional and restrictive in their views differ on other dimensions from persons who are more flexible and open on issues.

5. The possible responses were "very important," "important," "somewhat important," "not very important," and "of no importance." The scale satisfies the standard of unidimensionality, since factor analysis yielded only one factor. The highest score on each item was given to the "very important" responses.

6. There is, of course, the question of the validity of the scales measuring the concomitants of modernization. We can only claim that they have face validity and that they withstood the tests of factor analysis and item-to-scale correlations. For all four scales factor analysis yielded only one factor, thereby indicating the desired unidimensionality.

Chapter 11: Sorting the Indicators of Modernization

1. The designation "high" is arbitrary. The scale scores for each variable were collapsed into three or four categories—"high," "middle," and "low," or "high," "upper middle," "lower middle," and "low." In each case approximately one-fifth to one-third of the cases were arbitrarily assigned the "high" category. Thus, "high" means only "the highest category." Reporting only the highs is more efficient in the use of space, but it does obscure the fact that the respondents were spread across the whole range of scale scores.

2. This criticism is particularly voiced by the editors and writers of the *Sword and Trumpet* periodical.

3. We raised the question of whether the high ratings among those with graduate education might have been due to the inclusion of many seminary-trained ministers in the graduate category. A comparison of scale intercorrelations with ministers excluded and

with ministers included was made. When ministers were excluded, the relationship be-tween education and religious variables was slightly reduced but not eliminated. Thus if all ordained persons were removed from the sample, the observed relationships would per-sist, although with slightly diminished strength.

4. This difference is probably not due to our inclusion of education in SES, since we obtained similar results for education alone and SES with education included.

5. The zero order correlation of residence (urbanization) with secularism (r=.02), in-dividualism (r= -.06), and materialism (r= -.03) was statistically significant only in the case of individualism. When education and SES were controlled via partial correlation analysis, no significant correlation between residence and individualism or between residence and materialism resulted. However, a small but statistically significant correlation (r=.09) be-tween residence and secularism was obtained, indicating that secularism is slightly related to urbanization when the effects of education and SES are removed.

6. Religious research in the United States in the 1980s has shifted away from denomi-national surveys toward the use of national polls that identify the religious affiliation of re-spondents and permit cross-tabulations of religion with other social and religious variables. Primary among such polling agencies are the National Opinion Research Center (NORC) at the University of Chicago and the American Institute of Public Opinion (Gallup Organi-zation) at Princeton University. Religious research is easier in Canada since its national de-cennial census includes religious affiliation. Demographers in the United States have made many attempts, so far unsuccessfully, to have religious affiliation included in the U.S. de-cennial census.

7. A simple zero-order correlation coefficient between age and church attendance (and church participation) would show no relationship, due to the curvilinear nature of the relationship. Thus the percentage distributions present a much clearer picture of the varia-tion in attendance rates—and church participation in general—among the different age cat-egories than a correlation coefficient would give.

Bibliography

Ainlay, Stephen C.
1990a   "Communal Commitment and Individualism." In Leo Driedger and Leland Harder, eds., *Anabaptist-Mennonite Identities in Ferment*. Elkhart, Ind.: Institute of Mennonite Studies.

1990b   "The 1920 Seminary Movement: A Failed Attempt at Formal Theological Education in the Mennonite Church." *Mennonite Quarterly Review* 66:325-51.

Argyle, Michael
1959   *Religious Behavior*. Glencoe, Ill.: Free Press.

Bellah, Robert N., Richard Madsen, William M. Sullivan, Ann Swidler, and Steven M. Tipton.
1985   *Habits of the Heart*. New York: Harper & Row.

Bender, Harold S.
1944   "The Anabaptist Vision." *Church History* 13:3-24.

1945   "The Mennonite Conception of the Church and Its Relation to Community Building. *Mennonite Quarterly Review* 19:90-100.

1962   *These Are My People: The New Testament Church*. Scottdale, Pa.: Herald Press.

Bender, Ross T.
1982   *Christians in Families*. Scottdale, Pa.: Herald Press.

Bender, Thomas
1982   *Community and Social Change in America*. Baltimore: Johns Hopkins University Press.

Berger, Peter L.
1967   *The Sacred Canopy*. Garden City, N.Y.: Doubleday.

1977   *Facing up to Modernity*. New York: Basic Books.

Berger, Peter L. and Brigitte Berger
1975   *Sociology*. Second edition. New York: Basic Books.

Berger, Peter L., Brigitte Berger and Hansfried Kellner
1973   *The Homeless Mind*. New York: Random House.

Berger, Peter L. and Thomas Luckmann
1966   *The Social Construction of Reality: A Treatise in the Sociology of Knowledge*. Garden City, N.Y.: Doubleday.

Bibby, Reginald W.
1987   *Fragmented Gods: The Poverty and Potential of Religion in Canada*. Toronto: Irwin Publishing.

Braght, Thieleman J. van
1964   *Martyrs Mirror: A Story of Fifteen Centuries of Christian Martyrdom from the Time of Christ to A.D 1660*. Scottdale, Pa.: Mennonite Publishing House.

Breasted, James H. and Carl F. Huth
1961   *European History Atlas: Ancient, Medieval and Modern European World History*. Chicago: Denoyer-Geppert.

Breault, Kevin D.
1989   "New Evidence on Religious Pluralism, Urbanism, and Religious Participation." *American Sociological Review* 54:1048-53.

Breton, Raymond
1964   "Institutional Completeness of Ethnic Communities and Personal Relations to Immigrants." *American Journal of Sociology* 70:193-205.

Brinkley, David
1990   Commentary on "This Week with David Brinkley," ABC, November 25.

Burgess, Ernest W. and Harvey J. Locke
1953   *The Family*. Second edition. New York: American Book Co.

Burgess, Ernest W. and Paul Wallin
1953   *Engagement and Marriage*. Chicago: J. B. Lippincott.

Campbell, Thomas C. and Yoshio Fukuyama
1970   *The Fragmented Layman*. Philadelphia: Pilgrim Press.

Campolo, Anthony, Jr.
1971   *A Denomination Looks at Itself*. Valley Forge, Pa.: Judson Press.

Cherlin, Andrew J.
1981   *Marriage, Divorce, Remarriage*. Cambridge: Harvard University Press.

Clasen, Claus-Peter
1972   *Anabaptism: A Social History, 1525-1618*. Ithaca, N.Y.: Cornell University Press.

Coenen, W. L. C.
1920   *Bydrage tot de Kennis van de maatshappelijke verhoudingen van de zestiendeeeniwische Doopera*. Amsterdam.

Currie, Raymond, Leo Driedger and Rick Linden
  1979   "Abstinence and Moderation: Mixing Mennonite Drinking Norms."
         Mennonite Quarterly Review 53:263-81.

D'Antonio, William V. and Joan Aldous
  1983   *Families and Religions: Conflict and Change in Modern Society.* Beverly
         Hills: Sage Publications.

Dewey, Richard
  1960   "The Rural-Urban Continuum: Real but Relatively Unimportant."
         American Journal of Sociology 66:60-66.

Driedger, Leo
  1977   "The Anabaptist Identification Ladder: Plain Urban Continuity in Di-
         versity." *Mennonite Quarterly Review* 51:278-91.

  1980   "Nomos-Building on the Prairies: Construction of Indian, Hutterite
         and Jewish Sacred Canopies." *Canadian Journal of Sociology* 5:341-56.

  1984   "Multicultural Regionalism: Toward Understanding the Canadian
         West." In Tony Rasporich, ed., *Making of the Modern West: Western Cana-
         da since 1945.* Calgary: University of Calgary Press.

  1986a "Community Conflict: The Eldorado Invasion of Warman." *Canadian
         Review of Sociology and Anthropology* 23:247-69.

  1986b "Mennonite Community Change: From Ethnic Enclaves to Social Net-
         works." *Mennonite Quarterly Review* 60:374-86.

  1987   *Ethnic Canada: Identities and Inequalities.* Toronto: Copp Clark Pitman.

  1988   *Mennonite Identity in Conflict.* Lewiston, N.Y.: Edwin Mellen Press.

  1989   *The Ethnic Factor: Identity in Diversity.* Toronto: McGraw-Hill Ryerson.

  1989   "Urbanization of Mennonites in Post-War Canada." *Journal of Menno-
         nite Studies* 7:90-110.

  1990   *Mennonites in Winnipeg.* Hillsboro, Kan.: Kindred Press.

Driedger, Leo and Leland Harder, eds.
  1990   *Anabaptist-Mennonite Identities in Ferment.* Elkhart, Ind.: Institute of
         Mennonite Studies.

Driedger, Leo and J. Howard Kauffman
  1982   "Urbanization of Mennonites: Canadian and American Comparisons."
         Mennonite Quarterly Review 56:269-90.

Driedger, Leo, J. Winfield Fretz and Donovan Smucker
  1978   "A Tale of Two Strategies: Mennonites in Chicago and Winnipeg."
         Mennonite Quarterly Review 52:294-311.

Driedger, Leo, Michael Yoder, and Peter Sawatzky
  1985   "Divorce Among Mennonites: Evidence of Family Breakdown." *Men-
         nonite Quarterly Review* 59:367-82.

Dueck, Al
    1988   "Psychology and Mennonite Self-Understanding." In Calvin W. Redekop and Samuel J. Steiner, eds., *Mennonite Identity*. Lanham, Md.: University Press of America.

Duvall, Evelyn Millis
    1971   *Family Development*. Philadelphia: J. B. Lippincott.

Dyck, Cornelius J., ed.
    1967   *An Introduction to Mennonite History*. Scottdale, Pa.: Herald Press.

Dyck, Cornelius J.
    1980   *From the Files of MCC*. Scottdale, Pa.: Herald Press.

Dyck, Cornelius J., ed.
    1980   *Witness and Service in North America*. Scottdale, Pa.: Herald Press.

Dyer, Everett D.
    1979   *The American Family: Variety and Change*. New York: McGraw-Hill.

Eisenstadt, Samuel N.
    1968   "Social Institutions." In David L. Sills, ed., *International Encyclopedia of the Social Sciences* 14:409-29. Macmillan and The Free Press.

Epp, Frank H.
    1974   *Mennonites in Canada, 1886-1920: The History of a Separate People*. Toronto: Macmillan.

    1977   *Mennonite Peoplehood: A Plea for New Initiatives*. Waterloo, Ont.: Conrad Press.

    1982   *Mennonites in Canada, 1920-1940: A People's Struggle for Survival*. Toronto: Macmillan.

    1983   *Partners in Service: The Story of Mennonite Central Committee Canada*. Winnipeg: Mennonite Central Committee Canada.

Falwell, Jerry, ed.
    1981   *The Fundamentalist Phenomenon*. Garden City, N.Y.: Doubleday.

Fast, Erna J.
    1980   "Observations on Concepts of Ministry." In Dorothy Yoder Nyce, ed., *Which Way Women?* Akron, Pa.: Peace Section, Mennonite Central Committee.

Finke, Roger and Rodney Stark
    1988   "Religious Economies and Sacred Canopies: Religious Mobilization in American Cities, 1906." *American Sociological Review* 53:41-49.

Folsom, J. K.
    1943   *The Family and Democratic Society*. New York: John Wiley & Sons.

Francis, E. K.
    1951   "The Mennonite Commonwealth in Russia 1789-1914: A Sociological Interpretation." *Mennonite Quarterly Review* 25:173-82.

1955   *In Search of Utopia: The Mennonites in Manitoba.* Altona, Man.: D. W. Friesen.

Fretz, J. Winfield
1955   "Community." *Mennonite Encyclopedia* 1:656. Scottdale, Pa.: Mennonite Publishing House.

1974   *The Mennonites in Ontario.* Waterloo, Ont.: Mennonite Historical Society of Ontario.

1989   *The Waterloo Mennonites: A Community in Paradox.* Waterloo, Ont.: Wilfred Laurier University Press.

Friedmann, Robert
1944   "On Mennonite Historiography and on Individualism and Brotherhood." *Mennonite Quarterly Review* 18:117-22.

1949   *Mennonite Piety Through the Centuries.* Goshen, Ind.: Mennonite Historical Society.

Friesen, Duane K.
1986   *Christian Peacemaking and International Conflict: A Realist Pacifist Perspective.* Scottdale, Pa.: Herald Press.

Fullerton, J. Timothy and Bruce Hunsberger
1982   "A Unidimensional Measure of Christian Orthodoxy." *Journal for the Scientific Study of Religion* 21:317-26.

Gallup, George, Jr.
1982   *Religion in America.* Princeton, N.J.: Princeton Religion Research Center.

1985   *Religion in America.* Princeton, N.J.: The Gallup Report, May 1985.

Gallup, George, Jr. and Sarah Jones
1989   *100 Questions and Answers; Religion in America.* Princeton, N.J.: Princeton Religious Research Center.

Gans, Herbert J.
1988   *Middle American Individualism.* New York: Free Press.

Gendron, Bernard
1977   *Technology and the Human Tradition.* New York: St. Martin's Press.

Glock, Charles Y. and Rodney Stark
1965   *Religion and Society in Tension.* Chicago: Rand McNally.

Glock, Charles Y., Benjamin B. Ringer, and Earl R. Babbie
1967   *To Comfort and to Challenge.* Berkeley: University of California Press.

Goode, William J.
1964   *The Family.* New York: Prentice-Hall.

Goodsell, Willystine
1934   *A History of Marriage and the Family.* Revised edition. New York: Macmillan.

Granovetter, Mark S.
1973   "The Strength of Weak Ties." *American Journal of Sociology* 78:1370-77.

Haddon, Jeffrey K.
1969   *The Gathering Storm in the Churches*. Garden City, N.Y.: Doubleday.

Hadden, Jeffrey K. and Anson Shupe
1988   *Televangelism: Power and Politics on God's Frontier*. New York: Henry Holt.

Hamm, Peter M.
1987   *Continuity and Change Among Canadian Mennonite Brethren*. Waterloo, Ont.: Wilfred Laurier University Press.

1990   "The Sacred and Secularization." In Leo Driedger and Leland Harder, eds., *Anabaptist-Mennonite Identities in Ferment*. Elkhart, Ind.: Institute of Mennonite Studies.

Harder, Lydia
1990   "Discipleship Reexamined: Women in the Hermeneutical Community." In Harry Huebner, ed., *The Church as Theological Community: Essays in Honour of David Schroeder*. Winnipeg: CMBC Publications.

Herberg, Will
1955   *Protestant-Catholic-Jew*. Garden City, N.Y.: Doubleday.

Hershberger, Guy F., ed.
1957   *The Recovery of the Anabaptist Vision*. Scottdale, Pa.: Herald Press.

Hershberger, Guy F.
1958   *The Way of the Cross in Human Relations*. Scottdale, Pa.: Herald Press.

Hertzler, Daniel
1971   *Mennonite Education: Why and How?* Scottdale, Pa.: Herald Press.

Hoge, Dean R. and David A. Roozen
1979   "Research on Factors Influencing Church Commitment." In Hoge and Roozen, eds., *Understanding Church Growth and Decline, 1950-1978*. New York: Pilgrim Press.

Holman, Thomas B. and Wesley R. Burr
1984   "Beyond the Beyond: The Growth of Family Theories in the 1970s." In David C. Olson and Brent C. Miller, eds., *Family Studies Review Yearbook*, Volume 2. Beverly Hills: Sage Publications.

Horsch, James E., ed.
1990   *Mennonite Yearbook & Directory, 1990-91*. Scottdale, Pa.: Herald Press.

Hostetler, Beulah Stauffer
1987   *American Mennonites and Protestant Movements*. Scottdale, Pa.: Herald Press.

1990   "Nonresistance and Social Responsibility: Mennonites and Mainline Peace Emphasis, ca. 1950 to 1985." *Mennonite Quarterly Review* 64:49-73.

Hostetler, John A.
1974   *Hutterite Society.* Baltimore: Johns Hopkins University Press.

Huebner, Harry, ed.
1990   *The Church as Theological Community: Essays in Honour of David Schroeder.* Winnipeg: CMBC Publications.

Hunter, James Davison
1983   *American Evangelicalism.* New Brunswick, N.J.: Rutgers University Press.

Hunter, James Davison and Stephen C. Ainlay, eds.
1986   *Making Sense of Modern Times: Peter L. Berger and the Vision of Interpretive Sociology.* New York: Routledge & Kegan Paul.

Jagger, Alison M. and Paula Rothenberg Struhl
1984   *Feminist Frameworks.* Second edition. New York: McGraw-Hill.

Johnson, Otto, executive ed.
1990   *Information Please Almanac.* Boston: Houghton Mifflin.

Johnson, Roger A., ed.
1983   *Views from the Pews.* Philadelphia: Fortress Press.

Juhnke, James C.
1975   *A People of Two Kingdoms: The Political Acculturation of the Kansas Mennonites.* Newton, Kan.: Faith and Life Press.

1979   *A People of Mission: A History of General Conference Mennonite Overseas Missions.* Newton, Kan.: Faith and Life Press.

1988   "Mennonite History and Self Understanding: North American Mennonitism as a Bipolar Mosaic." In Calvin W. Redekop and Samuel J. Steiner, eds., *Mennonite Identity.* Lanham, Md.: University Press of America.

1989   *Vision, Doctrine, War: Mennonite Identity and Organization in America, 1880-1930.* Scottdale, Pa.: Herald Press.

Kauffman, J. Howard
1960   "A Comparative Study of Traditional and Emergent Family Types Among Midwest Mennonites." Unpublished Ph.D. dissertation, University of Chicago.

1961   "Interpersonal Relations in Traditional and Emergent Family Types Among Midwest Mennonites." *Marriage and Family Living* 23:247-52.

1966   "A Philosophy of Rural Life for Today's World." Unpublished paper. Copy in Mennonite Historical Library, Goshen College, Goshen, Ind.

1979   "Social Correlates of Spiritual Maturity Among North American Mennonites." *Sociological Analysis* 40:27-42.

1989   "Dilemmas of Christian Pacifism Within a Historic Peace Church." *Sociological Analysis* 49:4, 368-85.

Kauffman, J. Howard and Leland Harder
   1975   *Anabaptists Four Centuries Later: A Profile of Five Mennonite and Brethren in Christ Denominations*. Scottdale, Pa.: Herald Press.

Kaufman, Edmund G.
   1931   *The Development of the Missionary and Philanthropic Interest Among the Mennonites of North America*. Berne, Ind.: Mennonite Book Concern.

Kaufman, Gordon D.
   1979   *Nonresistance and Responsibility, and Other Essays*. Newton, Kan.: Faith and Life Press.

Kephart, William M.
   1981   *The Family, Society, and the Individual*. Fifth edition. Boston: Houghton Mifflin.

Klaassen, Walter
   1973   *Anabaptism: Neither Catholic nor Protestant*. Waterloo, Ont.: Conrad Press.

   1990   "The Quest for Anabaptist Identity." In Leo Driedger and Leland Harder, eds., *Anabaptist-Mennonite Identities in Ferment*. Elkhart, Ind.: Institute of Mennonite Studies.

Klapp, Orrin
   1975   "Opening and Closing in Open Systems." *Behavioral Sciences* 20:251-57.

Klassen, Peter J.
   1989   *A Homeland for Strangers: An Introduction to Mennonites in Poland and Prussia*. Fresno, Calif.: Center for Mennonite Brethren Studies.

Klippenstein, Lawrence, ed.
   1979   *That There Be Peace: Mennonites in Canada and World War II*. Winnipeg: Manitoba CO Reunion Committee.

Koontz, Ted
   1989   "Mennonites and 'Postmodernity.' " *Mennonite Quarterly Review* 63:401-27.

Krahn, Cornelius
   1980   "Dutch Mennonites Prospered in 'Golden Age.' " *Mennonite Weekly Review* 58:6-8.

   1981   *Dutch Anabaptism: Origin, Spread, Life, and Thought*. Scottdale, Pa.: Herald Press.

Kraus, C. Norman
   1990   "Shifting Mennonite Theological Orientations." In Leo Driedger and Leland Harder, eds., *Anabaptist-Mennonite Identities in Ferment*. Elkhart, Ind.: Institute of Mennonite Studies.

Kraybill, Donald B.
   1978   *Mennonite Education: Issues, Facts, and Changes*. Scottdale, Pa.: Herald Press.

1988   "Modernity and Identity: The Transformation of Mennonite Ethnicity." In Calvin W. Redekop and Samuel J. Steiner, eds., *Mennonite Identity: Historical and Contemporary Perspectives*. Lanham, Md.: University Press of America.

1990   "Modernity and Modernization." In Leo Driedger and Leland Harder, eds., *Anabaptist-Mennonite Identities in Ferment*. Elkhart, Ind.: Institute of Mennonite Studies.

Kraybill, Paul N.
1974   "North American Inter-Mennonite Relationships." Unpublished paper. Copy at Mennonite Historical Library, Goshen College, Goshen, Ind.

Kreider, Robert S. and Rachel Waltner Goossen
1988   *Hungry, Thirsty, a Stranger: The MCC Experience*. Scottdale, Pa.: Herald Press.

Lenski, Gerhard
1963   *The Religious Factor*. Garden City, N.Y.: Doubleday.

Leslie, Gerald R.
1979   *The Family in Social Context*. Fourth edition. New York: Oxford University Press.

Levy, Marion J.
1972   *Modernization: Latecomers and Survivors*. New York: Basic Books.

Lichdi, Diether Goetz, ed.
1990   *Mennonite World Handbook: Mennonites in Global Witness*. Carol Stream, Ill.: Mennonite World Conference.

Lindley, Susan Hill
1980   "Feminist Theology in a Global Perspective." In Dorothy Yoder Nyce, ed., *Which Way Women?* Akron, Pa.: Peace Section, Mennonite Central Committee.

Loewen, Harry, ed.
1988   *Why I Am a Mennonite: Essays on Mennonite Identity*. Scottdale, Pa.: Herald Press.

MacMaster, Richard K.
1985   *Land, Piety, Peoplehood: The Establishment of Mennonite Communities in America, 1683-1790*. Scottdale, Pa.: Herald Press.

Manual of Doctrine and Government.
1973   Revised edition. Nappanee, Ind.: Evangel Press.

Mennonite Church and General Conference Mennonite Church
1985   *Human Sexuality in Christian Life*. Newton, Kan.: Faith and Life Press.

Mennonite Confession of Faith
1963   Scottdale, Pa.: Herald Press.

Miller, Delbert and William H. Form
  1980   *Industrial Sociology: Work in Organizational Life.* Third edition. New York: Harper & Row.

Miller, Marilyn and Anne Neufeld Rupp
  1980   "Co-Pastoring in Mennonite Churches Today." In Dorothy Yoder Nyce, ed., *Which Way Women?* Akron, Pa.: Peace Section, Mennonite Central Committee.

National Center for Health Statistics
  1990   "Advance Report of Final Natality Statistics, 1988." *Monthly Vital Statistics Report* 39/4 (supplement). Hyattsville, Md.: U.S. Public Health Service.

National Opinion Research Center
  1989   *General Social Surveys, 1972-1989: Cumulative Codebook.* Storrs, Conn.: Roper Center for Public Opinion Research.

Newman, William M.
  1973   *American Pluralism: A Study of Minority Groups and Social Theory.* New York: Harper and Row.

Niebuhr, H. Richard
  1929   *The Social Sources of Denominationalism.* New York: World.

Nyce, Dorothy Yoder, ed.
  1980   *Which Way Women?* Akron, Pa.: Peace Section, Mennonite Central Committee.

Nyce, Dorothy Yoder
  1980   "Women in Pulpit Ministry in 19th Century US." In Dorothy Yoder Nyce, ed., *Which Way Women?* Akron, Pa.: Peace Section, Mennonite Central Committee.

Nye, F. Ivan and Felix Berardo
  1973   *The Family: Its Structure and Interaction.* New York: Macmillan.

Ogburn, William F.
  1933   *Recent Social Trends in the United States.* New York: McGraw-Hill.

Packull, Werner O.
  1979   "The Demise of the Normative Position." *Studies in Religion* 8:313-29.

  1990   "Between Paradigms: Anabaptist Studies at the Crossroads." *Conrad Grebel Review* 8:1-22.

Peachey, Paul
  1954   *Die soziale Herkunft der schweizerischen Täufer in der Reformationszeit.* Karlsruhe.

  1963   *The Church in the City.* Newton, Kan.: Faith and Life Press.

Penner, Horst
  1978   *Die ost- und westpreussischen Mennoniten in ihrem religioesen und socialen Leben in ihren kulturellen und wirtschaftlichen Leistungen.* Weierhof, Germany: Mennonitischer Geschichtsverein.

Quin, Bernard, Herman Anderson, Martin Bradley, Paul Getting, and Peggy Schriver.
1982 *Churches and Church Membership in the U.S.* Atlanta: Glenmary Research Center.

Ramseyer, Robert L., ed.
1979 *Mission and the Peace Witness: The Gospel and Christian Discipleship.* Scottdale, Pa.: Herald Press.

Redekop, Calvin
1976 "Institutions, Power, and the Gospel." In John Richard Burkholder and Calvin Redekop, eds., *Kingdom, Cross, and Community.* Scottdale, Pa.: Herald Press.

1989 *Mennonite Society.* Baltimore: Johns Hopkins University Press.

1990 "Sectarianism and the Sect Cycle." In Leo Driedger and Leland Harder, eds., *Anabaptist-Mennonite Identities in Ferment.* Elkhart, Ind.: Institute of Mennonite Studies.

Redekop, Calvin and Urie Bender
1988 *Who Am I? What Am I?: Searching for Meaning in Your Work.* Grand Rapids: Zondervan.

Redekop, Calvin W. and Samuel J. Steiner, eds.
1988 *Mennonite Identity: Historical and Contemporary Perspectives.* Lanham, Md.: University Press of America.

Redekop, John H.
1987 *A People Apart: Ethnicity and the Mennonite Brethren.* Winnipeg: Kindred Press.

Reimer, James
1990 "Toward a Christian Theology from a Diversity of Mennonite Perspectives." *Conrad Grebel Review* 6:147-59.

Reiss, Ira L.
1980 *Family Systems in America.* Third edition. New York: Holt, Rinehart and Winston.

Roof, Wade Clark and William McKinney
1985 "Denominational America and the New Religious Pluralism." *The Annals of the American Academy of Political and Social Science.* Volume 480, July 1985.

1987 *American Mainline Religion.* New Brunswick, N.J.: Rutgers University Press.

Ropp, Martha
1980 "The Role of Women in the Church." In Dorothy Yoder Nyce, ed., *Which Way Women?* Akron, Pa.: Peace Section, Mennonite Central Committee.

Rossi, Peter H. and Andrew M. Greeley
1964 "The Impact of the Roman Catholic Denominational School." *The School Review* 72:1, 34-51.

Rothenberg, Stuart and Frank Newport
  1984   *The Evangelical Voter: Religion and Politics in in America*. Washington,
         D.C.: The Free Congress Research and Education Foundation.

Ruth, John
  1984   *Maintaining the Right Fellowship*. Scottdale, Pa.: Herald Press.

Sawatsky, Rodney J.
  1977   "History and Ideology: American Mennonite Identity Definition
         through History." Unpublished Ph.D. dissertation, Princeton Univer-
         sity.

  1987   *Authority and Identity: The Dynamics of the General Conference Mennonite
         Church*. North Newton, Kan.: Bethel College Cornelius H. Wedel His-
         torical Series.

  1990   "Response." In Leo Driedger and Leland Harder, eds., *Anabaptist-
         Mennonite Identities in Ferment*. Elkhart, Ind.: Institute of Mennonite
         Studies.

Schlabach, Theron F.
  1980   *Gospel Versus Gospel*. Scottdale, Pa.: Herald Press.

  1988   *Peace, Faith, Nation: Mennonites and Amish in Nineteenth-Century America*.
         Scottdale, Pa.: Herald Press.

Schludermann, Shirin and Eduard
  1990   "Beliefs and Practices of Students in Mennonite and Catholic
         Schools." *Journal of Mennonite Studies* 8:173-88.

Schulz, David A.
  1982   *The Changing Family*. Third edition. Englewood Cliffs, N.J.: Prentice-
         Hall.

Smucker, Joseph
  1980   *Industrialization in Canada*. Scarborough, Ont.: Prentice-Hall.

Sorokin, P. A.
  1941   *Social and Cultural Dynamics*. New York: American Book Co.

Stark, Rodney
  1990   "Response." In "The Past, Present, and Future of Religion: Themes in
         the Work of Rodney Stark." *Journal for the Scientific Study of Religion*
         29:385-86.

Stark, Rodney and Charles Y. Glock
  1968   *American Piety: The Nature of Religious Commitment*. Berkeley: University
         of California Press.

Stark, Rodney, Daniel P. Doyle, and Lori Kent
  1980   "Rediscovering Moral Communities: Church Membership and
         Crime." In Travis Hirschi and Michael Gottfredson, eds., *Understanding
         Crime: Current Theory and Research*. Beverly Hills, Calif.: Sage Publica-
         tions.

Stark, Rodney and William Sims Bainbridge
1985   *The Future of Religion.* Berkeley: University of California Press.

Stayer, James M., Werner O. Packull, and Klaus Deppermann
1975   "From Monogenesis to Polygenesis: The Historical Discussion of Anabaptist Origins." *Mennonite Quarterly Review.* 49:83-121.

Toennies, Ferdinand
1965   *Community and Society.* Translated and edited by Charles P. Loomis. New York: Harper & Row.

Toews, John A.
1975   *A History of the Mennonite Brethren Church: Pilgrims and Pioneers.* Fresno, Calif.: Board of Christian Literature, General Conference of Mennonite Brethren Churches.

1981   *People of the Way: Selected Essays and Addresses.* Edited by Abe J. Dueck, Herbert Giesbrecht, and Allen R. Guenther. Winnipeg: Historical Committee, Canadian Conference of Mennonite Brethren Churches.

Toews, John B.
1981   "The Emergence of German Industry in the South German Colonies." *Mennonite Quarterly Review* 55:289-371.

1982   *Czars, Soviets and Mennonites.* Newton, Kan.: Faith and Life Press.

Toews, John B., Abram G. Conrad, and Al Dueck
1985   "Mennonite Brethren Church Membership Profile, 1972-1982 " *Direction* 14:2.

Toews, Paul
1990   "Response." In Leo Driedger and Leland Harder, eds., *Anabaptist-Mennonite Identities in Ferment.* Elkhart, Ind.: Institute of Mennonite Studies.

Turner, Joan and Lois Emery
1983   *Perspectives on Women in the 1980s.* Winnipeg: University of Manitoba Press.

Turner, Jonathan H. and Leonard Beeghley
1981   *The Emergence of Sociological Theory.* Homewood, Ill. Dorsey Press.

Unrau, Ed
1991   "MB Debate on 'Peace' Sets Worrisome Tone." *Mennonite Mirror* 20:30.

Urry, James
1989   *None but Saints: The Transformation of Mennonite Life in Russia, 1789-1889.* Winnipeg: Hyperion Press.

Vogt, Ruth
1990   "World Conference Also Notable for the Issues It Didn't Discuss." *Mennonite Mirror* 20:30.

Weber, Max
1978   *Economy and Society.* 2 volumes, Edited by Guenther Roth and Claus Wittich. Berkeley: University of California Press.

Wellman, Barry
1975   "The Community Question: The Intimate Ties of East Yorkers." *American Journal of Sociology* 84:1201-31.

Wiebe, Katie Funk
1979   *Women Among the Brethren: Stories of Fifteen Brethren and Krimmer Mennonite Brethren Women.* Hillsboro, Kan.: Board of Christian Literature, General Conference of Mennonite Brethren Churches.

Woudstra-Gorter, Johanna
1980   "Mennonite Female Ministers in the Netherlands." In Dorothy Yoder Nyce, ed., *Which Way Women?* Akron, Pa.: Peace Section, Mennonite Central Committee.

Wuthnow, Robert
1981   "Two Traditions in the Study of Religion." *Journal for the Scientific Study of Religion* 20:16-32.

1983   "Sources of Doctrinal Unity and Diversity." In Roger A. Johnson, ed. *Views from the Pews.* Philadelphia: Fortress Press.

1988   *The Restructuring of American Religion.* Princeton, N.J.: Princeton University Press.

1989   *The Struggle for America's Soul: Evangelists, Liberals, and Secularism.* Grand Rapids: Eerdmans.

Yinger, J. Milton
1970   *The Scientific Study of Religion.* New York: Macmillan.

Yoder, John H.
1984   *The Priestly Kingdom: Social Ethics as Gospel.* Notre Dame, Ind.: Notre Dame University Press.

1969   "A People in the World: Theological Interpretation." In James L. Garrett, Jr., ed. *The Concept of the Believer's Church.* Scottdale, Pa.: Herald Press.

Yoder, Michael L.
1985   "Findings from the 1982 Mennonite Census." *Mennonite Quarterly Review* 59:307-49.

Zimmerman, Carle C.
1947   *Family and Civilization.* New York: Harper and Bros.

Index

The Authors

J. HOWARD KAUFFMAN is a native of Ohio. He graduated from Goshen College (Indiana) in 1947. He studied at Michigan State University and received a Ph.D. in sociology from the University of Chicago.

Kauffman taught sociology at Goshen College from 1948 to his retirement in 1984. He and his students have surveyed a variety of Mennonite and local community populations. He was project director of the 1972 Church Member Profile (Mennonite) and the current Church Member Profile II. His publications include articles in professional journals and *Anabaptism Four Centuries Later* (with Leland Harder, Herald Press, 1975). He has served the *Mennonite Historical Society* as president, treasurer, and member of the board of editors of the *Mennonite Quarterly Review*.

Kauffman has filled various roles in such church-related agencies as the Mennonite Committee on Peace and Social Concerns, Mennonite Commission on Christian Education, Study Commission on Church Organization, and the Family Life Committee of the National Council of Churches. He was instructor in family life seminars sponsored by the World Council of Churches in Barbados, Ghana, and Botswana.

He is past president of the Rural Life Association and of the Indiana Council on Family Relations. He is a member of the National Council on Family Relations, the American Sociological Association, and the Society for the Scientific Study of Religion.

Kauffman is married to Verda Lambright Kauffman and has four children and nine grandchildren.

LEO DRIEDGER is professor of sociology at the University of Manitoba in Winnipeg, Manitoba, where he has taught for twenty-five years. His teaching and research specialties are in minority relations, urban sociology, and the sociology of religion.

Driedger has published extensively in most scholarly sociological journals in North America and has authored, co-authored, and edited a dozen books. Recent publications include *Ethnic Canada* (Copp Clark, 1987), *Aging and Ethnicity* (Butterworths, 1987), *Mennonite Identity in Conflict* (Mellon, 1988), *The Ethnic Factor* (McGraw-Hill, 1989), *Mennonites in Winnipeg* (Kindred, 1990), *Anabaptist-Mennonite Identities in Ferment* (IMS, 1990), *Ethnic Demography* (Carleton, 1990), and *The Urban Factor* (Oxford, 1991).

Work in the church took Driedger to more than fifty countries when he was on the boards of the Mennonite Central Committee (Manitoba, Canadian, International) and numerous committees for many years. He has served on the Executive boards of the Canadian and General Mennonite conferences as well as their service, peace, and social concerns committees.

Darlene and Leo Driedger have two children. They have lived in Winnipeg for twenty-seven years, where they are deeply involved in local Mennonite congregational life and service.